VICTORIA: THE FORT

Victoria:
The Fort

Derek Pethick

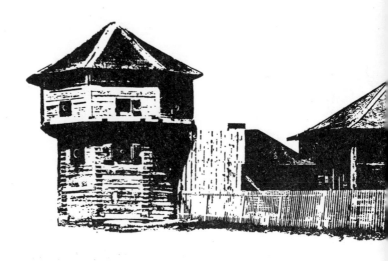

Mitchell Press Limited

Printed in Canada

MITCHELL PRESS LIMITED
Vancouver, Canada

FOR ROBBYN

IT is not long—not very many years—before all those who came hither in 1842 will lay their bones in the silent grave. The pioneers will be gone, no more to return. Victoria—the Colony—will live and grow whilst the Island remains anchored in the sea; but the men who made her—who first raised our flag here—who gave her language, laws, religion and the Anglo-Saxon race but twenty years ago, will soon be gone. Whilst they live and we live, we owe a duty to posterity to mark the era of the settlement of our adopted country. Who will take the initiative?

AMOR DE COSMOS
The Daily British Colonist,
November 20, 1862.

Contents

Foreword

The residents of Victoria have many reasons to be proud of their city; it is impossible to be unaware of its striking geographical setting and many fine parks and gardens. Most of its citizens doubtless are also aware that Victoria has an interesting history, and some at least know that it played an important part in the development not only of the Province of British Columbia but also in the creation of the Dominion of Canada itself. It is the purpose of this volume, and of the two which are to succeed it, to fill in some of the details of the city's unfolding story, and relate them, where appropriate, to the larger record of the nation.

My thanks are due for assistance in the preparation of this work to the staff of the Provincial Archives; also to Mr. Donald Abbott and Mr. Peter Macnair of the Provincial Museum, Victoria and to Dr. Donald Mitchell of the University of Victoria for giving me valuable advice regarding the opening chapter. I must also not neglect to record my gratitude to Professor Reid Elliott of the University of Victoria for help in disentangling Victoria's complex fiscal problems during its first two years as a city. Naturally all opinions expressed regarding these topics are my own responsibility.

Care has been taken in the preparation of this account to avoid errors. If any are detected and brought to the author's or publisher's attention, they will be privately acknowledged and discreetly corrected in subsequent editions, if any.

DEREK PETHICK

The Mists of Time

When, in the last quarter of the eighteenth century, the white man first encountered the natives of Vancouver Island, he may well have assumed, if he thought about the matter at all, that they had been there since time immemorial. Today, of course, we know better. Thanks to the patient labours of geologists and anthropologists, we are beginning to form a picture of the origins of the dark-skinned natives who gazed with awe at the "winged canoes" that glided into Nootka Sound less than two centuries ago, bringing to this remote corner of the world the many mixed blessings and calamities which together make up the all-devouring culture of the West.

They had been there, in fact, perhaps no more than ten or twelve thousand years.[1] Before that, much of the northern part of the continent had lain in the iron grip of the Great Ice Age. A large part of Alaska, however, was relatively free from ice, and, moreover, was at that time joined to Siberia by the "Bering land bridge". It was thus in effect a part of Asia, and it was comparatively easy for the ancestors of our present North American Indians to move dry-shod into what is now the "New World", following, no doubt, the gradual expansion of animal life into this area.

From time to time, as the Ice Age slowly came to an end, slight ameliorations in the climate of this region opened up corridors between the Continental (or Keewatin) ice sheet and the Cordilleran sheet centred in British Columbia. These passages, nearly all east of the Rocky Mountains, permitted a further migration into what is now the United States and the countries farther south. Here during many centuries the newcomers developed their own distinctive cultural traditions.

We must be careful, however, not to imagine that those who participated in these movements thought of themselves as "migrating". Probably very few humans felt during this period that they or any of their ancestors had lived anywhere but where they were then. The eastward expansion of the human frontier during the average lifetime would be imperceptible.

It was only with the final retreat of the ice fields, some ten or twelve thousand years ago, that what is now called British Columbia became habitable, and it is likely that most of the ancestors of our present Indians came here not from the north but the south.

There is considerable supporting evidence for the Asiatic origin of the earliest inhabitants of North America. For example, the silent testimony of the fossil record: all human remains in the new world are of the fully modern *homo sapiens* type, and the ape-like ancestors of man exist neither living nor as fossils.

Even everyday observation confirms this view of the origin of the first North Americans. The Indian differs sharply from the Europeans with their mixture of fair and dark hair and their variation in stature and skin colour; he is on the other hand closely allied in appearance with the races of Asia. He has similar skin to that prevailing throughout the Far East, uniformly black hair, broad face, and even in some cases the "Mongolian fold" of the eyelid. He is often, indeed, to the casual observer, difficult to distinguish from a Chinese.[2] His hands and feet are slightly smaller on the average than the European's, and he has yet to have a pair of blue eyes. We might note also the "Mongolian spot", a bluish-black mark that appears at birth on the backs of Mongolian children, and is also found on the bodies of about 40% of the Coast Indian infants. His Asiatic origin is thus evident, and the routes by which he arrived here are slowly being identified.

Of his early life on this continent, our knowledge is still fragmentary, and for the purposes of this narrative, not essential. We may well then move forward to a point of time roughly two centuries ago, and sketch rapidly the main outlines of the culture which subsequent events, and the contact with another culture, have since laid in ruins.[3]

Three language-families of Indians were to be found on the Island: the Kwakiutl[4] in the north-east, the Coast Salish[5] who inhabited the extreme south and much of the east coast, and the Nootka[6] who occupied most of the west coast. The two first-named also occupied corresponding areas on the mainland, while in the case of the Nootka, the Makah Indians of Cape Flattery in the present state of Washington belonged linguistically and culturally in the same group.

The main livelihood of the Coast Indians was in fishing, and since fishing grounds and clam beds dependably produced food, they had little compulsion toward nomadic wandering. Thus, on favorable sites for beaching canoes, digging clams and obtaining drinking water they built permanent dwellings and settlements. A striking feature of these was the long rectangular house. It was often as much as one hundred feet in length—one house which stood near Seattle for many years was over five hundred feet long—and held several related families. It was usually built near the water, within easy reach of the indispensable canoes. In selecting the site some attention was given to the fact that it might have to be defended, though some authorities maintain that there is no evidence of fortified villages. There were, however, "refuges", though these were usually at some distance from the village itself. The remains of stockades have been found, though it is possible that this form of military sophistication was only developed after the white man appeared in this area.

The buildings were strongly constructed: massive cedar posts were sunk in the ground, and on these rested the roof-beams. Some of these were of a remarkable size: for example, the roof-beams in Chief Maquinna's house at Friendly Cove, V.I., were a hundred feet in length, and no less than five feet in diameter at the butt. When we consider that the wheel and the pulley were unknown, the lifting of these massive timbers into place is a remarkable feat in itself.

Nails were also unknown, but by remarkable ingenuity this difficulty was surmounted. The planks forming the walls were tied in place with rope made from cedar, while the roof might be of either planks or bark, held down by stones or other pieces of wood. The roofs of the Nootka long-houses were gabled, but those of the Salish were of three types: in the north they were mostly gabled, while in the south the slightly-pitched shed roof was usual; there were also in the Fraser Canyon houses of a semi-subterranean variety. Smoke was permitted to escape from the first two types by moving aside a roof-plank with a long pole.

One interesting aspect of this type of construction was that when the tribe migrated temporarily, for example during the berry-picking season, the walls might be quickly dismantled and used to cover a second framework at the tribe's new camping-ground.

Each building was partitioned off inside, sometimes by finely woven mats, so that some privacy was afforded, though for certain important occasions the divisions could be removed to provide a large communal meeting-place. Over a series of fires in the centre of the house, the occupants cooked their meals, while racks for drying fish or clothing were suspended from the roof.

Each family had its allotted place, where it slept on benches and kept its belongings in chests fashioned with great ingenuity and accuracy from cedar planks.

Food was served in wooden dishes, usually hollowed out with adzes. Many of these were carved (especially in the north) to represent a well-known bird or animal; considering that the artist's tool was sometimes only the tooth of a beaver, the skill displayed is remarkable. Spoons were carved or moulded from horn or wood, and even here an effort was made to produce something that would be artistic as well as useful.

The clothing of the Indians varied according to the social status of its wearer. A blanket or a cape made from cedar bark sufficed for the poorest folk, while on special occasions one who belonged to the "best people" of his time and place might luxuriate in furs.

A curious feature of the life of southern Vancouver Island

Indians was the raising of dogs for wool. This was a small white dog, now extinct,[7] from whose wool, mixed with the wool of mountain goats and often bird down, excellent blankets were woven.

Novel but useful articles of clothing were conical hats, woven from spruce roots or cedar fibre, and designed to protect the wearer from sun and rain. Among the Nootka Indians, skilful designs were woven into the fabric, usually portraying the most dramatic feature of the life of the tribe, the pursuit of the whale.

Feet and legs usually went bare, the moccasin being unsuited to the damp coastal climate.[8] In unusually wet weather, however, socks and mittens are said to have made an appearance.

Nose-pins (sometimes six inches long) and ear-rings gave the men who affected them a striking appearance, while the women wore anklets, bracelets and necklaces. The Coast Salish bound the heads of their babies, producing a flattened forehead; slaves, however, (usually captured prisoners of war) were strictly forbidden to practise this art.

The people around Quatsino Sound, on the other hand, bound their children's heads in such a way as to make them grow up to a high point in the middle. We should not, of course, assume from this that the Coast Indians differed from the rest of mankind, except in detail; in pursuit of their vision of the "proper", the "in-thing" or the "good life", there have been few peoples anywhere at any time not prepared to undergo personal discomfort or inflict it on their children.

The staple diet of all the Indians of the coast was largely drawn from the sea. Salmon, cod, halibut, whales, seals, shellfish and waterfowl paid tribute to their tables, and were often smoked and dried for winter use or in preparation for big feasts. Deer were sometimes killed with bow and arrow or trapped in pitfalls,[9] and the diet was varied or augmented by roots, berries or the inner bark of the hemlock.[10]

Agriculture is everywhere a later development than hunting or fishing, and the Indians, well provided by nature with food, had no reason to engage in it. A little tobacco was perhaps grown in the Queen Charlotte Islands,[11] but the Indians had not yet discovered the uncertain glories of fermented liquor.

By means of ingenious nets, birds were often trapped as they alighted. Clams were dug from the sand of beaches at low tide. Oolichan oil was used as a condiment.

The most striking feature of life among the Nootkas was the hunting of whales. Canoes holding eight men would be launched into the great ocean, armed with harpoons attached to ropes made of cedar bark. The head of the harpoon was skilfully designed; the sharp edge of a mussel shell facilitated initial penetration, while barbs made from antlers or whalebone held the weapon fast. With this primitive equipment, the Nootkas would manage to kill animals weighing as much as seventy tons and then tow them laboriously to land. Often, of course, the contest would end very differently, and a single sweep of the flukes of the enraged animal would mean empty places in the long-house that night.[12]

The harpooner was a man of great prestige in the community, much as a celebrated athlete might be today. Before setting out on an expedition, he had to withdraw to a special house, containing the skulls and, it was believed, the spirits of former harpooners, and there purify his spirit and pray for success. The parallel of a medieval knight praying all night in the dim silent chapel under the symbols of his calling for good fortune in the combats of the morrow is not perhaps far-fetched. Likewise, ceremonies in which he cleansed his body by bathing in certain special ponds and then scourged himself with hemlock branches, will also readily bring counterparts to mind from other times and places.

The social structure of the Indians was highly interesting, that of the Kwakiutl being in some respects more complex than that of the Salish. There was a definite hierarchy of society, similar in some ways to that prevailing some centuries ago in the Scottish highlands. The matter is, however, rather difficult to unravel. Some students distinguish sharply differentiated classes—nobles, commoners and slaves—while others believe that it would be more accurate to speak of a "continuous hierarchy". One has only to consider the task confronting a Martian anthropologist undertaking a similar analysis of contemporary white North American society to realize the practical difficulties involved in complex questions of this sort.[13]

We may, however, say that the chiefs were the heads of several

groups of loosely-related families—or, as we might say, of clans—
and were responsible for erecting the dwellings of their clan, and
representing it on public occasions. Various symbols of status—the
use of certain crests, the right to sing certain songs, or to hunt and
fish in prescribed territories—were inherited and jealously guarded.
The slaves, at the bottom of the social pyramid, had no rights at
all; their owner might even kill them as a gesture of "conspicuous
consumption".

A certain amount of social mobility existed, and by means of
accumulating wealth and making lavish gifts, especially at the
great feasts or potlatches, a man might rise in rank. As in
nineteenth century English society, a rich man could by a nice
calculation of munificence be eventually considered a gentleman,
and even in rare cases under the mellowing influence of time
and money become an aristocrat.

The four major crises of life—birth, puberty, marriage and
death—were marked, as in nearly all societies, by appropriate
rituals and ceremonies. Again, as in the case of young English
aristocrats, cold baths and whipping were thought to impart to the
future rulers of the tribe important psychic attributes. At the close
of adolescence special festivities customarily marked the transition
to adult status.

We might note in this connection the Salish "spirit quest". In
this, those in search of either a spiritual experience or unusual
powers in the fields of medicine or warfare would discipline their
bodies by means of fasting, bathing and continence. Eventually
they might have an encounter with a spiritual being who would
bestow the desired qualities on them, and whom they would to
some extent control.[14]

Polygamy was permitted, though was apparently not common.
The status of women among the coast tribes was high; though the
man owned the hunting and fishing equipment, the woman owned
all the household furnishings.

Perhaps the most striking feature of life among the Indians was
the custom of the "potlatch". The origins of this institution are
now lost in antiquity, but it likely rose out of either the practice of
exchanging gifts between families at the time of a betrothal or the

formal presentation to the tribe of a new chief on the occasion of the death of an old one. With the passage of time, the attendant ceremonies increased in complexity and acquired significance.

The outward features of these great communal feasts—the songs, the dances, the oratory and the interchange of gifts—were of course easily noted by observers from the outside world; it was some time, however, before their correct interpretation was established. This was largely owing to the frequent intrusion, especially since the coming of the white man to the north-west coast of America, of two other features which were actually not essential to the original social custom. One of these was the practice of using the occasion of the potlatch for the repayment of loans made during the previous year. As the rate of interest was usually 100%, the idea grew up among the earliest white observers of the ceremony that it was the established custom to distribute at the potlatch gifts double in value to those received at the previous potlatch, when the current host was then the guest.

Another misleading "clue" was the rise toward the close of the 19th century, especially among the Southern Kwakiutl, of an abnormal aberration of the ceremony—the "rivalry potlatch". In this, various chiefs would strive to outdo each other in demonstrating their wealth and importance, and one method of achieving this which they employed was the public destruction of their own property, such as canoes, blankets or oolichan grease. This wasteful development of the original form of the ceremony was one of the reasons for the banning of all potlatches for many years.[15]

In this connection, we should note one interesting type of property: the "copper". These sheets of copper, usually shaped like a shield, were of no great value in themselves, but were important symbols of wealth. Each one had a name and had probably changed hands several times at previous potlatches, perhaps for as much as 5000 blankets or ten slaves. A chief could demonstrate his opulence and his contempt for his rivals by publicly breaking a "copper" in pieces and then presenting pieces of it to his rivals.[16]

It has also been suggested[17] that the potlatch, especially among the Coast Salish, was a device for the redistribution of wealth. At some times, it is argued, those living in certain areas would have a surplus of foodstuffs, while others would be experiencing want. The transfer of goods at the potlatch would help to correct this imbalance, and the obligations incurred would be discharged when the luck of the harvest changed in the other direction.

Wayne Suttles suggests that an extension of this function of the potlatch may have in time developed. Some groups, through greater industry or a better habitat, would build up consistent surpluses of "wealth goods", i.e., valuables other than food; the potlatch provided a means whereby these could be reintroduced into the economic bloodstream of the larger community.

Another theory about the potlatch is that advanced by Helen Codere. She maintains[18] that the potlatch was developed as an emotional and social substitute for warfare; much of her argument is based on the fact that in the speeches accompanying the ceremony references to warfare are remarkably numerous. Other students of the subject, however, feel that this was largely a matter of "big talk", and should not be taken too literally.

It seems beyond much doubt that the core of the potlatch ceremony was the public assertion of status and rights. When the host distributed gifts to his guest, he not only asserted his own social position and privileges, but was careful to give his assent to theirs. This he did by such means as observing a certain order of precedence and using honorific names when addressing them. In this way it was made clear beyond dispute just "who was who". As two contemporary students of this phenomenon put it, "In fine, it is clear that the potlatch must be regarded as a formal procedure for social integration, its prime purpose being to identify publicly the membership of the group and to define the social status of this membership."[19]

Turning from the social customs of the Indians to those traditional ways in which man expresses his highest aspirations—art and religion—we find much to engage our attention.

The art of the Coast Indian[20] has fortunately not been obliterated by his conquerors, and this is a tribute to its undoubted excellence and fascination. Totem poles[21] are of course famous from one end of the planet to the other; their features are too well known to describe. We might perhaps note, however, that their style is "impressionistic"—that is, it suppresses unnecessary detail—and that they do not, as is widely believed, "tell a story"; they are rather a series of family crests, usually of the chief who had the pole carved. Some might be as much as fifty feet in height, while others were much shorter, and were used as house-posts to support the main beams of the long-houses.

The ingenuity, symbolism and symmetry employed in carving the totem pole were continued in a wide range of other objects. Bowls, clubs and masks on display in our modern museums reflect the sense of proportion and design of their makers, "which yet survive, stamped on these lifeless things", and it should be a source of pride for white man and Indian alike that this art, once in danger of extinction, has in our own day been successfully revived, notably in Thunderbird Park, Victoria, by Mungo Martin and Henry Hunt.

If art reflects man's conception of beauty and his efforts to trap its fleeting image in matter, religion is the vehicle through which he expresses his relationship with the unseen powers which lurk behind the world of the senses. We should, however, perhaps use the word "animism" rather than "religion" in describing the Indian view of the universe. There were thought to be many supernatural beings, inhabiting either animals or natural phenomena, such as the sun or the thunderstorm. These might be propitiated by suitable offerings or ceremonies, and the concept of taboo was deeply ingrained. Ritual cleansing of the body was often practised, especially during the hunting or fishing season, as a means of ensuring good luck. The first salmon of the season was normally accorded special reverence, while the Nootka, if they killed a bear, would seat it at their table to show that they bore and expected no ill will.

The medicine man combined two offices usually separated in the white man's world, those of priest and doctor. He professed to be able to foresee the future, and accompanied expeditions against other tribes as a sort of chaplain. He ventured to diagnose and treat disease, by means of reciting magical formulas and creating an alarming din with whistles, drums and rattles.[22] Usually illness was seen as resulting from the intrusion of some foreign object which the shaman ceremoniously removed.

Belief in the existence of a soul was universal; it could escape from the body during sleep or sickness, but could be captured by the medicine man and restored to its owner. At death, it was believed to go to the rather shadowy land of the spirits.

The burial of the dead differed among the various tribes. A dead slave might simply be thrown into the sea; ordinary citizens might be placed in a cedar chest in a high tree. A great chief, dressed in his finest robes, would have his body publicly displayed for some time before his burial. A memorial pole, serving the same function as our modern tombstone, would often be set up near the grave-box. Sometimes when the family of a deceased man had increased its social standing, his bones would be collected, cleaned and reburied at a later date.[23]

Such, then, in broad outline, was the economic, social and spiritual framework within which the Indians of the B.C. coast passed their lives only two centuries ago. It was, all things considered, deserving of much respect. Cut off from any advanced civilization, its members had nevertheless successfully come to terms with their environment. The sea and forest had been made to yield up their harvest, and provision made for times of scarcity. Social duties had been parcelled out, with perhaps as much justice as ever exists anywhere.[24] Theories of the powers behind events had been formed, corresponding perhaps—who can tell?—as closely with ultimate reality as such theories ever do.

So within this scheme of things the years and no doubt the centuries had passed. In the summer the tribe might hunt for berries or the elusive wild deer, or wives might strain their eyes toward the ocean's rim where their menfolk battled leviathan; while children would play, as in all times and places, heedless of more than the day's pleasure and the gifts of sun and air. In the winter in the long-house, tales, perhaps slightly tall, would be told around the fire, and stirring deeds of former times recounted. At the great feasts, the cycle of birth, marriage and death would once more unfold, immemorially old yet ever new; while the struggle for social status, to become one of the favoured few regarding with disdain those outside the magic circle of wealth or power, would, as always everywhere, continue unabated. So it had been since the oldest could remember—for the tribes had no written records—and so perhaps might ever have continued.

Yet, all unknown to the native dwellers on this distant rim of the world, even as they lovingly and laboriously carved a club for stunning fish or carefully fashioned a basket in which to carry blueberries, on the other side of the globe a revolution—perhaps the most far-reaching in history—was in progress. Bursting out of their narrow peninsula on the western edge of Asia, the tribes of Europe, armed with the compass and the cannon, were falling headlong on the rest of the planet in an insatiable quest for power, wealth and knowledge. Eventually the two cultures would come in contact, and in the brief unequal contest the European way would triumph and the other be left in ruins. It is to this high drama, this tragedy without villain or hero, that we now must turn our attention.

FOOTNOTES

[1] Recommended works on this topic are: Gordon Willey, *An Introduction to American Archaeology*, Prentice-Hall, Englewood Cliffs, New Jersey, 1966, Vol. 1; H. M. Wormington, *Ancient Man in North America*, Denver Museum of Natural History, Denver, Colorado, 4th edition, 1957; K. MacGowan, *Early Man in the New World*, Macmillan, New York, 1950.

[2] The presence of some Mongolian features in North American Indians does not necessarily relate to the original entry into North America. Matings across the Bering Strait have continued ever since there were human beings living on both sides of it, and this has remained a means, however slight, for the interchange of genes.

[3] Among general works on the Indians of the Northwest Coast, perhaps the best are Philip Drucker, *Indians of the Northwest Coast*, McGraw-Hill Book Co., 1955 and *Cultures of the North Pacific Coast*, Chandler, San Francisco, 1965; Diamond Jenness, *The Indians of Canada*, National Museum of Canada, Ottawa, 3rd edition, 1955; Harold Driver, *Indians of North America*, U. of Chicago Press, 1961.

[4] A detailed study of the Kwakiutl is to be found in *The Kwakiutl of Vancouver Island* by Franz Boas, American Museum of Natural History Memoir No. 8, 1909. His *Kwakiutl Ethnography* (U. of Chicago Press, 1967) is a new work edited by Helen Codere from a manuscript unfinished at his death. The reader might also find interesting *Potlatch and Totem* by W. M. Halliday, Dent, Toronto, 1935.

[5] Detailed studies of the Coast Salish are to be found in *The Coast Salish* by H. G. Barnett, U. of Oregon Press, 1955, and *Indians of the Urban Northwest*, ed. Marian Smith, Columbia University Press, New York, 1949.

[6] See *The Northern and Central Nootkan Tribes* by Philip Drucker, Bureau of American Ethnology, Bulletin 144, 1951.

[7] They existed for a considerable time after the arrival of the white man. See J. R. Anderson, "Notes and comments on early days and events in British Columbia, Washington and Oregon". MS in Provincial Archives, Victoria, p. 168.

[8] Moccasins were, however, used in winter by the Coast Salish of the mainland.

[9] Deer were especially important to the Coast Salish, and were so abundant that no special "power" was necessary to be a deer hunter.

[10] The camas was particularly important to the Songhish of the Victoria area. Some believe that the word "Camosun" is derived from it.

[11] There is some dispute as to whether smoking as we know it was ever indulged in.

[12] See Douglas Leechman, *Native Tribes of Canada,* W. J. Gage and Co., Toronto, n.d. pp. 278-283; also Philip Drucker, *Cultures of the North Pacific Coast,* Chandler Publishing Co., San Francisco, 1965, pp. 132-144.

[13] See, for example, Helen Codere's "Kwakiutl Society: Rank without Class" in the *American Anthropologist,* Vol. 59, pp. 473-486, and Wayne Suttles' paper "Private Knowledge, Morality and Social Classes Among the Coast Salish", *American Anthropologist,* 1958 (Vol. 60).

[14] See P. Drucker, *Cultures of the North Pacific Coast,* Chandler Publishing Co., San Francisco, 1965, pp. 85-86.

[15] For abnormal aberrations of conviviality in a non-Indian society, see Charles and Mary Beard, *The Rise of American Civilization,* Macmillan, New York, 1930, Vol. II, p. 392. Speaking of the upper levels of American society in the late 19th century, the authors record: "At a dinner eaten on horseback, the favorite steed was fed flowers and champagne; to a small black and tan dog wearing a diamond collar worth $15,000 a lavish banquet was tendered; at one function, the cigarettes were wrapped in hundred dollar bills; at another, fine black pearls were given to the diners in their oysters; at a third, an elaborate feast was served to boon companions in a mine from which came the fortune of the host."

[16] Coppers do not, however, seem to have been used in the Salish area.

[17] Notably by Wayne Suttles in his article in Vol. 62, pp. 296-305, of the *American Anthropologist.*

[18] In her *Fighting With Property,* American Ethnological Society Monograph No. 18, 1950.

[19] Philip Drucker and Robert Heizer, *To Make My Name Good,* U. of California Press, Berkeley and Los Angeles, 1967, p. 8.

[20] Recommended books on Indian art are Franz Boas, *Primitive Art,* Dover Publications, New York, 1955; R. B. Inverarity, *Art of the Northwest Coast Indians,* U. of California Press, Berkeley, 1950; Bill Holm, *Northwest Coast Indian Art; An Analysis of Form,* U. of Washington Press, 1966.

[21] See *Totem Poles* by Marius Barbeau, two vols., National Museum of Canada, Ottawa, 1950.

[22] See *The Coast Salish* by Homer G. Barnett, U. of Oregon Press, Eugene, 1955; *Travels in British Columbia* by C. E. Barrett-Lennard, London, 1862; *Vancouver Island and British Columbia,* by Matthew Macfie, London, 1865.

[23] For a fuller account of Indian religious beliefs, see *The Indians of Canada,* by Diamond Jenness, King's Printer, Ottawa, 1932, pp. 167-199.

[24] Perhaps with more. J. R. Anderson (Notes and Comments, p. 171), gives us this vignette of an Indian chief: "Like all natives he loved rum and led the simple life. If he wanted a salmon he had to catch it like any other of his subjects, and as for clams it was the duty of the Queen to dig them up."

CHAPTER TWO

Explorers
and
Fur Traders

The fair breeze blew, the white foam flew,
The furrow followed free;
We were the first that ever burst
Into that silent sea.

How long this fateful clash of cultures had been in the making, no one can say beyond dispute. Europe had lain in a long sleep and now was awake; this was henceforth to be the dominating theme of world history, and all beyond that was a matter of details for historians to quarrel over. Some would place the time of rebirth—the Renaissance, as it came to be called—as early as 1100 A.D., when the towns of Northern Italy first felt a quickening of their economic pulse, and here and there man began seeing the universe as an object not of dread but of wonder and desire. For a time the pace had been hesitant; it was in the fifteenth century that the strides became those of a giant. The Atlantic was still feared, as indeed it still is today; yet few believed any longer that those who sailed westward into the sunset would drop without warning into everlasting nothingness. Rather they would come, after many adventures—so whispered in men's hearts the 'wild surmise'—back to the port from which they had set out, signed with fame—nay, immortality—and laden perhaps with the fabled and immeasurable riches of Cathay.

The Portuguese had opened this latest chapter of history. The farthest west of all the countries of Europe, it seemed the least favorably sited. Between it and the rest of the European continent lay Spain, a stronger power. Expansion in that direction seemed impossible. The only navigable sea, as Ptolemy, prince of geographers, had asserted in the second century A.D., was the Mediterranean. The Atlantic was an endless waste of waters; those who ventured too far on its stormy waves were destined not to return.

But was the famous geographer of Alexandria correct? What if he had been wrong? What if somewhere in the Atlantic new lands lay waiting for the taking? If so, then Portugal was the most favored of the nations; given a leader in the great quest, immortal fame might be hers.

An event first takes shape as a dream, and in this case the dreamer was at hand. He has come down to us as Prince Henry the Navigator.[1] He had early distinguished himself in wars against the Moors, and might have gone on from there to yet further martial glories. Yet one day, perhaps as he sat watching the gray waves endlessly breaking against the rock-shod foot of Europe, he decided that the cannon's mouth held but a bubble reputation and that his life would henceforth be dedicated to a sterner, more desperate campaign: against the unknown sea.

So at Sagres, a small port in southwest Portugal, he erected an observatory, and there for half a century till his death in 1460 he directed his great attempt to conquer his chosen enemy. He himself lived to see no great reassuring triumph, but he prepared the way for his successors. In 1471 the first ship creeping down the coast of Africa reached the Equator; in 1483 the mouth of the Congo was reached; in 1486 Bartholomew Diaz rounded the Cape of Good Hope.

Hardly had these deeds become the excited talk of every street-corner when like a thunderbolt fresh tidings struck the astonished mind of Europe. A Genoese mariner, Christopher Columbus, sailing under the Spanish flag, had crossed the Atlantic safely and found land, fertile and friendly, in the West. In 1498 Vasco Da Gama went on to become the first European to reach India by sea.

From then on, the pace of exploration was almost beyond comprehension; only we who live in the "space age" have known anything to equal it.² In 1498 Cabot reached Newfoundland, in 1500 Brazil and Madagascar were discovered, and in 1509 the Portuguese cast anchor at Malacca. In 1513 Nunez de Balboa climbed the isthmus of Panama and from a "peak in Darien" became the first of our race to behold the immeasurable prairie of the Pacific. Finally, in 1522, after a voyage of three years, in which four of the five ships which had set out together from Seville in 1519 were lost, the lone survivor, manned by a ghost-crew of eighteen, limped back up the river to Seville, first craft in history to circumnavigate the globe.

These were the great years; the years when the main outlines of the continents were at last laid bare; but the age of discovery, once opened, had no ending. Later voyages could never equal these in daring, but piece by piece they filled in the picture, as geographers were forced almost yearly to revise their maps.

As the new lands were discovered, their wealth flowed back to Europe to create there the first truly modern states and empires. Portugal, which had begun the race, fell behind—her natural resources were not great enough to sustain the struggle; but Spain, France, England and Holland yearly sent out fresh ships to take possession of still unclaimed parts of the planet, and by the eighteenth century among them disputed the mastery of the globe.

Everywhere they brought trade; everywhere, they overwhelmed local cultures with their superior wealth, organization and power. Everywhere they established outposts of Europe, of its religion, its customs, its science. And somewhere, in this relentless onrush of power, the Middle Ages melted back into the shadows and the Modern Age began. It was an age which though still owing a formal allegiance to heaven, in practice was to rely on strength guided only by its own will and reason. Henceforth, though few as yet dared to say it, man's mind would be man's fate.

The earliest visitor to the waters of northwest America was Sir Francis Drake in the sixteenth century. Setting out around the world, he had captured some Spanish ships and plundered their settlements in South America. His ship was laden with booty, and he began to wonder if he dared return eastward around Cape Horn. He had heard what everyone in those days had heard, that there was a passage from the Atlantic to the Pacific across the top of North America, and he decided to return to Europe by this convenient route. With this in mind, he sailed up the coast of North America in 1579 past San Francisco and (some estimate) almost to Cape Flattery.[3] Then fog and rain drove him back, and he returned to England across the Pacific without having seen either what is now Vancouver Island or the coast of British Columbia. It is curious to reflect that had he persevered a few days longer, the residents of B.C. might in days to come have boasted that they or their forebears had lived there under both of the royal Elizabeths.[4]

No Englishman returned to this area for almost two hundred years. The next visitor may have been a Greek called Juan de Fuca. He claimed to have found the fabled passage to the East from the Pacific in 1592, and to have drawn a map of it. That his tale had any truth in it is highly dubious; but later geographers gave him the benefit of the doubt in naming after him the strait to the south of Vancouver Island.[5]

Explorers now appeared from a far different quarter. In 1740 two Russians, Bering and Chirikoff, sailed eastward from Siberia.[6] Vitus Bering discovered Mt. St. Elias (18,000 ft.) on the mainland of North America, but later lost his life and was buried on lonely Hyack Island, while Chirikoff survived to tell of sighting land about 46° north latitude and following the coast northward. Moreover he brought back with him furs, and thenceforth there were always Russian ships trading with the Indians along the north B.C. coast. None of these, however, so far as is known, landed on Vancouver Island.[7]

News of these Russian expeditions eventually reached the ears of the government at Madrid.[8] At this time there were Spanish outposts well established in California at San Diego and Monterey, and it was decided to extend the arc of Spanish power northward. Accordingly in the spring of 1774 the *Santiago* under the command of Juan Josef Perez Hernandez set out from the balmy shores of California toward the northern mists where the fabulous furs were known to come from. On board were two Franciscan friars, and on July 17 one of them saw from a distance through the fog the Queen Charlotte Islands.[9] Later, in the latitude of 54°, the mainland also was sighted, but although Haida braves approached the ship in their canoes, no attempt was made to land and soon afterward the ship turned back.

On August 8, beset by sickness among his crew, the Captain decided to anchor briefly in a large bay on the western coast of what would someday be known as Vancouver Island. This bay he named "San Lorenzo"; although there is some dispute about the matter, it is assumed by many to be the one later named "Nootka Sound" by Captain Cook.[10] Perez did not, however, leave his ship (although he traded with the natives for furs) and so he missed the distinction of becoming the first white man to set foot upon the Island.

A second Spanish expedition was sent north in 1775. (On the other side of the continent, the "embattled farmers" had just "fired the shot heard round the world", serving notice that colonialism in North America was doomed). Two vessels sailed from San Blas: the *Santiago,* with Heceta in charge and Juan Perez as his first lieutenant; and the *Sonora,* under Captain Don Juan de la Bodega y Quadra.

On July 14, 1775, Heceta and some of his crew landed briefly in what is now the State of Washington, and, after erecting a cross, took possession of the country for Spain; this, it is claimed, makes them the first white men to set foot in the Pacific Northwest. The *Santiago* sighted Vancouver Island, but did not land there. Perez died on the way home, and several of Quadra's crew were killed by Indians, but otherwise the voyage was successful, the *Santiago* returning to San Blas on August 29. The *Sonora,* although only thirty-six feet long, on November 20 had continued alone almost as far as Alaska.[11]

Meanwhile, yet a third imperial power was converging on this remote and mist-shrouded corner of the world. As a result of her victories over the French in both India and North America (the battle of the Plains of Abraham had been fought only fifteen years before Perez dropped anchor at Nootka), Britain was now an imperial power of equal rank with Spain. Portugal was clearly no longer in this category; Holland, although it held the fabulously rich East Indies, seemed unable or disinclined to strike for the trident of the seas. The final struggle, then, seemed destined to be fought out between England, France and Spain. Actually, the power of Spain had begun its long melancholy descent from the times of Ferdinand and Isabella to the days of Admiral Dewey, but this was more apparent in retrospect than at the time. Spain still had many possessions, and was reckoned a foe to be feared. Thus the winner of the approaching contest for world mastery seemed still in doubt.

This was not, however, the sole motive that led the ships of Europe to voyage into distant seas. Science was becoming not only the handmaiden of commerce but the ornament of the mind, and the desire to learn more about the exotic and often bizarre forms of life—human, animal, or botanical—with which the newly-found continents abounded, provided an additional impetus to exploration.

Both factors weighed in the selection of the leader of the first British expedition to reach the shores of northwest America. Captain Cook was widely recognized as a man alert to new developments—he had drastically reduced the death-rate from scurvy on his ships, and had begun to make navigational use of the new Harrison chronometer. Also, he had already completed two successful voyages around the world, during which his careful and detailed observations had enlarged in many ways the knowledge of mankind.

On this third great voyage, with two ships, the *Resolution* and *Discovery,* he visited New Zealand and numerous smaller islands in the South Seas, noting the customs, appearance and beliefs of the natives, before sailing across the Pacific in the spring of 1778. His orders were to examine closely the northwest coast of America, as far north as 65°; to find if possible a river leading into Hudson's or Baffin Bay, and if this was determined not to exist, to proceed to Kamchatka in Siberia. (Some idea of the importance attached to the Northwest Passage may be gained from the fact that Parliament, in 1745, had offered £20,000 for its discovery.)[12]

Britain's first venture in North Pacific settlement was at Nootka on Vancouver Island's west coast

Capt. Juan Francisco de la Bodega y Quadra

Captain George Vancouver, R.

Captain James Cook, R.N.

It is interesting to note that with Cook on this voyage were two other men destined to achieve fame, though of rather different sorts: William Bligh (later of the *Bounty*), a subordinate officer, and George Vancouver, then a midshipman, but whose name would someday be given to the largest island and one of the largest cities on the Pacific Coast.

On March 22 Cook passed (and named) Cape Flattery, and then proceeded northward to anchor at Nootka (which he at first called King George's Sound) on March 29, 1778. Here he remained for a month, while extensive repairs were made to his ships, and where he wrote a detailed and penetrating account (most of the data for which was compiled by the ship's surgeon, Dr. Anderson) of the countryside and its natives.

One feature of the Pacific Coast immediately attracted his notice —one which later residents of Vancouver Island would also be careful to give wide circulation:

> The climate, as far as we had any experience of it, is infinitely milder than that on the east coast of America, under the same parallel of latitude. The mercury in the thermometer never, even in the night, fell lower than 42°; and very often in the day it rose to 60°. No such thing as frost was perceived in any of the low ground; on the contrary, vegetation had made a considerable progress; for I met with grass that was already above a foot long.[13]

Another feature of the Island (though Cook did not yet know it to be an island) which he noted was someday to provide the basis for its most important industry:

> The trees, in general, grow with great vigour, and are all of a large size.[14]

Elsewhere he records ". . . the largest pine-trees that I ever saw."[15]

The general luxuriance of the area and the variety of its flora also impressed Cook—the more so, perhaps, after the long toilsome weeks crossing the Pacific:

> About the rocks, and verge of the woods, we found strawberry plants, some raspberry, currant, and gooseberry bushes, which were all in a most flourishing state; with a few small

black alder-trees. There are likewise a species of sow-thistle; goose-grass; some crow's-foot, which has a very fine crimson flower; and two sorts of *Anthericum;* one with a large orange flower, and the other with a blue one. We also found in these situations, some wild rose-bushes, which were just budding; a great quantity of young leeks with triangular leaves; a small sort of grass, and some water-cresses, which grow about the sides of the rills; besides great abundance of *Andromeda.* Within the woods, besides two sorts of underwood shrubs unknown to us, are mosses and ferns.[16]

Cook was careful to give a detailed description of the birds and animals to be found in the district, observing, for example, that the humming birds were just beginning to move north. Raccoons, martens, squirrels, deer, foxes and bears were also noted. One sentence in this connection cannot be omitted, as it was to have a greater effect on at least some of his future readers than any other in his account. Concerning the sea-otters, abundant in the area, he wrote:

The fur of these animals, as mentioned in the Russian accounts, is certainly softer and finer than that of any others we know of; and therefore the discovery of this part of the continent of North America, where so valuable an article of commerce may be met with, cannot be a matter of indifference.[17]

Turning his attention to the natives themselves, Cook essayed a generalized portrait of them:

The persons of the natives are in general under the common stature, but not slender in proportion, being commonly pretty full or plump, though not muscular. Neither doth the soft fleshiness seem ever to swell into corpulence, and many of the older people are rather spare or lean. The visage of most of them is round and full, and sometimes, also, broad, with large prominent cheeks; and above these the face is frequently much depressed, or seems fallen in quite across the temples, the nose also flattening at its base, with pretty wide nostrils, and a rounded point. The forehead rather low, the eyes small, black, and rather languishing than sparkling, the mouth round with large round thickish lips, the teeth tolerably equal and well set, but not remarkably white. They have either no beards at all, which was most commonly the case, or a small thin one upon the point of the chin, which does not arise from any natural defect of hair on that part, but from plucking it out more or less; for some of them, and particularly the old men, have not only considerable beards all over the chin, but whiskers or mustachios, both on the upper lip and running thence toward the lower jaw obliquely downward.

Their eyebrows are also scanty and always narrow, but the hair of the head is in great abundance, very coarse and strong, and without a single exception black, straight, and lank, or hanging down over the shoulders. The neck is short; the arms and body have no particular mark of beauty or elegance in their formation, but are rather clumsy; and the limbs in all are very small in proportion to the other parts, and crooked or ill made, with large feet badly shaped, and projecting ankles. This last defect seems, in a great measure, to arise from their sitting so much on their hams or knees, both in their canoes and houses . . . .

The women are nearly of the same size, color, and form, with the men, from whom it is not easy to distinguish them, as they possess no natural delicacies sufficient to render their persons agreeable; and hardly any one was seen, even amongst those who are in the prime of life, who had the least pretensions to be called handsome.[18]

After he had become more familiar with them, Cook also ventured a character analysis:

They seem to be a docile, courteous, good-natured people; but notwithstanding the predominant phlegm of their tempers, quick in resenting what they look upon as an injury; and, like most other passionate people, as soon forgetting it . . . . [4]

Their other passions, especially their curiosity, appear in some measure to lie dormant. For few expressed any desire to see or examine things wholly unknown to them; and which to those truly possessed of that passion would have appeared astonishing. They were always contented to procure the articles they knew and wanted, regarding everything else with great indifference, nor did our persons, apparel, and manners, so different from their own, or even the extraordinary size and construction of our ships, seem to excite admiration, or even engage attention. One cause of this may be their indolence, which seems considerable. But, on the other hand, they are certainly not wholly unsusceptible of the tender passions; if we may judge from their being so fond of music, which is mostly of the grave or serious, but truly pathetic sort.[19]

A brisk trade soon developed between the white men and the Indians; furs were eagerly exchanged for nails, looking-glasses and buttons, both sides no doubt marvelling at the credulity of the other.[21] Not all the items offered by the natives were, however, acceptable:

> But the most extraordinary of all the articles which they brought to the ships for sale were human skulls, and hands not yet stripped of the flesh, which they made our people plainly understand they had eaten, and, indeed, some of them had evident marks that they had been upon the fire. We had but too much reason to suspect from this circumstance, that the horrid practice of feeding on their enemies is as prevalent here as we had found it to be at New Zealand and other South Sea Islands.[21]

Two items which were destined by an odd chance later to have a modest place in the records of international diplomacy also made their appearance. Cook himself, or at any rate his government, may have come to wish they had not:

> But what was most singular, two silver table-spoons were purchased from them, which, from their peculiar shape, we supposed to be of Spanish manufacture. One of these strangers wore them round his neck by way of ornament.[22]

These lines, or at least the event they described, were later to be used by the Spanish as evidence that their claims to Vancouver Island were prior to those of the British.[23]

It is worth noting, however, that Cook noticed several items of iron and brass in the possession of the Indians, and expressed the opinion that their acquisition was by no means recent. They must either have come to this remote place, he conjectured, by being passed from hand to hand northward along the coast from Mexico, or by a similar process westward from the Hudson's Bay forts in eastern North America.

After a month, in which his ships were repaired and extensive observations made of all aspects of the area, on April 26, 1778, the *Resolution* and *Discovery* set sail. Cook had become the first

British subject to set foot in what is now British Columbia; but it was an honor he did not live long to enjoy. Having sailed northward as far as the Bering Strait and thus finally demonstrated that the Northwest Passage, or "Strait of Anian" was a myth, on February 14, 1779, he returned to the Sandwich Islands where he was slain by natives. The weapon which reputedly did the deed is now on display in the Provincial Archives, Victoria.

Cook's ships, however, continued their memorable voyage, and after further adventures returned safely to London on October 4, 1780.

Much had been accomplished in the enlargement of several fields of human knowledge; but what perhaps attracted most attention, or at least had the most far-reaching results, was Cook's suggestion that large profits might be expected from the Nootka fur trade.

Taking the hint, two ships, one appropriately named the *Captain Cook* (Captain Lowrie) and the other the *Experiment* (Captain Guise) sailed from Bombay in 1785 and arrived in Nootka in July of the following year;[24] the *King George* (Captain Portlock) and *Queen Charlotte* (Captain George Dixon) arrived in Canton in November 1787 with 2500 furs;[25] Captain James Hanna sailed the sixty-ton *Sea Otter* in this period with over 500 pelts from Nootka to Macao, where they sold for $20,000;[26] while Captain Charles Barkley had an even more remarkable odyssey. In August 1786 at the age of 25 he sailed from England in the *Imperial Eagle* of 400 tons. Stopping first at Ostend, he raised the Austrian flag (so that he would not need a license from the East India Company to trade in far eastern waters) and then met and married Miss Frances Hornby Trevor, then aged 17. The young couple next sailed for Nootka, arriving there in July 1787. The captain named Barkley Sound after himself and Frances and Hornby peaks after his bride.[27] He then acquired 800 pelts, which he took to China and sold for $30,000.[28] His wife, who was the first white woman to set foot in what is now British Columbia, wrote two interesting accounts of these events; one is in the Provincial Archives, but the other is apparently lost.[29]

About this time, also, the *Columbia Rediviva* and the *Lady*

Washington arrived in Nootka from Boston, and wintered there 1788-89.[30]

A more complicated series of events was set in motion when John Meares, a retired lieutenant in the Royal Navy, arrived in Nootka in May 1788, bringing with him fifty Chinese laborers. With their aid he constructed the first ship launched in this part of the world. Named the *Northwest America,* and launched on September 20, 1788, it was a vessel of forty tons.

Meares also acquired (or so he afterwards maintained) a piece of land from the famous chief Maquinna on which he built a fortified house.[31] He could hardly have foreseen that around this transaction an angry controversy between two of the greatest powers of Europe would revolve.

It was apparent from this increasing activity that the fur trade with the Orient was a profitable business, and that Nootka was an excellent location for its headquarters. Spain therefore resolved to take firm possession of the area. To this end Esteban Jose Martinez, an experienced sailor who had been in these waters in 1788, was sent to set up a military post there. He arrived in February 1789, to find that the bay, unknown only fifteen years before, was now a busy harbor sheltering the ships of a number of nations. By June 24 Martinez had nearly completed a substantial fort, complete with gun emplacement. In a solemn ceremony he formally took possession of Nootka Sound and its environs for Spain.

This was, of course, what would be called in modern jargon a "unilateral declaration". A little over a week later, a British Captain, Colnett, arrived from China, claiming he had orders from the King of England to take possession of the area. Martinez thereupon seized Colnett's ship and ran up the Spanish flag; shortly afterward, when another British ship arrived, Martinez captured it as well.

As a result of these actions, before many months had passed, this remote bay was the focus of a quarrel between the great powers of Europe and might well have become the Sarajevo of a global conflict. For some months it seemed that Nootka was about to achieve the melancholy distinction of a similar place in the history books, and only after a series of diplomatic notes, claims, counter-claims and agreements was war averted.

It was July 1789 when the British ships had been seized. (That same month, the fall of the Bastille signalled the start of the French Revolution). It was January 1790 before the British government became aware of the matter. At first it was undecided as to what line to adopt, William Pitt the Prime Minister (then aged 30) fearing that Britain might find herself at war with both Spain and its ally, France. The Revolution, however, was rapidly reducing France to impotence, and Pitt decided to stand firm. On April 30 he mobilized the navy,[32] and in a solemn statement to the House of Commons of the 5th of May informed the members that British ships and property had been seized at Nootka, and British officers and men sent as prisoners to Mexico. A motion was passed by the House supporting a rapid increase in armaments,[33] and it seemed that war might be near.

Wiser counsels prevailed, however; Spain agreed to release the ships and men, and pay an indemnity of 210,000 Spanish dollars.

Stability seemed restored, and Spain employed it in actively exploring the area. In 1790 the *Princesa Real* (formerly the *Princess Royal)* seized earlier from the British and about to be returned to them by agreement, under Manuel Quimper[34] charted parts of the Straits of Juan de Fuca, visited Equimalt Harbor (which he named Puerto de Cordova)[35] on July 19, and took formal possession of areas in the vicinity of what are now called Sooke Inlet[36] and Royal Roads.[37]

The following year Rosario Strait and Haro Strait[38] were explored by Jose Maria Narvaez in the *Santa Saturnina*. He entered Nanaimo harbor, determined the main outlines of the Gulf of Georgia, discovered Port Angeles, became the first white man to visit what is now the present harbor of Vancouver,[39] and may perhaps have entered the mouth of the Fraser River.

1792 saw the *Sutil* and *Mexicana* under Captains Galiano and Valdez[40] at Neah Bay, Boundary Bay and Esquimalt.[41] This latter area Galiano described as "fertile, covered with trees and plants, and these growths are almost the same as those of Nootka, but wild roses are most abundant".[42] Although neither ship was over fifty feet long, and held only about fifty men between them,[43] their work in constructing charts contributed much to European knowledge of these coasts, and the names of their captains have with justice been given to islands in the area.

Another remarkable navigator and explorer now enters the story—one also destined to leave his name writ large on the map. Captain George Vancouver, who had once sailed under Captain Cook, had been despatched to Nootka with the ships *Discovery* and *Chatham,* with instructions to receive the restored British property and to learn what he could of developments there. He was also to survey as much of the north Pacific coast as he could, and of course keep an eye out for the Northwest Passage.

Vancouver had been born on June 22, 1757, and was to die, probably from overwork, before his forty-first birthday. At this time, however, he was at the height of his career, and reaching North America in 1792, set to work energetically. Puget Sound[44] and the San Juan archipelago were explored, and their present names given to the Gulf of Georgia and Point Grey.[45] On June 22 Vancouver encountered the Spanish ships *Sutil* and *Mexicana,* with whom he exchanged friendly greetings; then the four little vessels proceeded for some distance together. Later, after taking leave of the Spaniards, he explored Queen Charlotte Sound and South Bentinck Arm, and finally, sailing this time down the west coast of the Island,[46] dropped anchor on August 28 at Nootka, now under the control of that most civilized and cultivated gentleman, Senor Don Juan Francisco de la Bodega y Quadra.

The two men soon developed an amicable relationship, which Vancouver signalized by calling what he now knew to be a very large island "The Island of Quadra and Vancouver". Much dining and wining went on between the two commanders, and on one occasion Quadra treated Vancouver to a memorable repast:

> A dinner of five courses, consisting of a superfluity of the best provisions, was served with great elegance; a royal salute was fired on drinking health to the sovereigns of England and Spain, and a salute of 17 guns to the success of the service in which the *Discovery* and the *Chatham* were engaged.[47]

The courtly Spaniard also sent Vancouver two sheep, some

cabbages and a cask of rum, as well as hot rolls every morning.[48] During this period the two leaders paid an official visit to the famous chief Maquinna, where they were royally received.[49] Vancouver also discovered that even the more equivocal aspects of civilization were now represented on the island: a Mr. Magee, master of the merchant ship *Margaret* of Boston, was found to be happily pursuing a profitable avocation as the area's first bootlegger.[50]

The two congenial commanders, however, were unable to agree on their rights in the Nootka area, and decided to refer the matter to their respective governments. Lieutenant Broughton, in charge of the *Chatham,* was sent on the long voyage back to England for instructions. On the way, he sailed up the Columbia River and took possession of it for England. In the meantime, Vancouver went south to San Francisco and then wintered in the Sandwich Islands.

In the spring of 1793 he was back at Nootka, and spent a busy summer exploring the B.C. coast as far north as the Portland Canal. Then, after a second winter in the Sandwich Islands, he spent his final season in B.C. waters, by which time it was established beyond all doubt that the Northwest Passage or "Strait of Anian" was imaginary—or at least that it was well north of 60° latitude.[51]

In the meantime, back in Europe, negotiations were under way between Madrid and London. The two governments, both alarmed by events in France, were moving closer together, and it was agreed that Spain would withdraw its settlement from Nootka, that the British flag would be raised there, and that in future both countries would merely visit there. On March 23, 1795, commissioners met there for a ceremony in which British possessions were restored, and not long after the Spanish fort was dismantled.[52]

So ended Nootka's few brief years of glory. Walls crumbled, the grass crept over the ruins; overhead, the seagulls screamed forlornly; curious Indians explored the buildings where once the strange white tribes had lived. In the long-houses, as the smoke swirled upward, another tale was added to the legends told around the fire; and far away in Spain a few would treasure in their hearts the memory of a land where from great snow-capped mountains the rivers rushed down to the blue sea.

Meanwhile, the same outward thrust of Western Europe, with its triple-pointed quest for power, wealth and knowledge, that had brought Quadra and Vancouver half way around the world, was operating in the continent at their back. From the moment that the first colonists had settled in New England, the tide of humanity had moved westward, halting for a moment at a river or a mountain range, then lapping over it and moving on.[53] In the course of time, it came to be realized that, led by the trader and the explorer, it must come at last to the Pacific, and it was in fact in 1793, while the Spanish were trying to preserve some of the courtly manners of sunny Castile under the damp skies of Nootka, that Alexander Mackenzie was inscribing his name and immortal achievement— "From Canada, by land"—on a great rock near Bella Coola.[54]

He had been the first; but soon, painfully working their way across the sea of mountains, or venturing their lives in frail canoes on fierce rivers as they surged through deep gorges to the sea, came others. Mackenzie, in the employ of the North West Company (formed in 1784, with headquarters at Montreal) had reported that there was an abundance of fur in the land beyond the great mountains, and Simon Fraser,[55] another employee of the Company, was chosen to continue his work. In one of the most difficult and dangerous journeys on record, he made his way in 1808 to the Pacific Coast, discovering and naming the Thompson River and then, after terrible hazards and hardships, he reached the mouth of the great river to which he gave his name, and from which he glimpsed the mountains of Vancouver Island.

Another who made his way toward the great sea in the search for furs was David Thompson,[56] who on July 15, 1811, reached the mouth of the Columbia River, where he found already established an American expedition, sent by John Jacob Astor, a rising merchant of New York. The ownership of this area was not yet decided, and the two groups mingled amicably.

Rapidly, in the next few years, a network of trading posts spread throughout the Northwest. Furs were sent not only eastward toward Europe but occasionally westward across the Pacific to Canton. The American company under Astor did not prosper, and soon the North West Company had a virtual monopoly in the area.

With trade came wealth, and at some of the larger depots, such as Spokane House, most of the amenities were available.

Keen rivalry developed, however, with the Hudson's Bay Company, and it was soon apparent that the palmy days of the North West Company were over. Rather than see both companies perhaps go bankrupt, in 1821 they joined forces. The North West Company disappeared from history, and from now on, its former arch-rival, given exclusive trading rights by the British Government in the regions between the Great Lakes and the Pacific, dominated the scene. The Company also had posts eventually, we might note, as distant as the Sandwich Islands and Yerba Buena on San Francisco Bay, and had friendly relations with Russian fur-traders in Alaska.

The likelihood that territory south of 49° North would eventually come under American control (since this had been agreed upon as the boundary between British and American territory from the Rockies to the Great Lakes) now became a decisive factor in the thinking of the Company's superior officers. New forts were constructed, notably Fort Langley in the Fraser Valley in 1827, which (in restored form) may be visited by the tourist of today. A few retired employees of the Company took to cultivating patches of land, and agriculture had its modest beginnings. But fur was king, and the long trade-route from the B.C. interior to Europe was, though none perhaps called it so then, the lifeline of Empire.

At this time the Chief Factor of the Hudson's Bay Company at Fort Vancouver (in the present state of Washington) was John McLoughlin. Tireless and ambitious, he devoted himself to creating an efficient commercial empire in the northwest. One thing, however, he could not do: prevent the steady influx of American settlers into the Valley of the Columbia. Some day, he came to realize, this part of the world would be under the American flag. It was important, therefore, to find a centre of operations to the north of Fort Vancouver, one which, with luck, would remain under British control.[57]

To select such a site, he delegated one of his ablest lieutenants to search the shores of the Gulf of Georgia. His choice of lieutenant and the lieutenant's choice of a new trading centre were to prove fateful for some, at least, of the world's inhabitants; for the man whom McLoughlin chose was James Douglas, and the site that he selected was one day to be known as the City of Victoria.

FOOTNOTES

[1] An excellent account of Prince Henry and the explorations he inspired is to be found in Stefan Zweig's *Conqueror of the Seas,* Viking Press, 1938.

[2] The whole period 1500-1900 is placed in a larger perspective in Walter Webb's *The Great Frontier* (Boston, Houghton Mifflin, 1952).

[3] A discussion of the question may be found in R. P. Bishop's "Drake's course in the North Pacific", *BCHQ,* Vol. III, No. 3, July 1939.

[4] Drake has, however, been given credit for good intentions: the highest mountain on Vancouver Island (Mt. Golden Hinde, 7219 ft.) is named after his ship.

[5] Judge Howay describes him as merely a "fortunate liar" (*BCHA 1st annual report of proceedings,* 1923, p. 17). See also his (unrepentant) views in *BCHA 3rd annual report of proceedings,* 1925, p. 22-28. No reference to Juan de Fuca has yet been discovered in the Spanish archives.

[6] For accounts of Russian explorations in the Siberia-Alaska area see H. H. Bancroft's *History of Alaska 1730-1885* (San Francisco, 1886). Also J. R. Masterson and Helen Brower: *Bering's Successors 1745-1780* (U. of Washington Press, 1948).

[7] Gregori Ivanovich Shelekhov in 1784 established at Three Saints Bay on Kodiak Island, the first permanent Russian trading station in North America. (Galbraith, J. S., *The Hudson's Bay Company as an Imperial Factor, 1821-1869,* U. of Toronto Press, 1957, p. 114.

[8] The standard work on Spanish explorations in this area is Henry R. Wagner, *Spanish Explorations in the Strait of Juan de Fuca,* Fine Arts Press, Santa Ana, California, 1933.

[9] M. Ormsby, *British Columbia: A History,* Macmillan Company of Canada, 1958, p. 7.

[10] Wagner says "There is no evidence that he ever entered Nootka Sound or what was afterwards known as the Port of Nootka." (*Spanish Explorations,* p. 1).

[11] Wagner declares Quadra "reached the coast of Alaska" (*Spanish Explorations,* p. 1).

[12] Scholefield and Howay, *British Columbia from the earliest times to the present,* 4 vols., S. J. Clarke, Vancouver, 1914, Vol. I, pp. 75-76. The act had originally only applied to the ships of private owners, but was amended to include ships of the Royal Navy.
See also Bancroft, *History of British Columbia,* San Francisco, 1890, pp. 3-4.

[13] *The Three Famous Voyages of Captain James Cook 'Round the World,* Ward, Lock, Bowden and Co., London, n.d. p. 867.

[14] *Voyages*, p. 867.

[15] *Ibid.*, p. 863.

[16] *Ibid.*, p. 867.

[17] *Ibid.*, p. 869.

[18] *Ibid.*, pp. 871-2.

[19] *Ibid.*, pp. 875-6.

[20] Judge Howay, in his first presidential address to the B.C. Historical Association (October, 1923) says: "About 1500 sea-otter skins were thus obtained at a cost of, perhaps, sixpence each. Six of the very finest, says Captain King, were purchased for a dozen large glass beads." (*BCHA, first annual report of proceedings*, 1923, pp. 18-19).

[21] Cook, *Voyages*, p. 859.
Judge Howay denied this (Scholefield and Howay, *British Columbia from the earliest times to the present*, Vancouver, 1914, Vol. I, p. 125). The evidence, however, is all against him. James Strange, who visited Nootka in 1786, declared that cannibalism was prevalent. (See "James Charles Stuart Strange and his expedition to the north-west coast of America in 1786", by John Hosie, *4th annual report of BCHA.*) Strange was personally offered three human hands and a head (p. 50).
See also Mayne, *Four Years in British Columbia and Vancouver Island*, London, 1862, pp. 256-7 and 287; Macfie, *Vancouver Island and British Columbia*, London, 1865, p. 436; *Journal of Service of Lt. C. W. Wilson, R.E.*, PABC, entry for June 28, 1859.

[22] Cook, *Voyages*, p. 864.

[23] A letter from the Spanish ambassador in London to the British Foreign Secretary, dated Feb. 10, 1790, dealing with the "Nootka Sound Controversy" and mentioning the spoons, may be found in J. S. Marshall and C. Marshall, *Vancouver's Voyage*, Mitchell Press Ltd., Vancouver, 1967, p. 188.

[24] The surgeon of the *Captain Cook*, John Mackay, being ill, was left with the natives for a year. He learned their language and when picked up later declared his belief that the area was not part of continental America (Bancroft, *History of B.C.*, p. 5). Bancroft calls him McKey.

[25] Dixon gave their present names to Dixon Strait and the Queen Charlotte Islands.

[26] John S. Galbraith, *The Hudson's Bay Company as an Imperial Factor, 1821-1869*, U. of Toronto Press, 1957, p. 116.

[27] John T. Walbran, *British Columbia Coast Names, 1592-1906*. Published for the Geographic Board of Canada, Ottawa, 1909, pp. 33 and 35.

[28] M. Ormsby, *British Columbia: A History*, p. 14.

[29] See *BCHA, 4th report of proceedings*, pp. 33-36.
A cairn on Gonzales Hill, Victoria, gives Barkley credit for discovering the Straits of Juan de Fuca, and Commander John Meares, R.N., credit for being the first to enter it in 1788. The hill was given the name Gonzales by Quimper in 1790.

[30] Some dramatic events in which the *Lady Washington* was involved are

detailed in B. A. McKelvie, *Tales of Conflict*, Vancouver Daily Province, 1949, pp. 6-9.

[31] An account of the entire Nootka controversy is given in Marshall and Marshall, *Vancouver's Voyage*, Mitchell Press, Vancouver, 2nd edition, pp. 53-78. A full statement by Meares of his claims may be found in Begg, *History of British Columbia*, Toronto, 1894, pp. 28-31. Also Marshall and Marshall, *Ibid.*, pp. 189-195. See also *The Dixon-Meares Controversy*, ed. F. W. Howay, Ryerson Press, Toronto, 1929.

[32] Ormsby, *British Columbia: A History*, p. 18.

[33] On May 5, after a royal message, the House almost unanimously voted a grant of £2,000,000." (*Ibid.*, p. 18). Scholefield and Howay (*British Columbia from the earliest times to the present*, Vol. I, p. 150), declare £1,000,000 was voted on June 10, 1790, "to enable His Majesty to act as the exigency of affairs might require."

[34] Quimper Street, Victoria, is named after him.

[35] H. D. Parizeau, "Hydrographic Survey of the Northwest Coast of British North America from the earliest discoveries to the present time," *BCHA, 4th annual report*, pp. 10-19.
"In the year 1888 there died out in Esquimalt an ancient Indian woman whom they called 'Old Jane'. She had lived to the great age of well over one hundred years, for some of the coastal tribes are remarkable for their longevity, and she could distinctly recall the first ship which ever sailed into Esquimalt harbour . . . " (N. Lugrin and J. Hosie, *The Pioneer Women of Vancouver Island, 1843-1866*, Victoria, 1928, p. 190.

[36] Wagner, *Spanish Explorations*, p. 16.

[37] *loc. cit.*
See also L. B. Robinson, *Esquimalt, "Place of Shoaling Waters"*, Quality Press, Victoria, 1947, p. 15.

[38] Named after Quimper's first mate, Gonzalo de Lopez de Haro. (Robinson, *Esquimalt*, p. 15).

[39] Robinson, *Ibid.*, p. 16.

[40] Both later fought at the Battle of Trafalgar in 1805. (Robinson, *Ibid.*, p. 17).

[41] Robinson, *loc. cit.*

[42] Robinson, *loc. cit.*

[43] Scholefield and Howay, *History of British Columbia*, Vol. I, p. 165.

[44] Puget Sound was named after Peter Puget, 2nd Lieutenant of the *Discovery* (Walbran, p. 404); Point Roberts was named after Captain Henry Roberts, the previous captain of the *Discovery*, with whom Vancouver had sailed with Cook in the *Resolution* (Walbran, p. 425). Vancouver gave their present names to Mt. Rainier "after my friend Rear-Admiral Rainier", and the Hood Canal "after the Right Honourable Lord Hood".

[45] The Gulf of Georgia was named after King George III; Point Grey after Captain George Grey, R.N. (Walbran, p. 218); Point Atkinson after an unknown "particular friend", (Walbran, p. 26).

[46] It is not strictly speaking correct to say that Vancouver circumnavigated

the Island. He was, however, the first to demonstrate that it was an island.

[47] Vancouver, *A voyage of discovery to the North Pacific Ocean,* London, John Stockdale, 1801, 6 vols. Vol. 2, Ch. 10, pp. 336-7.

[48] See Marshall and Marshall, *Vancouver's Voyage,* p. 65.

[49] An interesting account of Maquinna is given in *Maquinna the Magnificent* by B. A. McKelvie (Vancouver Daily Province, 1946. Copyright Southam Company, Ltd.)

[50] Marshall and Marshall, *Vancouver's Voyage,* p. 65.

[51] The Northwest passage was eventually found by Roald Amundsen who, with six companions in the 47-ton sloop *Gyoa* sailed from Oslo on June 16, 1903 and reached Nome on the Bering Sea on August 31, 1906. See article by T. A. Rickard, "The Strait of Anian", *BCHQ,* V. 3, July, 1941.

[52] A few Spanish relics from Nootka and Esquimalt have been found. See Robinson: *Esquimalt: place of shoaling waters,* Quality Press, Victoria, 1947, p. 21.

[53] See L. J. Burpee, *The Search for the Western Sea: The Story of the Exploration of North-Western America.* Rev. ed., Toronto, Macmillan, 1935.

[54] See A. P. Woollacott, *Mackenzie and his voyageurs, by Canoe to the Arctic and the Pacific, 1789-1793.* J. M. Dent, London and Toronto, 1927.

[55] See Scholefield and Howay, *History of British Columbia,* I., 235-282. Also *Letters and Journals of Simon Fraser, 1806-1808,* ed. W. K. Lamb, Toronto, Macmillan, 1960.

[56] See David Thompson, *Narrative, 1784-1812* (ed. R. Glover, Toronto, Champlain Society, 1962).

[57] Curiously enough, when the boundary was finally decided in 1846, McLoughlin elected to remain to the south of it, and became the "Father of Oregon", dying in Oregon City in 1857.

The Bastion at Victoria showing part of the original log palisade

Donald Ross

Roderick Finlayson

Governor Richard Blanshard

CHAPTER THREE

The
Fort

The site we intend to build upon is well adapted to the purpose of scttlcment; it lies about half a mile off the main strait of De Fuca, in a snug sheltered cove from 5 to 10 fms. deep, accessible at all seasons to vessels, which may anchor within 50 feet of the bank on which the Fort will stand. A narrow canal passes the Fort and runs 5 miles into the interior of the Island, affording, at one point, a water power of incalculable force, and abundance of Pine with other valuable timber on its bank. The place itself appears a perfect "Eden", in the midst of the dreary wilderness of the Northwest coast, and so different is its general aspect, from the wooded, rugged regions around, that one might be pardoned for supposing it had dropped from the clouds into its present position.[1]

Such were the first impressions of James Douglas, set down after a preliminary survey of the site in the summer of 1842, the year before he dropped anchor at Clover Point and began the establishment of the earliest permanent settlement on Vancouver Island.

He himself had once been accustomed to far different scenes, for as a boy he had known life on the sugar plantations of South America. All the facts of his origin, however, are not yet established beyond dispute, and some mystery still surrounds the background of the man who was to become "the father of British Columbia".

John Douglas had been a Glasgow merchant with business interests in Demerara, British Guiana. Here he formed an alliance with a woman who may have been a Creole, but whose name is unknown to us; her famous son only mentioned her once, so far as is known, in all his writings, and then only to say that she died in July 1839.[2] This sort of arrangement was by no means uncommon in those days, and is paralleled by the Indian "wives" often taken by the fur-traders of North America until well on into the nineteenth century.[3]

Of this union there were at least three children: Alexander, born in 1801 or 1802; James, born in 1803; and Cecilia Eliza, born in 1812.[4] The birth certificates of these children have never been located, so there is perhaps a faint chance that James was not born in Demerara (Dr. Walter Sage, the distinguished author of *Sir James Douglas and British Columbia,* was told by Douglas' daughter that he was born in Lanarkshire);[5] however it seems almost certain that the future Chief Factor of Fort Victoria and Governor of British Columbia first saw the light of day in South America.

Certainly in the records of the Hudson's Bay Company he is described as a "West Indian" or a "Scotch West Indian",[6] and Letitia Hargrave, wife of the Chief Trader at York Factory, whose family was closely connected with the Company and well acquainted with its leading personalities, went so far as to declare in a letter written in 1842 to her mother that "Mr. Douglass is a *mulatto,* son of the renowned Mr. Douglass of Glasgow."[7]

A degree of uncertainty surrounds not only Douglas' origins, but also the exact date of his birth. In his own handwriting he gives it as June 5,[8] yet the family monument in Ross Bay Cemetery, Victoria, bears, cut into the enduring granite, the date August 15.

It is thus possible that the future governor of Vancouver Island, representative of Queen Victoria, and first citizen of the increasingly respectable nineteenth century society of the capital of British Columbia, was both illegitimate and part-colored, and rumors to this effect were in circulation throughout his career. This in turn may account for some conspicuous features of his character. Those who feel conscious of a deficiency in their backgrounds (Alexander

Hamilton and James Ramsay Macdonald are two names that come readily to mind) often exert themselves more than others in an effort to attain pre-eminence. This may have been one factor in making Douglas such a faithful and resolute servant of the Company and later of the Crown. On the other hand, the uncertainty of his origin may have been responsible for the unbending dignity with which he at all times comported himself in public life.

This latter aspect of Douglas was noted by many; for example, by Dr. J. S. Helmcken (later his son-in-law), who in his *Reminiscences* set down his first impressions (1850) of him:

> I saw Mr. Douglas—he did not impress me very favourably, being of a very grave disposition with an air of dignity—cold and unimpassioned. A dark complexioned man with rather scanty hair, but not too scanty—muscular—broadshouldered —with powerful legs a little bowed—common to strong men; in fact he was a splendid specimen of a man.[9]

1850, however, was still many years in the future and we must now trace the course of events that led from the hot climes of equatorial America to the balmier airs of southern Vancouver Island, and from such equivocal beginnings to posts of increasing dignity, responsibility, and power.

Young James Douglas and his brother both were sent to Scotland for their education (we shall see later the continuation of Cecilia's story), and both in due time entered the service of the North West Company. The elder brother, however, seemed unsuited to the work or the country, and after a short period abandoned both. With James, however, the story was very different. He had entered the service of the Company in 1819 as a clerk, and sailed in May of that year for the New World in the brig *Matthews,* arriving in Quebec from Liverpool on June 25.

The winter of 1819-20 he spent in the chilly climate of Fort William on the shore of Lake Superior. Promotion at first was slow, for in 1821 he was still only a "second class clerk". This was the year, we should note, in which the North West Company merged with the Hudson's Bay Company and so disappeared from history. For five years, from 1820 to 1825, he was at Ile-a-la-Crosse, on the upper waters of the Churchill River in Northern Saskatchewan,[10] and probably spent the summer of 1825 at Fort Vermilion in the Peace River District. The winters of 1826-27 and 1827-28 he spent at Fort St. James on Stuart Lake in what is now central British Columbia, where he married "after the custom of the country" Amelia,[11] daughter of Chief Factor Connolly, whose wife was of Indian blood. Amelia was then sixteen. (Later, when he was stationed at Fort Vancouver, their marriage would be solemnized by an Anglican clergyman,[12] but in the meantime the young couple were, as it would be phrased nowadays, "living common law", a fact that would in days to come provide yet further material for gossip in the burgeoning young settlement of Victoria.)

All the events of these early years cannot be given in detail, but one may be recounted that illustrates both the age and the man, and which in an unforeseen way brought him nearer his ultimate destiny.

In the year 1828, as previously noted, Douglas was stationed at the remote outpost of Fort St. James. Some years previously, in 1823, at the outpost of Fort George (now Prince George) two Indians, working for the company, enraged at what they considered an insulting reprimand by their two white overseers, attacked and killed them in the night, cut off their heads and disappeared. One of the two murderers eventually lost his life at the hand of another tribe, but the other remained at large. Diligent search was made for him by the Company, but for five years without success.

Then in the summer of 1828 Chief Quah (or Kwa), ruler of the Carrier Indians[13] in the Stuart Lake District, held a great feast not far from Fort St. James. William Connolly, Chief Factor at the Fort, was away at the time, and his son-in-law was left in charge. Word was secretly brought to him that the long-sought murderer was in the nearby village. Taking several men, Douglas searched the houses of the Indians and finally came upon the wanted man. What happened next is a matter of dispute. Father Morice in his *History of the Northern Interior of British Columbia*[14] who declared his account to be a "careful digest of all the accounts of the affair by disinterested native and surviving Hudson's Bay Company parties" says that "with hoes and the remnants of a camp-fire nearby, his assistants stunned the Indian and reduced his lifeless body to the condition of a shapeless jelly. Then, by order of Douglas, they passed a stout rope around his neck and proceeded to drag him in the direction of the Fort. 'The man he killed was eaten by the dogs; by the dogs he must be eaten,' declared the inexorable clerk.[15]

On the other hand, John Tod, who knew Douglas well, declared in his memoirs that the Indian "made a thrust at Mr. Douglas' head. The latter and the others shot at the man, but all missed him, whereupon one of the party, not Mr. Douglas, struck the murderer on the head with the barrel of his gun and killed him."[16] Tod makes no reference to the disposal of the corpse, but whether this was because no indignity was offered to it or from loyalty to an old associate, it is impossible to say.

Another account of the incident, by a presumably well-informed writer, John McLean, is even briefer: "He proceeded to the camp accompanied by two of his men, and executed justice on the murderer."[17]

None of these three accounts is that of an eyewitness. We do, however, have two references to the affair by one who was there— Douglas himself. Reporting at the time to Connolly, he mentioned the murderer "whom we dispatched on the first of the month, in the Indian village of this place, without confusion or any accident happening to any other individual",[18] while many years later in 1873, writing to his daughter regarding newspaper stories about the affair, he declared: "True, I seized the Indian, a noted murderer, as stated, and secured him after a desperate struggle, but I did not shoot him with my own hands; he was afterwards executed for his crime. It was a desperate adventure, which nothing but a high sense of duty could have induced me to undertake."[19]

Where the exact truth lies between these several versions is now impossible to determine. One may, however, note that all accounts except this last support the view that as soon as the murderer was apprehended, he was despatched in the presence of Douglas. When we reflect that standards of acceptable conduct changed greatly between the earlier and the later years of the nineteenth century, just as Douglas himself in this period changed from a fur-trader's assistant to Sir James Douglas, K.C.B., we are justified, I think, in concluding that in this paternal missive the supposedly immutable historical record has also undergone a metamorphosis in keeping with the standards of a more sophisticated age.

A similar variation is also perceptible in accounts of the sequel to this affair. All are agreed that one hot summer afternoon some time later Chief Quah (who felt that his rights as a host had been infringed) invaded the fort with some of his warriors, demanding trade goods with which to recompense the dead man's relatives. Douglas was overpowered—how strenuous a struggle first ensued is unclear—and forced to agree to these terms. Father Morice represents the chief's nephew as pointing a dagger at Douglas' heart, asking "Shall I strike?", and tells us that at this critical juncture two of the women in the fort threw down the ransom in the form of clothes and other trade goods from the balcony above, an action which satisfied the Indians and may have saved Douglas' life.[20]

McLean on the other hand declares that the interpreter's wife overawed the angry natives with a stirring harangue, which resulted in the freeing of Douglas and an "amicable conference."[21]

Tod declares that the Indians "rushed into the building, tied and threw all the men into a heap, and then, in spite of his desperate resistance, overpowered Mr. Douglas, and binding him hand and foot, deposited him writhing and shouting on the table of the mess hall", where after some hours of this enforced impotence, he agreed to his captor's terms. Tod makes no mention of any intervention by the women and says that "the incident was soon forgotten by us in the district, and by none more willingly than by the future Knight Commander of the Bath, whose just mind, I daresay, notwithstanding the ever present feeling of the 'ropes', appreciated Kwa's position in the premises."[22]

It is thus by no means clear just what happened that hot afternoon over a century ago, but it seems certain that relations remained tense. Late that same year, on December 9, 1828, while en route with two men to Fraser Lake, Douglas was surrounded by an angry band of about 120 Indians, who declared their intention of killing him. Deciding that flight might be even more dangerous than standing his ground, he boldly faced them down and after an interval of great tension succeeded by his unflinching attitude in convincing them that discretion was the better part of valor.

It was apparent, however, that future encounters of this sort could be expected, and Chief Factor Connolly decided it would be best if his son-in-law were stationed in a different area. Accordingly, with the approval of the higher officials of the Company, Douglas left the district of New Caledonia on January 30, 1830, and proceeded to Fort Vancouver, with the testimonial from Connolly that "wherever he may be placed he cannot fail of being essentially useful."[23]

At Fort Vancouver it soon became apparent that Douglas was living up to this estimate of his abilities. He was appointed second-in-command to the redoubtable John McLoughlin, and pursued his duties, mainly as an accountant, with efficiency and despatch. He also had his marriage officially solemnized according to the rites of the Anglican Church.[24]

The fur trade continued to prosper, half a million dollars worth of pelts being shipped to London each year.[25] In 1835, the same year that saw Douglas promoted to the rank of "Chief Trader",[26] the ship *Beaver*,[27] built in England and sent out around the Horn, became the flagship of the small HBC fleet, and steamed industriously between the Company's various posts on the Pacific Coast.

Under these favorable conditions Fort Vancouver, centre of operations for the whole Columbia district, blossomed, though in a somewhat rough and ready way, into a microcosm of the larger world. At the table in the great dining-hall, voyageurs just in from a long journey through uncharted wildernesses, where they had perhaps drunk

> *the gilded puddle*
> *Which beasts would cough at*,[28]

exchanged experiences over their wine with sea captains who had looked upon strange sights in the South Seas. Well-tilled fields outside the Fort provided the necessities of life, while sawmills and flour-mills made their contribution to the welfare of the inhabitants. Over all presided the genial McLoughlin, benevolent autocrat of this vast area over which as yet no other government held sway; while at his side, marked for destiny, awaiting his hour, stood his vigilant second-in-command.

Time passed; the Douglases soon had a small family;[29] far away, an old king died; in his place sat a girl of eighteen, destined after the longest reign in British history to see the dawning of the next century. Slowly but surely, by no man's single will, Europe was changing from the agricultural to the industrial system; factories were displacing handicrafts, masses of lost and driven humanity were draining down from the hills and dales into the Great Wen of London; while above the ignorant armies of capital and labor a new sign appeared in the sky—"Get on, get honour, get honest"— and thousands resolved in this new faith to conquer.

But on the far Pacific Coast these tidal waves washed up as scarce-felt ripples, and as year by year the pelts arrived at the Fort and were shipped out again to the greedy buyers of the world, it might well have seemed that as it was, so it would always be.

And so, indeed, for a few years more it continued. Slowly but steadily, Douglas rose in the estimation of his superiors. Sir George Simpson,[30] from 1826 to 1860 overseas governor-in-chief of all HBC territories, and tireless inspector of even its remoter posts, recorded his opinions of all the Company's officials in a confidential "Book of Servants' Characters" (now in the HBC archives in London). About Douglas he had this to say in 1832:

A Scotch West Indian; About 33 Years of Age, has been 13 years in the Service. — A stout powerful active man of good conduct and respectable abilities: — tolerably well Educated, expresses himself clearly on paper, understands our Counting House business and is an excellent Trader. — Well qualified for any Service requiring bodily exertion, firmness of mind and the exercise of Sound judgement, but furiously violent when roused. — Has every reason to look forward to early promotion and is a likely man to fill a place at our Council board in course of time.—Stationed in the Columbia Department.[1]

By this time, however, it had been realized, at least by the more perceptive directors of the Company's fortunes, that that part of the "Oregon Territory" south of 49° would almost certainly come under American control, and that sooner or later a substitute for Fort Vancouver would have to be found. An added factor in reaching this conclusion was that supply ships had been repeatedly wrecked on the bar at the mouth of the Columbia River.

As early as 1834, indeed, Governor Simpson had been told by the London Headquarters of the Company to find a suitable location on Puget Sound, and he in turn gave orders to McLoughlin to this effect. The mouth of the Fraser, at first favored by Simpson, was soon rejected, once it was realized that the river was virtually impassable.[32] Inevitably, this focused attention on Vancouver Island.

In the summer of 1837 Capt. McNeill in the indispensable *Beaver* explored the southern part of the Island. Before long, McLoughlin was informing his superiors that McNeill, who had apparently explored the vicinity of what are now Victoria, Esquimalt and Sooke, had "found an excellent harbour, of easy access with good anchorage, surrounded by a plain of several miles in extent, of an excellent soil".[33] In the spring of 1838 Douglas wrote enthusiastically to Governor Simpson:

> The plains are said to be fertile and covered with luxuriant vegetation; but judging from a sample of the soil brought here, I think it rather light and certainly not of the best quality, admitting even this disadvantage I am persuaded that no part of this sterile & rock bound coast will be found better adapted for the site of the proposed Depot or to combine, in a higher degree, the desired requisites of a secure harbour accessible to shipping at every season, of good pasture, and, to a certain extent, of improvable tillage land.[34]

Events did not immediately take shape, however, possibly due to the secret opposition of McLoughlin, who had considerable influence in the higher circles of the Company, and who visited London in the fall of 1838.[35] Some confirmation of this is given by McLoughlin's report to Governor Simpson in the spring of 1840, soon after his only visit to the Island in the fall of 1839:

> It is a very fine harbour, accessible at all seasons, but it is not a place suitable to our purpose . . .[36]

In 1840 Douglas believed for a time that a new post at the northern end of the Island might be best, as affording quicker relations with the Queen Charlotte Islands. With this view McLoughlin professed himself in accord.

For a time in 1840 Douglas was engaged in an even more distant area. He headed an expedition to Alaska, arriving in Sitka on May 25. Here he discussed matters of mutual interest with Governor Kopreanoff. It was agreed that the HBC should occupy the Russian post at the mouth of the Stikine River, that it should supply the Russians with wheat, butter and meat, and that a fair division of the fur trade should be effected. Douglas was not much impressed by what he saw of Russian management practices, considering that their fur-trading companies were over-staffed with naval officers, frequently replaced and with no great interest in the commercial success of their companies.

Later in the same year Douglas was at almost the southern end of the Pacific coast. Leaving Fort Vancouver on December 3, 1840, he arrived on New Year's Day 1841 at Monterey. One purpose was to decide whether the Company should establish a trading post on San Francisco Bay. Douglas discussed commercial matters with the Mexican authorities[37] through an interpreter,[38] and reached mutually advantageous agreements. In March of 1841 he was once more back at Fort Vancouver.[39]

It is interesting to note in passing that, like so many visitors from the more northerly part of the coast, Douglas was much beguiled by sunny California — almost, indeed, to the point of settling there. Writing to a friend on his return, he declared ". . . I would nevertheless cheerfully become a citizen of that country provided that I could do so in company with a party of friends respectable from their numbers, and powerful enough to restrain oppression".[40]

In 1841 Governor Simpson, the chief official of the Company in North America, made his memorable journey around the world,[41] in the course of which he visited nearly every outpost of the far-flung empire of fur. Reaching Fort Vancouver on August 25, he was welcomed by Douglas. The two men then went to Sitka, Alaska for talks with the Russians. In March of 1842 Simpson reported to his superiors in London:

The Southern end of Vancouver's Island forming the Northern side of the Straits of De Fuca, appears to be the best situation for such an establishment. From the very superficial examination that has been made, it is ascertained there are several good harbours, in that neighbourhood no place, however, has yet been found combining all the advantages required, the most important of which are, a safe and accessible harbour, well situated for defence, with water power for Grist and Saw Mills, abundance of Timber for home consumption and Exportation and the adjacent Country well adapted for tillage and pasture Farms on an extensive scale. I had not an opportunity for landing on the southern end of the Island, but from the distant view we had of it in passing between Puget's Sound and the Gulf of Georgia and the report of C. F. McLoughlin and others who have been there, we have every reason to believe there will be no difficulty in finding an eligible situation in that quarter for the establishment in question.[42]

Simpson also believed that establishing a post in this area would serve two other useful purposes: it would be a convenient centre for salmon and whale fisheries, and it would strengthen Britain's claim to the whole of Vancouver Island. To Douglas was assigned the task of re-examining the area and selecting the exact site for the post. He did so, and on July 12, 1842 submitted a detailed report to his superiors.[43]

Two possible sites which he examined and rejected were Sooke and Esquimalt, which he referred to under their Indian names (as he understood them) of "Sy-yousung" and "Is-whoy-malth". The former, he declared,

. . . is a spacious Inlet, extending more than Two Miles into the Country, where Shipping may lie at all Seasons of the Year in perfect Safety, as it is protected from every wind; there is, however, a strong Current setting through the Entrance with the Flood and Ebb that might detain and prove inconvenient to Vessels entering or leaving Port, otherwise it is unexceptionable as a Harbour.[44]

The latter, on the other hand,

. . . is the next Harbour to the Eastward, and appears on the Ground Plan accompanying this letter. It is one of the best

Harbours on the Coast, being perfectly safe and of easy Access, but in other respects it possesses no Attraction.[45]

By this, Douglas meant that there was no large level area on which to erect a fort and grow food for its inhabitants. In contrast, Victoria (which he called Camosack,[46] and other early settlers would call Camosun), seemed exactly suited to the needs of the Company:

> On the contrary, at Camosack there is a pleasant and convenient Site for the Establishment within Fifty Yards of the Anchorage, on the Border of a large Tract of clear Land, which extends Eastward to Point Gonzalo at the South-east Extremity of the Island and about Six Miles interiorly being the most picturesque and decidedly the most valuable Part of the Island that we had the good Fortune to discover . . .
>
> Being pretty well assured of the Capabilities of the Soil as respects the Purposes of Agriculture, the Climate being also mild and pleasant, we ought to be able to grow every Kind of Grain raised in England . . . . We are certain that Potatoes thrive and grow to a large Size, as the Indians have many small Fields in cultivation, which appear to repay the Labour bestowed upon them, and I hope that the other Crops will do as well.[47]

It is clear from this that the proximity of good agricultural land was the decisive factor in the selection of the site, and present-day residents of Saanich are thus entitled to remind the city-dwellers to the south of them that they owe their existence to the pleasant countryside beyond the metropolitan area!

Douglas, with his keen vision, was also able to see yet further possibilities for this area, which when he visited it was inhabited only by Indian fishermen:

> As a harbour it is equally safe and accessible and abundance of timber grows on it for home consumption and exportation. There being no fresh water stream of sufficient power, flour or saw mills may be erected in the Canal of Camosack[48] at a Point where the Channel is constricted to the breadth of Forty-seven Feet by Two Ridges of Granite projecting from either bank into the Canal, through which the Tide rushes out and in with a Degree of Force and Velocity capable of driving the most powerful Machinery, if guided and applied by mechanical Skill.[49]

Douglas was in fact enthusiastic about the whole project, and outlined his ideas to Sir George Simpson in a letter dated March 10, 1843:

> . . . I am confident that the place from its situation and accessibility, will eventually become a centre of operation, either to ourselves or to others who may be attracted thither, by the valuable timber and exhaustless fisheries of that inland sea.
>
> I would therefore purpose to make the stores roomy and substantial, and the Fort on a plan of at least 300 feet square, so that when it is up we may not be put to the expense and derangement of incessant changes and extensions.[50]

This was closely in accordance with the views of the Council, i.e., the North American top management of the Company, which, meeting at Norway House, had decided:

> That the New Establishment to be formed on the Straits de Fuca to be named Fort Victoria be erected on a scale sufficiently extensive to answer the purposes of the Depot; the square of the Fort to be not less than 150 yards; the buildings to be substantial and erected as far apart as the grounds may admit with a view to guarding against fire.[51]

Accordingly, setting out in the *Beaver*, Douglas reached Shoal Point about four in the afternoon of March 14, 1843. The events of the next few days may be followed in the pages of the diary which he kept, and which is now in the Provincial Archives, Victoria:

> Wednesday 15th March. Went out this morning with a boat and examined the wood of the north shore of the harbour; it is not good, being generally short, crooked and almost unserviceable. On the south shore, the wood is of a better quality and I think we will have no difficulty in getting enough for our purpose. Small wood for picketing is scarce, particularly cedar which answers better than any other kind for that purpose from the lightness and greater durability underground. We will probably have to bring such as we require from a distance . . .
>
> I am at a loss where to place the Fort, as there are two positions possessing advantages of nearly equal importance

though of different kinds. No. 1 has a good view of the harbour, is upon clear ground, and only 50 yds. from the beach, on the other hand vessels drawing 14 feet cannot come within 130 feet of the shore, we will therefore either have to boat cargo off and on at a great destruction of boats, and considerable loss of time or be put to the expense of forming a jettie at a great amount of labour. No. 2 on the other hand will allow of vessels lying with their sides grazing the rocks, which form a natural wharf, whereon cargo may be conveniently landed from the ship's yard, and in that respect would be exceedingly advantageous, but on the other hand, an intervening point intercepts the view so that the mouth of the Port cannot be seen from it, an objection of much weight in the case of vessels entering and leaving Port, another disadvantage is that the shore is there covered by thick woods to the breadth of 200 yards so that we must either place the Fort at that distance from the landing place, or clear away the thickets which would detain us very much in our building operations. I will think more on this subject before determining the point. The weather rather cloudy, but dry, and beautifully clear in the afternoon.

Thursday 16. The weather clear and warm. The gooseberry bushes growing in the woods beginning to bud.

Put 6 men to dig a well and 6 others to square building timber. Spoke to the Samose[52] to-day and informed them of our intention of building in this place which appeared to please them very much and they immediately offered their services in procuring pickets for the establishment, an offer which I gladly accepted, and promised to pay them a Blanket for every forty pickets of 22 feet by 36 inches which they bring. I also lent them 3 large axes, 1 half sqre head Do. and 10 half round head axes, to be returned hereafter, when they have finished the job.

Bought a few salmon today at 2 charges of ammunition each . . . .

Friday 17th. Clear warm weather. Frost last night . . . Saw a luminous streak in the heavens this evening, which lasted from dusk until 9 o'clock, when the moon rose and obscured it. Its highest altitude was at Betelguix in Orion, due south from the position we occupied at the time of its appearance, & extended from thence, in a continuous line to the south west point of the horizon, forming an arc of about 90 degrees . . . We cannot account for this phenomenon, unless we may suppose that it is produced by the reflection of the waters in the Straits of De Fuca, although it is difficult to account for its existence even on any such principle. It was also seen last night.[53]

Six men digging the well.

Saturday 18th. Men employed as yesterday. The well is now about 11 feet deep. The luminous appearance still visible in the same position it occupied last night. It faded away about 11 o'clock.

Sat. 18, Sun. 19, M. 20, T. 21. Fine weather. Luminous column still visible in its former position.

At this point the diary breaks off, and it is thought likely that Douglas, satisfied that the work had been satisfactorily begun, left to pick up the men from the two more northerly posts (Fort Durham on Taku Inlet and Fort McLoughlin on Millbank Sound) which were to be closed down.

However, by an interesting chance, we have yet another account of these earliest days of the Fort, one written by a very different sort of observer. Father J. B. Bolduc, a Roman Catholic priest, had been travelling throughout the far west of North America at this time, bringing the gospel to the pagan Indian tribes. Finding that Douglas was about to sail for Vancouver Island, he accompanied him on his voyage across the Straits. He was not, of course, as is sometimes claimed, the first priest to visit the Island—there had been Spanish priests at Nootka some seventy years before— but he was the first in the area now known as Victoria, and the pages of his journal devoted to his brief stay in this area make interesting reading, especially as his purpose in seeking out this remote corner of the continent was so different from the rest of his travelling companions, being focused not on furs but souls.

It was about four o'clock in the afternoon when we arrived there. At first we saw only two canoes; but, having discharged two cannon shot, the aborigines left their retreats and surrounded the steamboat. The following day canoes arrived from all sides. Seeing that there was no danger, I landed with the commander of the expedition and the captain. Yet it was only after several days, that is to say, when I had unmistakable proofs of their good dispositions, that I went to their village, situated at six miles from the harbor at the base of a charming little bay. Like almost all of the surrounding tribes, this one possesses a stockade fort of about 150 feet square. They fortify themselves to provide shelter from the Yougletas, a powerful and warlike tribe, part of which inhabit Vancouver Island itself, the rest inhabiting the continent to the north of the Fraser River. These ferocious enemies fall, usually at night, on the villages they wish to destroy, kill and massacre as many of the men as they can, and take the women and children as slaves. On top of posts in the fort one sees many human heads sculptured and painted in red or black, and occasionally both colors together.

On my arrival the whole village, men, women and children, arranged themselves in two lines to shake hands with me, a ceremony which they would not omit for a great deal. I counted 525 individuals, apart from absent ones. I assembled them all in the largest lodge, the chief's. I spoke to them of a God, Creator of all things, Rewarder of good acts, and punishing evil by eternal retribution . . . .

One day when I was speaking to them of baptism, and said to them that already several tribes had had their children baptized, an old man arose and said to me: "Your words are good; but we have been told that those that were baptized of the Kwaitlens and the Kawitshins (on the Fraser River) died almost immediately; however, as you say it is a good thing, we believe it. Since that will make us see the Master on high after death, baptize all those in our camp; do them this charity; they are to be pitied; almost all die." I told them that I would return on Sunday to baptize them, and that all ought to be there . . . .

The 18th being Saturday, I employed it for constructing a temporary altar for celebrating on land the Lord's day. M. Douglass gave me several of his men to help me in that work. Long fir branches formed the sides; the awnings of the steamboat the covering.

On Sunday early in the morning, more than 1200 natives from three large tribes, Kawitshins, Klalams and Tsamishes, assembled around the modest temple. Our bourgeois forgot nothing that could contribute to rendering the ceremony imposing; I was put even to choosing on board all that could serve as decoration. He was present in person at the mass, as well as several Canadians and two Catholic ladies. It was among this numerous gathering that, for the first time, our holy mysteries were celebrated on that ground, for so many

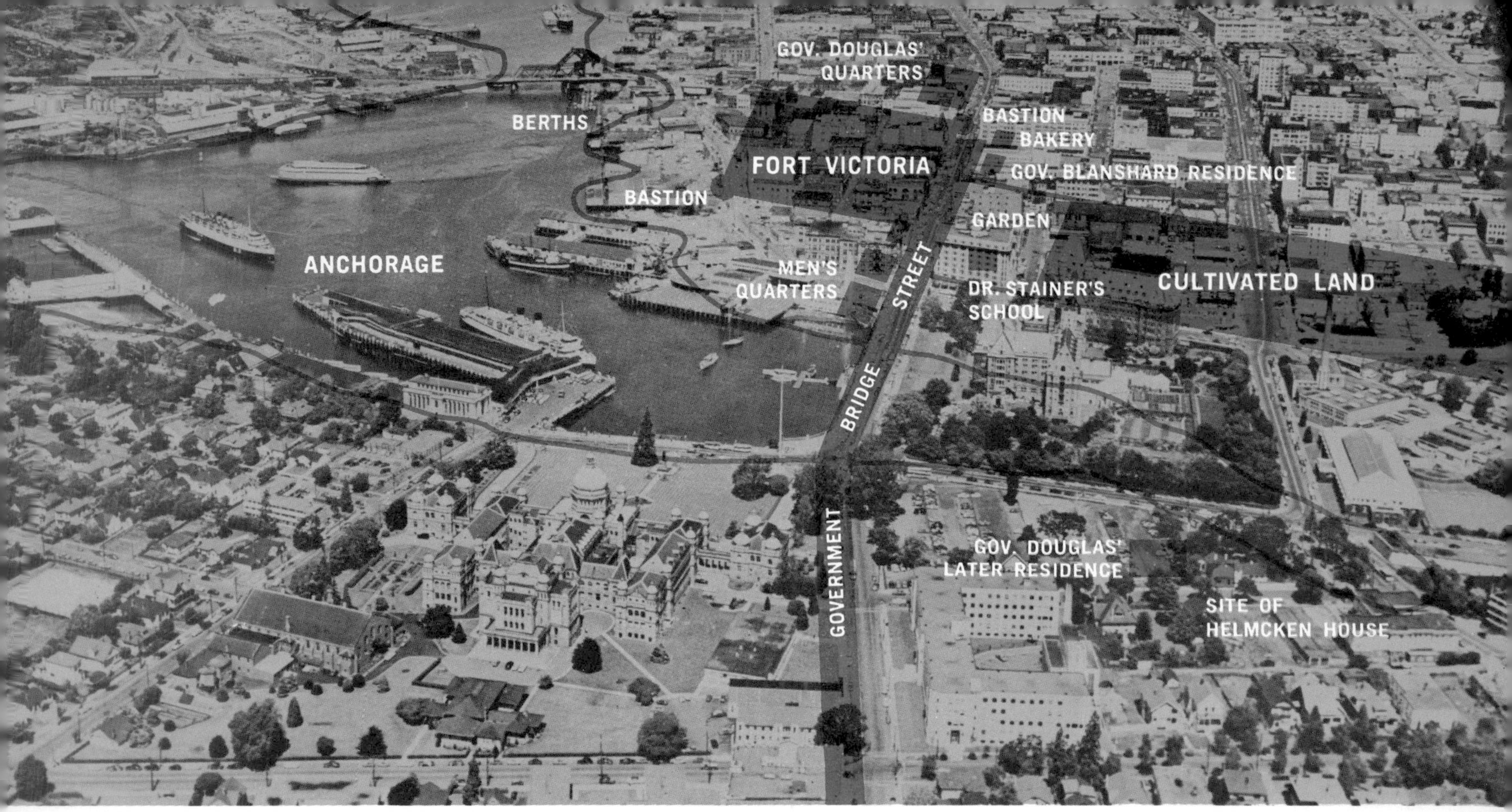
GOV. DOUGLAS' QUARTERS
BERTHS
BASTION BAKERY
FORT VICTORIA
GOV. BLANSHARD RESIDENCE
BASTION
GARDEN
ANCHORAGE
MEN'S QUARTERS
STREET
DR. STAINER'S SCHOOL
CULTIVATED LAND
BRIDGE
GOVERNMENT
GOV. DOUGLAS' LATER RESIDENCE
SITE OF HELMCKEN HOUSE

The overlay of this aerial of modern Victoria, with Empress Hotel and Parliament Buildings, the harbor shoreline and Government Street as landmarks will indicate where, in 1857, the old fort and its environs were located. Bastion Square today is all that formally marks the fort's site. A tidal estuary was where the Empress Hotel now stands. The New Provincial Museum and Mr. Helmcken's preserved house stand near where Governor Douglas built his residence.

Chief Maquinna

Sir Alexander Mackenzie

Simon Fraser

Dr. John McLoughlin

years the theater of hell's abominations. May Heaven effect that the Blood of the Lamb without stain make fertile this land, and cause it to produce an abundant harvest![54]

Later, however, when writing to his superior, Father Bolduc confessed a certain amount of doubt regarding the depth and permanence of these conversions:

> You see, sir, by this correspondence that the natives of Puget Sound show quite a zeal for prayer; yet they hardly understand the meaning of the word. If it had only been a matter of knowing some prayers, of singing canticles to be a Christian, there would not have been one not desiring to be one. But there is a major consideration that holds them back, that of morals. As soon as that chord is touched, their enthusiasm becomes indifference. The chiefs make vehement harangues to their people; but what impression can they produce, they who are the most guilty? I know several of the chiefs that have as many as five wives, others four, three, rarely fewer. I do not in any way mistrust Providence, but I have every reason to fear lest the moment of grace may be past for them as well as for many others who have not wanted to receive the good news. One may say without too much risk of being mistaken that there is not much to be expected of all the tribes inhabiting the shores of the ocean or at the mouths of the numerous rivers that empty into it.[55]

Both Father Bolduc and Douglas left the Island shortly afterward, the former to search for converts elsewhere in the great Northwest, the latter to proceed northward to pick up the men and supplies of Fort Durham on Taku Inlet and Fort McLoughlin on Millbank Sound, which the Company had decided to abandon. On the first of June, with the personnel of these two posts, Douglas returned. He now had under his authority about fifty armed white men, but realizing that in the event of trouble with the Indians this would be but a weak force, he set to work immediately to construct a defensible compound.

The weather was exceptionally favorable, and with the help of Indian labor the work went ahead rapidly.[56] Douglas himself had to return to his duties at the Company's main depot at Fort Vancouver; Charles Ross was placed in charge with Roderick Finlayson as his second in command.[57]

Douglas was of course kept fully informed of developments, and in November was able to describe the new Company outpost to Governor Simpson:

> It is in form a quadrangle of 330x300 feet intended to contain 8 buildings of 60 feet each, disposed in the following order say 2 in the rear facing the harbour and 3 on each side standing at right angles with the former leaving the front entirely open. The outhouses and workshops are to be thrown in the rear of the main buildings and in the unoccupied angles, so as not to disturb the symmetry of the principal square. So much for the plan now for the progress made in carrying it out. On the 21st September when we last heard from Ross the Pickets and defences were finished, and two of the buildings completed so far as to be habitable, and they were engaged in hauling out the logs of a third building.
>
> The climate of the place is pleasant, and I believe perfectly healthy.[58]

In January 1844 Ross also wrote to Simpson, and we glean a few more details of the Fort:

> Our progress in regard to the Establishment is as follows— a Quadrangle of 330 by 300 feet surrounded by stoccades, eighteen feet high—one Octangular Bastion of three stories erected—also two men's houses, and one Store each measuring 60 by 30 ft. with 17 ft. Posts & Pavilion roofs. These have been thoroughly completed, and an Officers' & main house of 60 by 40 ft. are rapidly advancing to the same end.[59]

Ross also makes reference to the first beginnings of farming on the Island. It had always been Company policy that posts should be as far as might be self-supporting; suitable seeds were supplied to those founding new settlements, but after that they were expected to maintain themselves. Ross had not been negligent in this regard:

> The farming is as yet little more than in embryo—there being only about five acres under cultivation and about the same quantity prepared for the Plough.[60]

Ross added some other interesting comments:

> Nothing can be finer than the climate and scenery of this place. The former, especially, surpasses anything I ever before

experienced—for from the month of June up to the present moment, we have scarcely yet had four & twenty hours of consecutive wet weather.[61]

The main purpose of the settlement was not, of course, neglected. In the first season, between 300 and 400 furs, mostly beaver and otter, were purchased from the Indians,[62] and it seemed likely this trade would increase.

The opening months of the fledgling settlement, then, were auspicious; the men on the spot, Douglas at Fort Vancouver, the higher authorities of the Company in the East and in London, might all be satisfied with the new venture.

The next year, 1844, saw some difficulties, but they were successfully surmounted. Charles Ross "died, much regretted, in March, and was buried in the old burying ground near the gully, on Johnson Street now",[63] and the command of the Fort devolved upon Roderick Finlayson, then only 26.[64] Almost at once he was faced with a serious crisis in his relations with the Indians, who formed a considerable settlement on the shores of what is now the Inner Harbour. Writing in his old age, Finlayson gave his account of this affair; beneath his matter-of-fact language one detects little sense of fear or danger, but it is hard to believe that some was not felt at the time.[65]

In 1844 mattters went on for some time smoothly enough after Mr. Ross died, when it was found that the natives killed some of our oxen feeding in the open spaces. I then questioned the Songees chief about this and demanded payment, as we could not allow our cattle to be killed in this way with impunity. He went away in a rage, assembled some Cowichan Indians to his village and the next move I found on their part was a shower of bullets fired at the fort, with a great noise and demonstration on the part of the crowd assembled threatening death and devastation to all whites. I had then to gather up our forces and man the bastions, and did not allow any of our men outside the Fort until I could settle the matter with the Indians. Noticing the chief's lodge, the largest among the others I directed the interpreter, a half-breed, to go outside, to pretend he had deserted from us, and to tell them as from himself that I was going to fire on the chief's lodge and to see that all inmates had left it in order to prevent bloodshed, and to make a sign to me, at the same time watching matters from the bastion, by twisting his handkerchief round, that all was vacant, which he did. I then fired a nine pounder with grape in, and pointed the gun to the lodge, which flew into the air in splinters like a bombshell, after this there was such howling that I thought a number was killed, and was quite relieved when the interpreter came round and told me none were killed but much frightened, not knowing we had such destructive arms. The chief, with some of his men, shortly after this, came to the gate and asked to see me, I went and assumed a warlike attitude and mentioned that unless the cattle killed were paid for I would demolish all their huts and drive them from the place. The reply was that he would pay and asked the price, which was named, and the next day payment in full in furs were made, when peace was restored and hand shaking took place I mentioned to them, through the interpreter, that we came here to trade peaceably with them and did not want war unless we were forced to, so ended this disagreeable affair.[66]

Another less serious incident took place a short time afterwards; this was also handled without difficulty:

Some time after this the belt of thick wood between the fort and Johnson Street in front of which the lodges were placed, took fire and we had some difficulty in extinguishing it as it was gaining towards the fort, and this fire having been caused by the Indians I wanted them to remove to the other side of the harbor which they at first declined to do, saying the land was theirs and after a great deal of angry parleying on both sides, it was agreed that if I allowed our men to assist them to remove they would go, to which I consented. This was the origin of the present Indian Reserve.[67]

So passed the first full year of the Fort's existence: its defence had been secured, and both farming and fur-trading were successfully under way. The next five years were a time of gradual progress, but no very striking developments—the charting of the main harbours in the area; a few visitors from the great outside world, and finally, in the course of time, the first independent settlers. Yet there is something of interest in all these matters, and it will not perhaps be amiss if they are accorded a few pages.

1845 saw the arrival of the first visitors to the area after the founding of the Fort. Two army officers, Lieutenants Warre and Vavasour, were sent out by the British government to make a first-hand report[68] on the military and economic potential of the colony. Although not very much impressed by the former, the latter struck them greatly. "The fisheries (salmon and sturgeon) are inexhaustible, and game of all descriptions is said to abound. The timber is extremely luxuriant, and increases in value as you reach a more northern latitude . . . The cedar and pine become of an immense size."

With regard to another matter, still one of controversy a century later, they ventured an analysis and a prediction:

> The total abolition of the sale of intoxicating liquors has done much for the good of the whole community, white population as well as Indian; and so long as this abstinence (which can hardly be called voluntary) continues, the country will prosper. When this prohibition is withdrawn and the intercourse with the world thrown open, such is the character of the dissolute and only partially reformed American and Canadian settlers, that every evil must be anticipated, and the unfortunate Indian will be the first to suffer.

Also in this year, H.M.S. *America* arrived in the harbour under the command of Capt. the Hon. John Gordon, brother of the Earl of Aberdeen, then Foreign Secretary of Great Britain. Also on board was Lieut. William Peel, son of Sir Robert Peel the Prime Minister. The officials of the Fort did their best to entertain their distinguished visitors, but without great success. Finlayson recorded that:

> We had some fine horses for the use of the Captain and his officers & we paid them every attention. We went out on one occasion to Cedar Hill (Mount Douglas) to shoot about the first of June. The country looked beautiful, with beautiful wild flowers. Capt. Gordon was a great deer stalker. We met a band of deer & had a chase after them on horseback. The deer ran for a thicket into which the horses with their riders could not penetrate and of course no deer were had.[69]

This incident seems to have soured the aristocratic Captain Gordon; his disillusion deepened to disgust when he learned that these benighted colonials caught their salmon by trolling, and not, as a gentleman should, with a fly. He has, however, a certain historical significance as the first of a long line of Britons to complain that Victoria was not English (or, in his case, Scottish) enough.

However, Capt. Gordon and Lieut. Peel in due course vanished below the horizon, the Fort breathed again, and the year 1846 brought rather more congenial visitors.

Among these were the officers and crew of the survey ships *Fisgard* and *Pandora*. The commander of the former was Capt. Duntze, while the brig *Pandora* was under the command of Lieut. James Wood. The two ships began the charting of Victoria and Esquimalt harbors. Here they did much good work, as well as lending their names to numerous natural features of the area, Duntze Head, Cole Island, Paterson Point, Ashe Head, Richards Island, Dunn's Nook and Rodd Hill being all named after various officers of these two ships.[70] H.M.S. *Herald* (which afterwards searched fruitlessly for Sir John Franklin) was also for a time in these waters.

For a time in 1846 it seemed as if this area, uninhabited by whites only four years before, might be the base for actual warfare. The boundary with the United States was still in doubt and it looked possible that it might be determined by force.[71] Six British warships anchored in the area for a time, ready to visit the Imperial wrath upon the insolent Republic; however, the boundary was amicably settled (with Fort Vancouver, as had long been expected, to the south of the line) and the war scare soon died down. It had been a profitable interlude while it lasted—the Company farms did a thriving business in supplying the warships with meat, flour and vegetables. (For beef the farms received 8c a lb., "which paid us well in those days".)[72]

A few whalers also called at Victoria during this period[73] and the *Vancouver* became the first HBC ship to sail directly from England (via the Horn) to Victoria. The steam vessel *Cormorant* also arrived in these waters, charged with the task of discovering if there were, as rumoured, good coal deposits in the middle part of the Island. In general, however, the port was still considered off the main world trade route.[74]

It was in 1846, also, that John McLoughlin finally retired from the HBC service and was succeeded by Douglas as Chief Factor. Fort Vancouver, however, was still the Company headquarters in the Northwest, though it was realized that this arrangement could not be of much longer duration.

The agricultural side of the Company's venture continued to develop in this period. There were several farms, notably the Fort Farm (where the city business district now stands), Beckly Farm (in southern James Bay) and the North Dairy Farm. There were three dairies, one at a place below "Church Hill" (the site of the present Anglican cathedral), one in the Gonzales area, and one at the North Dairy Farm. Each had 70 milch cows, which produced 70 kegs of butter in a season. Other farm products were oats, barley, peas and potatoes, while grain was shipped as far away as Sitka.[75] Forty bushels to the acre was not an uncommon yield.[76]

In this period, too, Finlayson went to the San Juan Islands where he set up a sheep farm and salmon fishery.[77] These latter ventures were, however, given up when controversy developed with the Americans over the ownership of the Islands.

There is a picture of the young settlement at this time given by Berthold Seemann, who as naturalist of H.M.S. *Herald,* was in Victoria in June 1846. Like countless residents of the area since, he evidently liked to stroll here and there as the fancy took him, and he gives us an account of both the scenery and the works of man:

> In walking from Ogden Point round to Fort Victoria, a distance of little more than a mile, we thought we had never seen a more beautiful country; it quite exceeded our expectation; and yet Vancouver's descriptions made us look for something beyond common scenery. It is a natural park; noble oaks and ferns are seen in the greatest luxuriance; thickets of the hazel and the willow, shrubberies of the poplar and alder, are dotted about. One could hardly believe that this was not the work of art; more particularly when finding signs of cultivation in every direction—enclosed pasture-land, fields of wheat, potatoes and turnips.
> . . . About 160 acres are cultivated with oats, wheat, potatoes, turnips, carrots, and other vegetables, and every day more land

is converted into fields. Barely three years had elapsed since the settlement was made, yet all the necessaries and most of the comforts of civilized life already existed in what was a wilderness. The company, when forming an establishment such as Victoria, provide the party with food for the first year, and necessary seed for the forthcoming season; after that time it is expected that the settlements will provide completely for their future subsistence. Of course the settlers have many facilities—the fertility of virgin soil, an abundant supply of the best seed, and that great inducement to industry, the desire of independence, and the assurance almost amounting to certainty, that success will attend their endeavours.

Seamann noted also:

. . . a trading house, in which smaller bargains are concluded, and tools, agricultural implements, blankets, shawls, beads, and all the multifarious products of Sheffield, Birmingham, Manchester and Leeds are offered at exorbitant prices. There being no competition, the company has it all its own way; it does not profess to supply the public; indeed, although it does not object to sell to people situated as we were, yet the stores are for the trade in furs, to supply the native hunters with the goods which they most value, as also for the use of its own dependents, who, receiving little pay, are usually in debt to the company, and are therefore much in its power. In fact, the people employed are rarely those to whom returning home is an object; they have mostly been taken from poverty, and have at all events food and clothing. The work is hard, but with health and strength this is a blessing rather than otherwise.[78]

The next year saw another visitor, though of a somewhat different kind. Paul Kane, an artist, was at this time wandering about North America, sketching and describing the various Indian tribes. In April 1847 he came to Victoria, and set down what he saw:

The appearance of the interior, when seen from the coast, is rocky and mountainous, evidently volcanic; the trees are large, principally oak and pine. The timbers of a vessel of some magnitude were being got out. The establishment is very large, and must eventually become the great depot for the business of the Company. They had ten white men and forty Indians engaged in building new stores and warehouses. On the opposite side of the harbour, facing the fort, stands a village

of Clal-lums Indians. They boast of being able to turn out
500 warriors, armed chiefly with bows and arrows. The lodges
are built of cedar like the Chinook lodges, but much larger,
some of them being sixty or seventy feet long.[79]

Some aspects of Indian life did not however excite much admiration in Kane:

> One morning while I was sketching, I saw upon the rocks
> the dead body of a young woman, thrown out to the vultures
> and crows, whom I had seen a few days previously walking
> about in perfect health. Mr. Finlayson, the gentleman in
> charge of Fort Victoria, accompanied me to the lodge she
> belonged to, where we found an Indian woman, her mistress,
> who made light of her death and was doubtless the cause of it.
> She told us that a slave had no right of burial, and became
> perfectly furious when Mr. Finlayson told her that the slave
> was far better than herself. "I," she exclaimed, "the daughter
> of a chief, no better than a dead slave!" and bridling up with
> all the dignity she could assume, she stalked out, and next
> morning she had up her lodge and was gone. I was also
> told by an eye-witness of a chief, who having erected a
> colossal idol of wood, sacrificed five slaves to it, barbarously
> murdering them at its base, and asking in a boasting manner
> who amongst them could afford to kill so many slaves.[80]

Kane seems to have attributed these deficiencies in Indian civilization to their faulty perceptions of theology:

> They do not believe in any future state of punishment,
> although in this world they suppose themselves exposed to
> the malicious designs of the skoocoom, or evil genius, to whom
> they attribute all their misfortune and ill luck.[81]

At the Fort 1848 was another year of quiet steady development.
This was not so in Europe, however; there it was to be in many
lands the "Year of Revolutions", and timorous souls feared even
for the throne of England. Yet, though the revolutions and their
British counterpart, the Chartist movement, were largely failures,
notice had been served that autocracy must yield to something
more democratic, and, as we shall see, all this was eventually,
though in a delayed and diffused way, to have its influence on
developments in the tiny settlement eight thousand miles away.

To most residents of the Fort, however, the main event of 1848 was the visit of Her Majesty's frigate *Constance,* which was the first British man-of-war to visit Esquimalt Harbour.[82] Her commander was Capt. George William Courtenay (after whom Courtenay Street, Victoria is named; Constance Avenue in Esquimalt is a reminder of his ship). He reported that 300 acres were under cultivation, and that the company farms held 80 cows and 24 brood mares.

By this time, too, we might note, there was a sawmill at Mill-stream,[83] and it was in this year, too, that the Fort received the accolade of having its portrait appear in the *Illustrated London News* (August 26, 1848).[84]

1849 was undoubtedly to prove the most important year since the construction of the Fort. Not only were there several interesting arrivals at Victoria,[85] notably the first resident chaplain-schoolmaster and the first independent colonists, but the government of the settlement was reorganized in keeping with its increasing importance.

The chaplain was the Reverend Robert Staines, who was to play a more active role in the affairs of the colony than his calling might suggest. Born in 1820, a graduate of Cambridge, he was a sound classical scholar and had taught with success at Derby Grammar School. He was pursuing his career in France when on the recommendation of a friend he was given the appointment at Fort Victoria. As the year was 1848 and revolution apparently impended in Europe, he lost no time in accepting the position.[86] He was not at that time an ordained clergyman, but in August of that year he "took holy orders" and on September 12th left (by way of the Sandwich Islands) for Victoria.

It is interesting to note that while en route to take up his duties he first heard of the California gold rush. "The sensation it had caused throughout the Pacific is almost inconceivable,"[87] he wrote to his friend Rev. Edward Cridge soon after his arrival at Victoria, unaware that in due time—after his own death, in fact—those now feverishly scrabbling for the precious metal in California would suddenly be diverted, like a swollen river, in the direction of Victoria, transforming it irrevocably and almost overnight from a fur-trading post to a city.

Gold did not, however, so far as we know, figure further in the young schoolmaster's thoughts. With the promise of a salary of £100 a year (plus £340 as a teacher, of which £40 was an allowance for a servant), he came ashore on March 17, 1849. With him was his wife,[88] a well-educated woman, proficient in music and French, who was to assist him in his teaching duties.

The first impressions received by this cultured pair must have been dismaying in the extreme. Roderick Finlayson many years later set down a description of what they found on their arrival:

> At this time there were no streets, the traffic cut up the thoroughfares so that every one had to wear sea boots to wade through the mud & mire. It was my duty to receive the clergyman, which I did, but felt ashamed to see the lady come ashore. We had to lay planks through the mud in order to get them safely to the Fort. They looked around wonderingly at the bare walls of the buildings and expressed deep surprise, stating that the Co. in England had told them this & that & had promised such & such. Anyway their rooms were fitted as best could be done.[89]

Despite this unpromising beginning, the Staines settled quickly into their duties. Their pupils took their lessons in the upper storey of one of the main buildings of the Fort—"Bachelor's Hall"— where they endured the rigors of unheated dormitories and Mr. Staines' uncertain temper, somewhat compensated for by occasional picnics and excursions into the countryside. One of the pupils in Victoria's first school, James Anderson, who was born in 1841, arrived at the Fort from Langley with his sister by canoe in 1850, and lived to become B.C.'s first deputy minister of agriculture, set down in 1925 a vivid account of these early days, and we shall have occasion to give extracts from it in a later chapter.

Another interesting newcomer in 1849 was Captain Walter Colquhoun Grant, who has the distinction of being Vancouver Island's first independent settler.[90] Born in Edinburgh in 1822 of a distinguished military family, he became a captain at an early age. When the Hudson's Bay Company began advertising in the English newspapers for settlers, Grant decided to try his luck in the new world. He applied for the position of surveyor in the colony, was accepted, and arrived in the *Harpooner* with eight workmen in the summer of 1849.[91]

From the beginning, however, his luck (or his own deficiencies) worked against him. Finding that the Company controlled all the choice land around the Fort, he established himself at Sooke,[92] 28 miles away. From this vantage-point he attempted simultaneously to farm on his own account and survey the Victoria area. He was clearly unprepared for conditions in the colony, as:

> He brought with him articles of every description which he thought to be necessary for an emigrant. Needless to say, the great majority of the articles were of no earthly use; sets of carriage harness, there being no carriages nor suitable horses, and similar useless articles of all descriptions. The cricket sets he brought and presented to the school, however, proved to be most acceptable and we unanimously voted Captain Grant a fine fellow.[93]

Despite his enthusiasm for cricket, however, his qualifications as either farmer or surveyor were tenuous, and his ventures soon came to grief, in the latter case much to the annoyance of Douglas. He had moreover mortgaged almost his entire first year's pay to buy equipment and steamship tickets. His gallant but ineffectual efforts to make some sort of success of things were to be spread over the next four years, and we shall have occasion to look at them again in a later chapter.

The year 1849 also saw a very different and unexpected group of visitors to the Fort. Though no one apparently realized it at the time, its residents were being given a foretaste of events a decade later. To Roderick Finlayson, however, in charge of the Fort, what he beheld seemed less an arrival than an apparition:

> In the Spring of 1849 a vessel appeared in the harbor, the crew of which wore red flannel shirts, and when they landed we took them to be pirates. I ordered the men to the guns, manned the bastions and made ready for defence. I then interviewed the men, from the gate, who told me they were peaceable traders, come from San Francisco, with gold, to trade for goods, as this was the only station on the northern coast where they could get the goods they wanted. Having satisfied myself that they were what they represented them-

selves to be, I let them in, and they then told me that gold
had been discovered in California in large quantities the
previous Fall, and that they had gold nuggets which they
would gladly exchange for goods. They produced several
nuggets, the value of which I at first felt doubtful of, but
brought one of the nuggets to the blacksmith's shop, and told
him and his assistant to hammer it on the anvil, which they
did, and flattened it out satisfactorily. I then referred to my
book on minerals, and found that the specimens appeared
to me to be genuine. I then offered them $11 per ounce for
their gold, which they accepted without a murmur, and having
thus mentioned my price and receiving no objections, I felt
doubtful but concluded to accept it, and the trade went on.
They then took in exchange such goods as were not required
for our own trade, such as old pots of iron, sea boots, blankets,
baize, etc., for which I got satisfactory prices. I thus traded a
considerable sum in gold nuggets, the amount of which I
cannot now call to mind, but, being doubtful as to the value
I put on the gold, I dispatched a canoe with eight hands,
to Puget Sound, and thence to the head depot at Vancouver,
with specimens of my trade, and asking whether I was right
or wrong. The answer was that I was right, and that more
goods would be sent me to carry on the trade. Afterward
another vessel came to trade in the same way, when one of
the traders offered me $1,000 per month if I would go and
take charge of his store in San Francisco, as clerks were scarce
there. Then my reply was that I declined with thanks, when
he mentioned "I guess you must be pretty well paid here."
I, at the same time, had a salary of £100 per annum from
the Company, which, of course, I did not tell him. I was,
however, under an engagement with the Company to give
twelve months' notice before quitting the service, so I remained
at my post. This, and several other vessels came from California to trade, from which considerable quantities of gold was
received in trade. After this our operations here got considerably disarranged, by numbers of our men leaving for
the California diggings, including the sailors from our ships,
when pay had to be considerably increased to induce them to
remain. We had to employ Indians as sailors to replace our
seamen in the ships and labourers on land.[94]

By far the most important development in the history of Victoria
to this point, however, was the transfer by Royal Grant early in

1849 of the entire Island to the Hudson's Bay Company. The Oregon Territory had passed irrevocably under American control in 1846, and the Company was anxious to gain a secure hold on the remaining part of the Northwest.[95] The original aim of its representatives, notably Sir John Pelly, was to acquire the whole of the territory north of 49° and west of the Rocky Mountains, but Lord Grey, speaking for the British Government, felt that Vancouver Island would be sufficient.

Not everyone in England, however, was partial to the new proposal. The Company did not apparently have a good "image" at that time; perhaps it was felt to be a relic of the age of monopoly in an era when Free Trade was in the ascendant.[96] At all events, there were numerous protests against transferring any land at all to the Company.[97]

This did not deter the British Government from ceding Vancouver Island to the Company on January 13, 1849, at the rather reasonable annual rent of seven shillings.[98] In return, the Company agreed to bring out colonists and sell them land at a fair price, using the proceeds (less 10% for the Company) to improve the colony; if no colony had been established within five years, then the British Government could resume control of the Island.

Even these proposals and conditions aroused sharp opposition in the British Parliament. One speaker, the Earl of Lincoln, denounced them for no less than four and a half hours, touching on a wide variety of matters from the Company's treatment of the Indians to its secrecy regarding its operations.[99] Not too many British M.P.'s, however, were keenly interested in the subject, a vote to censure the Government for its action was defeated 76 to 58,[100] and the Royal Grant was duly agreed to.[101]

The question of the first governor for the colony was also considered, and although both the officials of the Company and the British Government would have liked the position to go to Douglas as the best qualified man, the authorities in London felt it prudent to bow somewhat to the winds of public opinion, and a virtually unknown barrister, Richard Blanshard, was appointed to the post.

As we shall see, this choice of the totally inexperienced Blanshard over the Chief Factor with half a lifetime of service in the field was to create in the new colony in the following two years a highly awkward situation for all concerned. This unfortunate series of developments, however, still lay in the future; and in early June of 1849 Douglas was transferred from Fort Vancouver to Fort Victoria, there as Chief Factor of the all-powerful Company to await, with who knows what emotions, the coming of Governor Blanshard.

FOOTNOTES

[1] *The Hargrave Correspondence*, ed. G. P. Glazebrook, Toronto, The Champlain Society, 1938, p. 420.

[2] W. K. Lamb, "Some Notes on the Douglas Family", *BCHQ*, Vol. XVII, January-April, 1953, p. 43. See also W. N. Sage, *Sir James Douglas and British Columbia*, U. of Toronto Press, 1930, p. 363.

[3] John McLoughlin's wife, for example, had Indian blood. (Sage, *Douglas*, p. 54). There is a vivid description of her quoted in Bancroft, *History of British Columbia*, San Francisco, 1890, p. 300.

[4] That the elder Douglas was prepared to labor in a variety of vineyards is evinced by his marriage in 1809 to Jessie Hamilton of Glasgow. (Lamb, *op. cit.*, p. 43).

[5] Sage, *Douglas*, p. 14.

[6] Douglas MacKay, *The Honourable Company*, McClelland and Stewart, Toronto, 1937, p. 200. John Tod, in his *History of New Caledonia and the North West Coast* (MS in *PABC*) calls him "a native of the West Indies".

[7] M. A. McLeod (ed.), *The Letters of Letitia Hargrave*, Toronto, The Champlain Society, 1947, p. 132.

[8] Sage, *Douglas*, p. 14.

[9] J. S. Helmcken, *Reminiscences*, MS in *PABC*, II, 84. Douglas' daughter, Cecilia, whom Helmcken married in 1852, was also "of dark complexion" (*Ibid.*, II, 85-86).

[10] He is said to have fought a duel here in 1820 with an employee of the rival Hudson's Bay Company. Sage, *Douglas*, p. 20.

[11] Admiral Moresby, in *Two Admirals* (London, John Murray, 1909, p. 121) calls her an "Indian princess". Margaret Ormsby in *British Columbia: A History* (Macmillan, 1958, p. 94) terms her a "half-breed".

[12] His name was (appropriately) the Rev. Herbert Beaver.

[13] So called because a widow was forced to carry her husband's bones about with her for a year after his death.

[14] Toronto, 1904.

[15] Morice, *op. cit.*, pp. 137-140.

16 John Tod: "Career of a Scotch Boy", *BCHQ*, July-October, 1964, Vol. XVIII, Nos. 3 and 4. Tod's memoirs originally appeared in several installments of the *Victoria Daily Times* in the last quarter of 1905. The memoirs were composed from material taken down by G. M. Sproat and G. H. Wilson-Brown in Tod's home in Oak Bay. Tod himself died in 1882 and Wilson-Brown in 1904.

17 John McLean, *Notes of a twenty-five years' service in the Hudson's Bay Territory*, London, 1849. Reprinted by the Champlain Society, Toronto, 1932, pp. 162-164.

18 B. McKelvie, *"Tales of Convict"*, Vancouver Daily Province, 1949, p. 28.

19 J. R. Anderson, *Notes and comments on early days and events in British Columbia, Washington and Oregon*, MS in *PABC*, 1925, p. 236.

20 Morice, *History*, pp. 137-140.

21 McLean, *Notes*, p. 164.

22 *BCHQ*, July-October 1964, Vol. XVIII, Nos. 3 and 4, p. 166.

23 Chief Factor Connolly to Governor Simpson, February 27, 1829. Quoted by B. A. McKelvie, *Tales of Conflict*, p. 30.

24 This was the first marriage performed by the Rev. Herbert Beaver at Fort Vancouver. Beaver had been personally selected by Governor Simpson when on a visit to England in 1835-36, and sailed from London in February 1836 on the HBC ship *Nereide*. Travelling by way of Honolulu, he arrived at Fort Vancouver on Nov. 6, 1836. He and McLoughlin were at odds from the beginning. Beaver wanted the children of the district taught according to the Anglican catechism, despite the fact that most of them were Roman Catholics. He also disapproved strongly of the common-law marriages of many of the Fort's personnel. In a report to the higher officials of the Company he had the temerity to refer to Mrs. McLoughlin (who had been married to her husband in a civil ceremony conducted by Douglas) as "a female of notoriously loose character" and "the kept mistress of the highest personage in your service". When this report came to the attention of Mr. McLoughlin, he gave the clergyman a good thrashing (March 19, 1838). Beaver soon afterwards returned permanently to England, where he wrote an impassioned article in a Church of England magazine, denouncing McLoughlin as "this monster in human shape". See *Oregon Historical Society Quarterly*, XXXIX, March, 1938, pp. 22-38; and pp. 65-73.

25 R. Haig-Brown, *Fur and Gold*, Longmans, Toronto, 1962, p. 29.

26 Sage, *Douglas*, p. 70.

27 It was eventually wrecked off Prospect Point, Vancouver, in 1888. There is a model of the ship in the Provincial Archives. See "The Advent of the Beaver", *BCHQ*, July 1938, pp. 163-179.

28 Shakespeare, *Antony and Cleopatra*, I. iv.

29 The full list of Douglas' 13 children, as taken from the family tree in the Provincial Archives, is as follows:

Amelia	1829-1830
Alexander	1831-1834
John	1833-1833
Maria	1834-1835

Hudson's Bay Company's SS BEAVER, first steamer on the Pacific
Coast of North America

Douglas on the site of Fort Victoria

Model of the Fort

Fur Trade Buildings with stockade at centre

Cecilia	1834-1865
Ellen	1836-1837
Jane	1839-1909
Agnes	1841-1928
Alice	1844-1913
Margaret	1846-1848
Rebecca	1849-1849
James	1851-1883
Martha	1854-1933

[30] The background of Simpson, for over 30 years the dominant figure in the Company, remains obscure. He was illegitimate (J. S. Galbraith, *The Hudson's Bay Company as an Imperial Factor, 1821-1869*, U. of Toronto Press, p. 20), and the date of his birth is unknown. *The Dictionary of National Biography* gives it as 1792, but the date on his tombstone in Montreal is 1787 (Galbraith, *loc. cit.*). Simpson himself had numerous illegitimate children (Douglas MacKay, *The Honourable Company*, McClelland and Stewart, Toronto, 1936, p. 198).

[31] MacKay, *The Honourable Company*, p. 200.

[32] Simpson made a personal survey of the Fraser in 1828. (Galbraith, *Hudson's Bay Company*, p. 181).

[33] McLoughlin to Governor and Council, October 31, 1837. E. E. Rich (ed.), *The Letters of John McLoughlin*, 1st series, 1825-1838, Toronto and London, 1941, p. 214.

[34] *Ibid.*, p. 286-7.

[35] W. K. Lamb, "The Founding of Fort Victoria", *BCHQ*, April, 1943, p. 77.

[36] March 20, 1840, HBC Archives. Quoted by W. K. Lamb, "The Founding of Fort Victoria", *BCHQ*, Vol. VII, no. 2, April, 1943, p. 77.

[37] California did not become American territory until 1846.

[38] Douglas had some knowledge of Spanish. There is a letter written by him in that language in the Provincial Archives.

[39] For a full account of Douglas' expedition to California, including his own impressions, see *James Douglas in California, 1841*, ed. Dorothy Blakey Smith, The Library's Press, Vancouver, 1965.

[40] Letter to A. C. Anderson, dated Fort Vancouver April 20, 1841. Quoted in Sage, *Douglas*, p. 109.

[41] Described in his *Narrative of an overland journey 'round the world during the years 1841 and 1842*. 2 vols., London and Philadelphia, 1847.

[42] Written from Honolulu, March 1, 1842. Transcript in *PABC*.

[43] It may be found in the *Beaver* for March, 1943, pp. 4-7.

[44] *Beaver*, March, 1943, pp. 4-5.

[45] *Ibid.*, p. 5.

[46] Some controversy exists over the names "Camosack" and "Camosun". Some find their origin in an Indian word meaning "swiftly flowing water" —a reference to the Gorge. Others believe they refer to the camass plant, very common on the original site of Victoria. See Robinson, *Esquimalt*, p. 28; also Kane, *Wanderings of an Artist*, Toronto, Radisson Society, 1925, p. 144.

47 *Beaver,* March, 1943, p. 6.

48 i.e., the Gorge.

49 *Beaver,* March, 1943, p. 4.

50 HBC Archives. Quoted by W. K. Lamb in "The Founding of Fort Victoria", *BCHQ,* April, 1943, p. 85.

51 *Beaver,* March, 1943, p. 9.
See also R. Haig-Brown, *Fur and Gold,* Longmans, Toronto, 1962, p. 35.

52 Douglas evidently believed this to be the name of the tribe. Actually it was Songhees or Songhish.

53 This was actually "The Great Comet of 1843", seen throughout the Northwest.
Douglas was always much interested in natural phenomena. Dr. Helmcken reported "I have heard Mr. Douglas expatiate on the beauties and flowers, and how much he was enamoured by his first exploration of Victoria District and Beacon Hill. (*Reminiscences,* III, 39). Some claim that the broom which flourishes around Victoria was brought there by Douglas; certainly there was none before his arrival.

54 *Notices and Voyages of the Famed Quebec Mission to the Northwest.* Oregon Historical Society, Champoeg Press, Portland, 1956, pp. 193-4.

55 *Ibid.,* p. 198. It will be observed that the reverend father, like so many men of the cloth, considered the Christian ethic essentially a sexual one. This point of view finds no support in the four gospels, but no doubt its champions have other sources of revelation.

56 According to Bancroft, the Fort was built without the use of a single nail, boards and beams being held together with wooden pegs. (*History of British Columbia,* San Francisco, 1890, pp. 115-6).

57 A letter by Ross, headed 'Fort Albert", is one item in a complex controversy over whether Victoria ever had any other name. (See W. K. Lamb, "The Founding of Fort Victoria", *BCHQ,* Vol. VII, No. 2, April, 1943; also Sage, *Douglas,* p. 123).
Finlayson in his "History of Vancouver Island and the Northwest Coast" (MS in PABC), declares "In the year 1845, the name of Camosun, previously given to the Fort, was changed to Fort Albert by order from England and the succeeding year to that of Victoria. On each occasion the baptism was performed with the usual ceremonies of firing salutes." (p. 23). This would appear at first decisive testimony, but we should remember that this was a recollection written down many years after the events.
Bancroft declares that bills of lading and other shipping documents headed "Port Camosun" exist dated as late as 1847 (*History of British Columbia,* p. 46).

The Provincial Archives at Victoria has a letter from Governor Sale of the HBC, written April 7, 1927, from Hudson's Bay House in London, and addressed to the Provincial Library, which casts some light on the matter. It is perhaps worth quoting in full:

You will remember that when I was in Victoria last August you asked me whether we had any information amongst the Company's Records with regard to the original name of the City of Victoria; there is no doubt that it was always the intention at headquarters for the new establishment in the Straits of De Fuca to be named "Fort Victoria". A resolution to this effect was included in the Minutes of Council for the Northern Department of Rupert's Land which were held at the Red River Settlement in June, 1843, and instructions were accordingly conveyed to Chief Factor John McLoughlin in charge of the Western Department by letter from Sir George Simpson dated 21st June, 1843.

On examination, however, of a Log Book of the schooner *Cadborough* it would appear that when the fort was first established in 1843, it was called Fort Camosun and then Fort Albert pending definite instructions from headquarters. We find references to Fort Camosun in July, 1843, and to Fort Albert continuously from August to December of that year. As further proof that the Fort was designated Fort Albert between August and December, 1843, a letter from Chief Trader Charles Ross dated Fort Albert August 18th, 1843, is referred to in the Company's Minute Book during the following year.

From December 12th, 1843, onwards, however, the Fort is consistently referred to as Fort Victoria in this Log Book. This would allow time for Sir George Simpson's instructions to C. F. McLoughlin dated 21st June, 1843, referred to above, to be conveyed to Chief Trader Charles Ross, who was at that time in charge of the new Fort.

Chief Factor McLoughlin also states in a letter to Sir George Simpson dated Fort Vancouver, 20th March, 1844, that the new establishment at the south end of Vancouver's Island had been named Fort Victoria according to instructions received.

With regard to the origin of the name Fort Camosun, Sir George Simpson states in a letter to the Governor and Committee of the Hudson's Bay Company in London dated 21st June, 1843, that Chief Factor Douglas has "been successful in finding an advantageous situation for the new depot in the Bay of Camosack near the S.E. extremity of Vancouver's Island", and there is also a reference to the Camosack Canal. This was evidently the Indian name for the Bay, and appears to have meant "a deep narrow gorge" or "swift running water". We also find subsequent references to the Port and Harbour of Camosun or Camoosan, both in the Log of the *Cadborough* referred to above, and also in a letter from the Secretary of the Company in London to Captain A. C. Mott of the Barque *Vancouver* dated 4th September, 1844.

See also "The Colonial Postal System of Vancouver Island and British Columbia, 1849-1871" by A. Stanley Deaville, 3rd annual report of *BCHA*, pp. 46-47.

[58] Douglas to Simpson, November 16, 1843. In HBC Archives. Quoted by W. K. Lamb in "The Founding of Fort Victoria", *BCHQ*, April, 1943, p. 89.

[59] HBC Archives (Lamb, *Ibid.*, p. 90) There is a model of the Fort in the *Beaver* for March, 1943, p. 9.

[60] HBC Archives. Quoted by W. K. Lamb in "The Founding of Fort Victoria", *BCHQ*, April, 1943, p. 90.

[61] *loc. cit.*

[62] Douglas to Simpson, November 16, 1843, in HBC Archives. Quoted by Lamb, *Ibid.*, p. 89.

[63] Roderick Finlayson, *Biography*, Victoria, 1891, p. 11. Finlayson was mistaken in the month, which was June.

Ross died, according to W. K. Lamb, on June 27, 1844, "apparently of appendicitis". A monument to him was unveiled in Victoria on June 27, 1943, the 99th anniversary of his death. It stands in the old Quadra Street Cemetery (now Pioneer Square) where he is now buried. The monument was unveiled by his grandson, Mr. Francis Ross. (See *BCHQ*, July, 1943, pp. 220-221).

Ross Bay is named after him.

[64] Finlayson was married to Sarah Work, a daughter of John Work, by the Rev. John Staines in 1849; they had seven daughters and four sons. He became a Chief Trader in 1850, and a Chief Factor in 1859. He was a member of the Legislative Council of Vancouver Island from 1851 to 1863, retired from the HBC in 1872, was Mayor of Victoria in 1878, and died in 1892.

Finlayson Channel, and Roderick Island in it, are named after him. (Walbran, *British Columbia Coast Names*, p. 427).

[65] Perhaps, bearing in mind the nine-pounders, Finlayson merely displayed the "calm confidence of a Christian with four aces."

[66] Roderick Finlayson, *Biography*, Victoria, 1891, pp. 12-13.

[67] Finlayson, *Biography*, p. 13.

[68] Great Britain. Colonial Office. *Miscellaneous Papers Relating to Vancouver Island, 1848-1863*, pp. 7-8.

[69] Finlayson, *Biography*, p. 15.

[70] Details may be found in J. T. Walbran, *British Columbia Coast Names, 1592-1906*. Geographic Board of Canada, Ottawa, 1909. See also Robinson, *Esquimalt*, p. 40.

[71] It was finally determined on June 15, 1846 (with minor revisions in 1872). In this year, also, California became part of the American Union.

[72] Finlayson, *Biography*, p. 18.

[73] Five American whalers were at Royal Roads in 1845 (Bancroft, *History of B.C.*, p. 120) but ships engaged in this trade found the Hawaiian Islands more convenient for their purposes.

[74] Communication with England had, however, become more rapid. Until 1845 despatches from the Admiralty had to be taken around Cape Horn. In that year the mail route was shortened by the new Royal Mail Steam Packet Company's service via the West Indies to the old port of Chagres, then up the Chagres River to Cruces, then by mule transport to Panama. (F. V. Longtaff, *Esquimalt Naval Base*, Clarke & Stuart, Vancouver, 1941 (c. 1942), pp. 22-23.

[75] Scholefield and Howay, *History of B.C.*, I., 476.

[76] Finlayson, *Biography*, p. 16; *History of Vancouver Island and the Northwest Coast*, p. 22.

[77] Finlayson, *Biography*, p. 16.

[78] B. Seemann, *Narrative of the Voyage of H.M.S. Herald*, 2 vols., London, Reeve & Co., 1853, pp. 101-104.

[79] Paul Kane, *Wanderings of an artist among the Indians of North America*, Toronto, the Radisson Society of Canada, 1925, Chapter XIV, pp. 144-145.

80 *Ibid.,* p. 149.

81 *Ibid.,* pp. 150-151.

82 She was one of the most modern and powerful ships of her day, carrying 500 officers and men. Of 2132 tons, she carried 50 guns. (Robinson, *Esquimalt,* p. 44).

83 See article by W. K. Lamb, "Early Lumbering on Vancouver Island" in *BCHQ,* 1938.

84 This may not be the earliest reference to Victoria in the literature of other countries; some give the honor to Virgil's line:

Penitus toto divisos orbe Britannos
(The Britons completely cut off from the whole world)

85 We could include in this connection Douglas himself, who was transferred from Fort Vancouver in June of this year.

86 G. Hollis Slater, "Rev. Robert John Staines: Pioneer Priest, Pedagogue & Political Agitator", *BCHQ,* Vol. XIV, October, 1950, p. 191.

87 Letter in *PABC,* Victoria.

88 Some have claimed she was the first Englishwoman to land in Victoria. The honor probably goes either to a Mrs. Covington, who arrived from the Hawaiian Islands in 1848, or to Mrs. Annie Muir, wife of John Muir of Sooke, who came the same year. (Bancroft, *History of B.C.,* pp. 249-250).

89 Finlayson, *History of Vancouver Island and the Northwest Coast,* Victoria, n.d., p. 40.

90 For a fuller account of Capt. Grant, see W. E. Ireland, "Capt. Walter Colquhoun Grant, Vancouver Island's first independent settler", *BCHQ,* Vol. XVII, January-April, 1953.

91 James Yates, after whom Yates Street is named, also came out on the *Harpooner.* He eventually became a member of the opposition to Douglas.

92 Always called *Soke* in early accounts.

93 J. E. Anderson, "Notes and comments on early days and events in British Columbia, Washington and Oregon", MS in *PABC,* 1925, pp. 157-8.

94 R. Finlayson, *Biography, Victoria,* 1891, p. 21-22.

95 It seems possible that the HBC saw Vancouver Island not so much as a source of furs (which at this period were neither numerous nor valuable) but as a protective shield for its thriving fur-trade in New Caledonia (as the mainland of B.C. was then called). See Galbraith, *The Hudson's Bay Company as an Imperial Factor, 1821-1869,* pp. 284-285.

96 This was the point of view strongly put forward by the rising young politician W. E. Gladstone.

97 One factor in this decision was probably the financial stringencies arising from the "Year of Revolutions" (1848).

98 There were also two other groups interested in Vancouver Island. One, headed by James Edward Fitzgerald, was anxious to promote a joint stock company for the colonization of the Island. The other consisted of a group of British Mormons, who presented a memorial to Queen Vic-

toria, asking to be allowed to establish a settlement on the Island. Fitzgerald later wrote a work outlining his grievances against the Company,
entitled *Vancouver Island and the Hudson's Bay Company*. It attracted
some attention at the time. See article by John S. Galbraith in *BCHQ*,
July-October, 1952, "Fitzgerald versus the Hudson's Bay Company: the
Founding of Vancouver Island".
Regarding the Mormons, see Robinson, *Esquimalt*, pp. 31-32.

[99] Among his other accusations was that the Company had an "anti-coloniz-
ing spirit". (Sage, *Douglas*, p. 146. This charge will be looked at again
later; it is a question of considerable importance when interpreting the
early history of Vancouver Island. It is discussed at length in Galbraith,
The Hudson's Bay Company as an Imperial Factor, 1821-1869, pp. 283-
307, where the conclusion is reached that the Company was, at the very
least, unenthusiastic about large-scale colonization.

[100] Galbraith, *op. cit.*, p. 289.

[101] The terms of the Crown Grant are given in full in Scholefield and Howay,
British Columbia from the earliest times to the present, Vancouver, 1914,
I, 676-680. Also in Begg, *History of B.C.*, Toronto, 1894, pp. 186-188.
See also Sage, *Douglas*, pp. 158-159.

CHAPTER FOUR

Governor
Blanshard

The next two years were not in some ways to be very happy ones for the Fort. Behind lay seven years of progress, in which a defensible settlement had been built, farms developed to support its inhabitants, and trading operations with the natives expanded vigorously. Charles Ross, and after his untimely death Roderick Finlayson, had directed day-to-day affairs resourcefully, with Douglas giving over-all direction from Fort Vancouver. After 1851, there would be another time of advance in which Douglas, as the second Governor of Vancouver Island, would guide the growth of the colony as it evolved into a more complex society. Between these two eras, however, was a brief period when the almost impossible experiment was attempted of having a Governor, totally unfamiliar with the colony and its problems, in nominal control of it, with Douglas, from both ability and experience the real master of the situation, "merely" in charge of the all-powerful Company and its affairs.[1] As the Company and the Colony were virtually identical terms (Captain Grant and his workmen being almost the only inhabitants not in the employ of the former), this left remarkably little for the Governor to exercise his powers over, and it was a very short time indeed before this became painfully apparent.

Governor Richard Blanshard left Southampton on September

17, 1849,[2] and arrived on the 11th of March, 1850, in H.M.S. *Driver,* landing with a single body servant. It was a cold, late spring; snow still lay a foot deep on the ground as he made his way to the Fort. He was accorded a salute from the guns before a small crowd of onlookers, including a few naval officers. Douglas himself (then 46, with 30 years experience in posts of responsibility) read the proclamation which formally inaugurated the government of Vancouver Island.

Yet this, perhaps, was the high point of Blanshard's term of office. In the next few weeks he was to make a whole series of unpalatable discoveries: that he had almost no subordinate officials (such as courts, soldiers or policemen) to enforce his decrees; that Douglas was the real source of all authority; that it would be a considerable time before he received any salary;[3] and that in the meantime there was not even a place for him to stay.

Blanshard, a young barrister of 32, who had attended both Oxford and Cambridge, but who had no previous experience in the colonial service, struggled manfully with these obstacles, but from the very first they proved insuperable. He solved his accommodation problem by remaining on board ship until a suitable residence could be constructed for him, and was able later on to use seamen from the Royal Navy as a kind of temporary militia,[4] but the other difficulties were too much for him. Douglas was and remained the real colossus bestriding this little world,[5] and in the meantime the inexperienced young Governor had to support himself out of his own pocket[6] while finding almost no duties to exercise his talents upon.

The elements had thus been assembled of an unfortunate and embarrassing situation, where it is difficult to assign blame and more charitable perhaps to forgive and forget. In the long run, no serious harm was done to the colony, and this brief time of troubles between two happier periods proved merely the one step backward—or, possibly, sideways—before a whole series of steps forward.

It is difficult to understand just why Blanshard had been chosen by the British Government for the position, which, considering the remoteness and half-developed state of the colony, and the divided spheres of influence between Governor and Company, they must have known would be a trying one. Despite this, they had sent this totally inexperienced young man half way around the world into a situation which he would have to struggle with unaided.

Actually, his appointment had been in the nature of a last-minute substitution. It seems almost certain that the United Kingdom government had decided that the first governor of Vancouver Island should be Douglas himself, but that opposition in England to the turning over of the government of the Island to a man so closely identified with the Company which had been granted exclusive control of its economic life, caused the Colonial Office to revise its plans.[7]

As early as July, 1848 Earl Grey, the Colonial Secretary, had written to Sir John Pelly, Governor of the Company, asking his opinion as to the most suitable choice as first Governor of Vancouver Island. Sir John had promptly suggested Douglas, pointing out that he was a man of property, a Chief Factor of the Company, and a member of its board of directors for the region west of the Rocky Mountains.[8] He conceded, however, the unsuitability of having a governor drawn from the ranks of Company officials, and agreed that the arrangement he suggested should be temporary.

The authorities in England, more in touch with public opinion there than Sir John, decided to reject this suggestion, and appoint someone less likely to become the subject of controversy. In a letter to Douglas[9] dated August 4, 1849, Pelly explained the delicate situation:

> It was proposed to appoint you Governor pro tempore of the Island, but you will see by the Public press, that from the jealousy of some parties and the interested motives of others, how next to impossible it would have been to give you the situation.

Blanshard's willingness to accept the position is not entirely clear, but it is probable that he wished to rise in the world, and felt that almost any position would do for the lowest rung of the ladder; moreover, he was under the impression that he would be granted a thousand acres of land, which he pictured no doubt as a country estate on the English model.[10]

At all events, this "comparatively young man, of medium height, with aquiline aristocratic features, set off by a large military mustache"[11] did his best to cope with the totally novel situation in which he now found himself. In a few weeks, at a cost of less than $1600,[12] his house, located at what is now the corner of Yates and Government, was completed. Douglas reported to his superiors that it was "40x20 ft. with a kitchen 18x12 feet attached and a house 24x18 for his servants . . . It has a neat appearance and is on the whole the best finished building in Oregon."[13]

A month after his arrival, Blanshard wrote his second despatch to Earl Grey.[14] He recorded the circumstances of his arrival, the absence of any official residence, and his decision to remain on board the *Driver*. He reported that efforts had recently been made to discover coal of good quality in the northern part of the Island, but so far without success. He also made some comments on the land and native inhabitants that he had come to govern:

> The quantity of arable land, or land that can be made arable is, so far as I can ascertain, exceedingly limited throughout the Island, which consists almost entirely of broken ranges of rocky hills, intersected by ravines and valleys so narrow as to render them useless for cultivation. A Mr. McNeill, Agent for the Hudson's Bay Company at Beaver Harbour, who is considered to be better acquainted with the Indian population than any other person, estimates their number at the very largest at ten thousand, and these he considers to be steadily decreasing, although the sale of spirituous liquors has been for a considerable time prohibited, and the prohibition appears to be strictly enforced.[15]

Finally, he explained why, in his judgment, it was inappropriate to implement those of his instructions that directed him to appoint a council to aid him in his duties:

> As no settlers have at present arrived, I have considered that it is unnecessary as yet to nominate a council, as my instructions direct; for a council chosen at present must be composed entirely of the officers of the Hudson's Bay Company, few if any of whom possess the qualification of landed property which is required to vote for Members of Assembly, and they would moreover be completely under the control of their superior officers; but as no immediate arrival of

settlers is likely to take place, and my instructions direct me to form a Council on my arrival, I should wish for a further direction on this point before I proceed to its formation.[16]

In his next despatch,[17] Blanchard reported that the two Companies, the HBC and the Puget Sound Agricultural Association (which he referred to as "The Hudson's Bay Company under another name"), had begun surveying the land reserved for them, and he estimated the tract as about ten miles square. This took in all of what are now Victoria City and Esquimalt as well as a considerable part of Saanich, and Blanshard also took note of a development which he correctly saw would prove troublesome to the colony:

> I have received news from Oregon of the discovery of very rich gold mines on the Spokan River. The whole population of that territory are flocking to the spot. Should the favourable accounts of these mines prove correct, I fear that it will draw away all the Hudson's Bay Company's servants from Vancouver Island, and at present they form the entire population.[18]

It may be convenient at this point to quote part of a letter written by Douglas to a friend soon after Blanshard's arrival. Not only does it afford us sidelights on a variety of aspects of life in the Colony, but it makes us realize that not only the inexperienced young governor but also the resourceful Chief Factor often found them perplexing:

> Her Majesty's Sloop *Driver* arrived here on the 11th instant with His Excellency Richard Blanshard Esq. Governor of Vancouver Island, on board. Mr. Blanshard has neither Secretary nor troops being accompanied by a single body servant. I have not had time to become much acquainted but I may say that his quiet gentlemanly manner is prepossessing. He has not yet entered upon his Executive duties, further than reading his commission to the assembled states of this Colony. Captain Grant is still the only Colonist upon the island. Dodd, Sangster and other parties in the Company's service wish to become settlers but are scared at the high price charged for land say £1 per acre. I hope you will think differently on this subject. For my own part I am resolved to hesitate no longer but to make a purchase as soon as

possible. I would rather pay a pound an acre for land with a secure title and numerous other advantages than have a farm for nothing with two years torturing suspense. The barque *Cowlitz* from England arrived here a few days ago and we are now busy discharging her cargo. Nearly all the seamen on board ran from her at the Sandwich Islands from whence she came on with Sandwich Islanders who made a shift to get here but cannot be trusted on a coasting voyage. This is not our only difficulty. Two more ships are expected out in the course of this season with about 70 servant colonists whom we shall have trouble enough to keep and feed. The anxiety and suspense of this life is torturing; wealth is truly no compensation except it leaves one at liberty to seek a change . . . The school is progressing but not numerously attended. 6 boys and 11 girls is all the force we can yet muster. The children are boarding with Mr. Staines who is very kind to them; they are not so well accomodated as I wish but we shall go on improving . . .[19]

Not long afterward, Blanshard was faced with the first of a series of crises. Trouble broke out in the northern part of the Island among the coal miners at Fort Rupert, which had been founded the previous year. They felt they were not being adequately protected against possible attacks by Indian tribes, and had other assorted grievances—probably including the knowledge that gold miners in California were earning comparatively fantastic sums. Faced with this discontent (in which some have detected distant echoes of the Chartist agitation in England,[20]) the official in charge of the small settlement had put some of the miners in irons and was feeding them on bread and water. News of these developments reached Blanshard in Victoria, who went north in H.M.S. *Driver* to investigate. He listened sympathetically to the miners, and later decided to appoint the young fort doctor J. S. Helmcken as resident magistrate.[21] In a despatch to Lord Grey, Blanshard expressed the hope that as the doctor had only recently arrived in the colony, he would be impartial in his judgments.

Here we should give credit to Blanshard for good intentions, but of course through no fault of his, he was complicating matters as much as he was solving them; although Helmcken's duties would consist largely of adjudicating disputes between the company and its employees, he himself in the last analysis was another employee of the Company. Thus the problem of divided powers between the two sources of authority in the colony pursued its inhabitants even into this remote outpost.

Blanshard also recommended a duty on imported spirits, "as their introduction tends to demoralize the Indians to a most dangerous degree . . . " It was, however, impossible, he feared, to stop them from getting any: ". . . no liquor is given them by the Company on any pretence, but it is impossible to prevent their obtaining it from the merchant vessels that visit the coast."[22]

In view of the deepening distrust which Blanshard came to have toward the Company, it is interesting to note that at this stage he was prepared to speak well of it. He informed Lord Grey that contrary to some reports, it treated the natives well:

> I may here mention that the accounts which have been published respecting the barbarous treatment of the Indian population by the Hudson's Bay Company, are both from my own personal observation, and from all I have been able to gather on the subject, entirely without foundation. They are always treated with the greatest consideration—far greater than the white labourers, and in many instances are allowed liberties and impunities in the Hudson's Bay Company's establishments that I regard as extremely unsafe.[23]

A month later, however, Blanshard's view of the Company had changed sharply; the occasion was the most serious occurrence since his arrival in the colony:

> I have to inform your Lordship of the massacre of three British subjects by the Newitty Indians, near Fort Rupert. Want of force has prevented me from making any attempt to secure the murderers—indeed the only safeguard of the Colony consists in the occasional visits of the cruizers of the Pacific squadron, which only occur at rare intervals, and for short calls. The massacre of these men has produced a great effect on the white inhabitants, many of whom do not scruple to accuse the officers of the Hudson's Bay Company of having instigated the Indians to the deed by offers of reward for the recovery of the men (sailors who had absconded) dead or alive. I have not yet been able to enquire into the truth of this report, but it is very widely spread, and men say that

they ground their belief on what the Hudson's Bay Company have done before.

The establishment at Fort Rupert is in a very critical state. A letter I have received from Mr. Helmcken, the resident magistrate, states that the people are so excited by the massacre, which they charge their employers with instigating, that they have in a body refused all obedience both to their employers and to him as magistrate, that he is utterly unable to maintain any authority, as they universally refuse to serve as constables, and insist upon the settlement being abandoned . . .[24]

As a result of this state of affairs, Blanshard reported, Helmcken had resigned, and there was thus no effective authority at all in the northern part of the Island.

In the following month, Blanshard again asked for a garrison of regular troops to be stationed on the Island; two companies, he thought, would be sufficient.

He also alluded to Captain Grant; his isolated location at Sooke was due, Blanshard believed, to the Company having reserved to itself all the good land near the Fort.[25]

In his next despatch, however, Blanshard to some extent retracted his earlier allegations against the Company. He informed Lord Grey that Dr. Helmcken had been deceived as to some of the circumstances of the murders at Fort Rupert, and that there seemed no reason to suspect the HBC of having even an indirect part in them.

This despatch[26] was dated from Fort Rupert, where Blanshard had gone in H.M.S. *Daedalus*[27] commanded by Captain G. G. Wellesley.[28] His aim was to make a first-hand appraisal of the situation there. The tribe responsible for the crimes was identified, but refused to surrender the murderers and offered furs in payment. This was not satisfactory to the whites, and a naval party landed and thoroughly destroyed the Indian camp.[29]

At about this time Captain Grant, his venture into farming at Sooke unprofitable and his attempts at surveying the colony merely bizarre, left for the Sandwich Islands, and Blanshard was thus left for a brief period as the Governor of a colony without a single colonist.[30] This absence of settlers was not in some ways surprising;

the colonists had to pay £1 an acre for land, even though it was free, or at most a dollar an acre, in the neighbouring American territories; California was drawing the adventuresome to its new goldfields; and Vancouver Island was not on the main trade or travel routes of the world.

The situation must have seemed far from encouraging to Blanshard, whose health (perhaps as a result of malaria picked up in the tropics)[31] was already beginning to break down. Faced with this array of difficulties, he decided to resign, and on November 18, 1850 submitted his resignation to Lord Grey:

> I regret to inform your Lordship that I find myself compelled to tender my resignation as Governor, and solicit an immediate recall from this Colony, as my private fortune is utterly insufficient for the mere cost of living here, so high have prices been run up by the Hudson's Bay Company, and as there are no independent settlers every requisite for existence must be obtained from them;—my health has completely given way under repeated attacks of argue (sic) and shows no sign of amendment. Under the circumstances I trust your Lordship will at once recall me, and appoint some person as my successor whose larger fortune may enable him to defray charges which involve me in certain ruin; I trust that your Lordship will give directions that I may be furnished with a passage as far as Panama in one of H.M. ships, as my state of health will not bear the long voyage round Cape Horn, and being compelled to defray the expences of my passage out by the Hudson's Bay Company who repudiated the bills their Chairman had authorized me to draw has so straightened my private means, that I am unable to pay the heavy expenses of the route through California.[32]

The slow communications of those days, however, meant that many months would have to elapse before an answer could be received, and in the meantime he continued to fulfill his duties as best he could. His relations with Douglas, who perhaps felt that Blanshard had

> popped in between th'election and my hopes[33]

though cordial, were seldom easy. Douglas for example, wanted to reserve a large area of land around the Fort for the Company; Blanshard thought a much smaller area would be sufficient, and wrote to the Headquarters of the Company about the matter. His next despatch to Lord Grey also dealt with this latter question, and it is clear from it that by this time Blanshard's feelings toward the Company had hardened:

> I have written to Sir John Pelly, the Governor of the Hudson's Bay Company, requesting some information respecting a large tract of land called the Hudson's Bay Company's and Puget Sound Company's Reserve, but no notice of my letter has been taken yet. Their Agent here professes ignorance of every arrangement, but has admitted that they do not intend to pay for it. This tract contains I am informed nearly thirty square miles of the best part of the Island and they are already attempting to sell small Lots to their own servants at greatly advanced rates.
>
> I consider this an extremely unfair proceeding. The terms of the Grant of the Island expressly state that "all lands shall be sold except such as are reserved for public purposes" and in consideration of the trouble and expense they may incur the Hudson's Bay Company are allowed the very handsome remuneration of ten per cent on all Sales they may effect and on all Royalties, not satisfied with this they are grasping at the whole price of the land, by monopolizing this vast district, making it a free gift to themselves, and then selling it for their own profit, as they are attempting to do . . .[34]

Certainly it cannot be denied that the novel and slightly awkward situation in which Douglas found himself did not prevent him from promoting the Company's interests with energy and despatch. During this period he bought from the Indians considerable portions of their land, paying for choice areas in the region of Victoria, Albert Head and Sooke the grand sum of £150.3.4.[35]

Meanwhile, the Governor had found yet another cause for complaint about the Company, this time one which he could back with facts and figures:

> The Agent of the Hudson's Bay Company[36] has presented me an account for signature being a voucher of the balance between the amount expended by the Hudson's Bay Company on the Colony, and the receipts of duties, sales, royalties collected in the Colony.
>
> The account asserts that they have expended $2736 (Dollars) of which $2130 (Dollars) are for goods paid to

Indians to extinguish their title to the land about Victoria and Soke Harbour, the remainder also for goods paid also to Indians for work done for the Colony, provisions and ammunition for the same Indians. The receipts amount to $1489 (Dollars) (from which 10 per cent is to be deducted according to the Charter of Grant to the Hudson's Bay Company) and consists entirely of Royalties on Coal for the last two years, land there are none, as I have previously informed your Lordship. On examining the account I found that for the goods paid to the Indians a price was charged three times as great as what they are in the habit of paying them at for their own work; respecting this and some inaccuracies I detected in the Account I addressed a letter to the Agent; he corrected the errors but made no alteration in the prices, and in the course of the conversation gave me to understand that they did not expect the Charter of Grant to be renewed at the expiration of the five years (January 1854) and that they would be entitled to a reimbursement of their expenditure. At this rate they may continue for the next three years paying away a few goods to Indians to extinguish their claim to the Soil, and by attaching an ideal value to their goods they will at the end of that time appear as creditor of the Colony to an overwhelming amount, so that the foundation will be laid of a Colonial debt, which will for ever prove a burden.

I beg your Lordship to observe that, at the prices they usually pay goods at, the receipts are amply sufficient to cover the expenditure and to leave a balance in favor of the Colony . . .

I trust that your Lordship will lose no time in appointing my successor, as my health has been very bad for some months, and I feel it impossible to remain here much longer, on account of increasing weakness; my instructions direct that in the event of my death or absence, and there being no Lieutenant Governor, the Senior Member of the Council shall for the time assume the Government (Art. 40) but I have not been able to appoint a Council, as there is no one in the Island above the grade of a laborer except the servants of the Hudson's Bay Company, and I have previously stated to your Lordship my reasons for considering them unfit for Magisterial appointments, of any kind.[37]

As a result of Blanshard's suspicions of the Company (which events would show were widely shared in the Settlement), another complicating factor now entered into the life of the tiny colony. Those who resented Douglas' control of almost every aspect of life in the settlement were drawn together into what might be termed an opposition group; into this group Blanshard almost automatically gravitated, and the unhappy spectacle was presented of the Queen's representative taking sides in a factional dispute. Once again, it is difficult to apportion blame — the situation was merely working out its own inherent contradictions.

The two main figures in the opposition to the Chief Factor seem to have been Edward Langford, who had arrived in Victoria in May 1851 to become the bailiff of the newly established Esquimalt (or Colwood) Farm, and the Rev. Robert Staines, who had been the Fort chaplain and schoolmaster since his arrival in March 1849. Both these figures, and evidently a good many more, believed that the power of the Company was too great, and that the interests of the colonists were being neglected, and, indeed, discriminated against. As we shall see later, a full statement of their grievances was eventually drawn up and presented to Blanshard near the end of his term of office; considering that the signatories comprised nearly all the independent settlers in the colony, it is hard to reduce the matter, as some have tried to do, to the appetite for agitation of the Rev. Mr. Staines. Indeed, Blanshard himself believed that the Company had no real intention of bringing out settlers in any number from England; it is thus apparent that genuine grounds existed for criticism of the way things were being managed in the young colony, and Blanshard as the servant of the Crown, not the Company, was entitled to listen to this criticism and transmit the gist of it to his superiors. For all that, he had once again, through no fault of his own, been put in an awkward position, and he can hardly have regretted his decision to resign.

In the meantime, while waiting for Lord Grey and Sir John Pelly to reply to his communications, Blanshard continued to fulfil his duties as best he could, on one occasion summoning Douglas before him to point out that the privilege of signing the registers of sea-going vessels was his and not the Chief Factor's.[38]

From other despatches written during this period, we glean a few more details of life in the Colony. It will be observed how frequently Blanshard reverts to the question of the land claimed by the Company in the areas near Victoria, and the effect that this claim was likely to have on the future development of the Colony.

> One or two persons in the employment of the Hudson's Bay Company may have as they inform me agreed to purchase small plots of Land near Fort Victoria at very high rates, others who are willing to settle are deterred by the price.[39]

On March 29 he informed Lord Grey that:

> I have heard that fresh specimens of gold have been obtained from the Queen Charlotte's Islands. I have not seen them myself but they are reported to be very rich, the Hudson's Bay Company's servants intend to send an expedition in the course of the summer to make proper investigations.[40]

On April 28 he took up the question of the land grant again, saying that:

> ... these reserves effectually prevent any bona fide Colonists from settling.
>
> No Site for a Town has ever been mentioned, and indeed till the question of the Reserves is settled, it would be useless to select one, for by refusing to sell the land around it, taking it as their own and setting an extravagant price on it, as they have already done near Victoria they will completely isolate and prevent the occupation of any such Town.[41]

On May 12 Blanshard again criticized the prevailing arrangements in the colony, declaring:

> The whole tendency of the system pursued by the Hudson's Bay Company being to exclude free Settlers, and reserve the Island either as an enlarged Post of their own, or a desert.[42]

On June 10, Blanshard had further complaints against the Company to record. He enclosed a memorial from Andrew Muir, a Scottish miner, formerly an employee of the Company at Fort Rupert, in which it was charged by Muir that he had suffered severe and illegal treatment at its hands:

> I hereby charge the aforesaid William Henry McNeill, George Blenkinsop and Charles Beardmore that on Friday 3rd May 1850 at Fort Rupert aforesaid, the aforesaid William Henry McNeill, George Blenkinsop and Charles Beardmore

did illegally assault my person. I likewise charge them that they did illegally imprison me from Friday 3rd May 1850 aforesaid until Saturday 15th of June 1850 and keeping me in Irons and fed on bread and water during six days of the said period by which imprisonment I have sustained permanent and serious injury to my bodily health.

Muir, Blanshard informed Lord Grey, had left with several others for San Francisco, but had now returned in search of redress. Blanshard recommended that to protect the rights of residents of the Colony, a Chief Justice should be appointed. He also recorded a contingent of new arrivals in the colony, and the reception awaiting them at the hands of their new employers:

The ship "Tory" has just landed about one hundred and twenty persons, all with two exceptions servants of the Hudson's Bay Company, some have already been sent to Oregon, and some to other ports (posts?) of the Company, no preparations had been made here for their reception beyond erecting a couple of log houses or rather sheds, in these the remainder are huddled together like cattle as I have seen myself, to the number of thirty or thirty five in each shed, men and women, married and single without any kind of screen or partition to separate them, — as may be supposed great discontent exists already and will most certainly increase, — the result will probably be that they leave the colony and seek employment in Oregon.[43]

Shortly afterward, Blanshard was again brought into conflict with the Indians. In June of 1851, H.M.S. *Portland,* the flagship of the Commander-in-Chief, Pacific Station, came to Esquimalt. Borrowing some of its crew, Blanshard went north in H.M.S. *Daphne* to Beaver Harbor, where, to punish the tribe which had refused to surrender the murderers the previous year, a number of native houses and canoes were burned.[44]

Although Blanshard felt that in taking this action he was upholding the supremacy of law and order (as interpreted by the white man), the British Government saw matters in a different light. They had scant wish to endanger good relations with the main source of the colony's revenue by protecting isolated white men who chose to wander into the wilderness; thus when Blanshard's letter of resignation arrived, they did not delay in notifying him of their acceptance of it.

We should not conclude, however, that Blanshard's term of office was composed of nothing but misadventures. In three important respects—the expansion of agriculture, the attraction of new settlers, and the development of constitutional government—there was definite progress, and it is worth looking at each of these areas in turn.

Two large "Company" farms were founded in this period: "Viewfield" farm in 1850 and "Colwood" (or "Esquimalt") Farm in 1851.[45] The former consisted of some 600 acres in Esquimalt, over which an experienced man, Donald Macaulay, was in charge as bailiff. He had once known the more rigorous climate of Fort Simpson, and he and his wife had six daughters, one of whom eventually married the son of John Tod. The farm produced sheep, cows and pigs, and in later years cattle, which were driven along the Esquimalt and Admirals Roads to the slaughter-house at Craigflower Farm. Only the name of Viewfield Street survives as a reminder of the farm, but for a time it was a valuable adjunct to the Colony.

Colwood (or Esquimalt) Farm occupied the land where the members of the Royal Colwood Golf Club now consider their choice of irons; here the presiding figure was Captain E. E. Langford, who had arrived in the *Tory* in the spring of 1851 with his wife and five daughters. The Captain, it soon transpired, had ideas of his own about things, his main one being to create for himself, his family and his friends in this remote corner of the world the way of an English country gentleman — all at the Company's expense. This was to lead to a very pleasant existence for those invited to partake of his lavish hospitality, and very strained relations with his employers, who were unaware that the Age of Leisure had arrived. These developments, however, which are interesting enough to record in their proper place, came after Governor Blanshard had returned to England, and need not detain us here.

Settlement of the colony, though almost exclusively by employees of the Company, was also getting under way. In 1850 the *Norman Morison*, the HBC's annual supply ship, had brought out

80 men[46] (including J. S. Helmcken, who soon afterward became the Company doctor);[47] in June 1851 130 settlers arrived on the *Tory*.[48] However, considering that in 1853 there were only about 300 settlers in Victoria, 125 at Nanaimo, and a handful at Fort Rupert, it must be conceded that progress in this respect was far from rapid.

In the development of the colony towards self-government, however, one important step was taken. The malcontents of the settlement (or the independent settlers, as they understandably preferred to be known), learning that Blanshard had submitted his resignation and suspecting strongly that Douglas would be his successor, drew up a petition in which they set forth their grievances and made one practical suggestion for improvement. The document is worth quoting in full:

> To His Excellency Richard Blanshard, Esquire, Governor of Vancouver Island:
>
> May it please your Excellency:
>
> We, the undersigned inhabitants of Vancouver Island, having learned with regret that your Excellency has resigned the government of this colony, and understanding that the government has been committed to a chief factor of the Hudson Bay Company, cannot but express our unfeigned surprise and deep concern at such an appointment. The Hudson Bay Company being, as it is, a great trading body, must necessarily have interests clashing with those of independent colonists. Many matters of a judicial nature will undoubtedly arise, in which the colonists and the Company, or its servants, will be contending parties, or the upper servants and the lower servants of the Company will be arrayed one against the other. We beg to express in the most emphatical and plainest manner our assurance that impartial decisions cannot be expected from a governor who is not only a member of the Company, sharing its profits, his share of such profits rising and falling as they rise and fall, but is also charged as their chief agent with the sole representation of their trading interests in this island and the adjacent coasts.
>
> Furthermore, thus situated the Colony will have no security that its public funds will be duly disposed of for the benefit of the colony in general, and not turned aside in any degree to be applied to the private improvement of that tract of land

held by them, or otherwise unduly employed. Under these circumstances we beg to acquaint your Excellency with our deep sense of the absolute necessity there is, for the real good and welfare of the colony, that a council should be immediately appointed, in order to provide some security that the interests of the Hudson Bay Company shall not be allowed to outweigh and ruin those of the colony in general. We, who join in expressing these sentiments to your Excellency, are unfortunately but a very small number, but we respectfully beg your Excellency to consider that we, and we alone, represent the interests of the island as a free and independent British colony, for we constitute the whole body of the independent settlers, all the other inhabitants being, in some way or other, connected with and controlled by the Hudson Bay Company, as to be deprived of freedom of action in all matters relating to the public affairs of the colony, some indeed by their own confession, as may be proved if necessary. And we further allege our firm persuasion that the untoward influences to which we have adverted above are likely if entirely unguarded against, not only to prevent any increase of free and independent colonists in the island, but positively to decrease their present numbers.

We therefore humbly request your Excellency to take into your gracious consideration the propriety of appointing a council before your Excellency's departure; such being the most anxious and earnest desire of your Excellency's most obedient and humble servants, and Her Majesty's most devoted and loyal subjects.[49]

Acting on the recommendation contained in this document, on August 27, 1851,[50] Blanshard appointed his first (and last) Council. It consisted of James Douglas, John Tod and James Cooper, and met for the first time on August 30.

On the first of September, 1851, Douglas formally assumed office as the second governor of Vancouver Island, and later the same month Blanshard left its shores forever. It would perhaps be going too far to say that he left it in disgrace, but the fact that he was forced to pay most of his own passage home,[51] and was never given a similar appointment again, may be said to speak for itself.[52]

It was surely a harsher condemnation than he deserved. Without any real training for the position, he had struggled manfully while in personal ill health against an impossible set of circumstances, and it is hard to see where another man could have succeeded where he had failed.[53] While invested with the trappings of power and distinction, he was forced to live in the shadow of one of the most forceful figures in the history of the Island, a man, moreover, who believed, not without some reason, that the Governor's place was rightfully his own.[54]

Even the clock of history had been against Blanshard; the day had not yet arrived when the balance of power would be more evenly divided between the Company and the independent settlers. This was, in fact, though few guessed it at the time, just coming into sight above the horizon, as events in the next few years would disclose. In 1852 the discovery of coal at Nanaimo would mark the beginning of a new source of employment;[55] farming was steadily expanding; the number of immigrants was starting to increase; surveyors more practical than the muddle-headed Captain Grant already had arrived,[56] and sales of land were beginning to provide some revenue for the Colony.

Perhaps if Blanshard's health had held up better and he had "stuck it out", these factors might have been enough to make his term of office more successful. It was the misfortune, not the fault, of this well-meaning young barrister[57] that he was caught in the changing gears of history, and it is some satisfaction to know that one of Victoria's pleasantest streets is named after him,[58] and that in later years he inherited money, dying at the good old age of 77 worth £130,000.[59]

FOOTNOTES

[1] Douglas was to be "agent to the Company for all matters relating to the territory of Vancouver's Island", and Blanshard to be "confined to the administration of the civil government of the colony and to military affairs". (Archibald Barclay, secretary to the Governor and Committee, writing to Douglas, August 3, 1849. *PABC*).

[2] See W. E. Ireland, "The Appointment of Governor Blanshard", *BCHQ*, July, 1944, Vol. VIII, p. 223.

[3] Sir John Pelly, Governor of the Colony, after suggesting that Blanshard be paid £150 or £200 annually from the proceeds of land sales, on second thoughts decided that a salary could wait until money for it was

available from either taxes or royalties on coal. (Ormsby, *British Columbia: A History*, Macmillan, 1958, p. 98). The Governor's passage out had cost him £300; of this the Company paid £175 and he paid the rest. He also eventually paid for most of his journey home. (Bancroft, *History of B.C.*, p. 270).

[4] Blanshard was also commander-in-chief of the colony, and was appointed to the rank of vice-admiral.

[5] Bancroft outlines Blanshard's predicament with a kind of sour accuracy: "As their noble friend, Lord Grey, had taken the trouble to appoint him, and the appointee had taken the trouble to come so far over the two great oceans, they would treat him politely, that is, if he would be humble and behave himself; but as for his governing them, that was simply ridiculous. (Bancroft, *History of B.C.*, pp. 268-9).

[6] He was forced to pay the HBC's highest price for his personal purchases, as he was not an HBC employee. See "The Governorship of Richard Blanshard" by W. K. Lamb, *BCHQ*, January-April, 1950, p. 5.

[7] Douglas always contended that he had actually been appointed Governor pro tempore on May 12, 1849, and was entitled to pay at £300 per annum till March, 1850. (Lamb, *op. cit.*, p. 35). In a letter to Archibald Barclay, Secretary of the Company, on Dec. 10, 1849 (in the HBC Archives), Douglas speaks of "resigning" his office (as pro tem. governor). (Ireland, *op. cit.*, pp. 217-220). Douglas tried for some time to collect this "back pay" but his claim was finally disallowed by the British Government.

[8] Bancroft, *History of British Columbia*, p. 263-4.

[9] *PABC*, Victoria. Douglas in a letter to Pelly (April 3, 1850) agreed it was better that he should not be appointed Governor.

[10] It transpired that the thousand acres were to belong to the office and not to the man. "He might select, subdue and beautify the tract for his successors, should he so please, but he could not sell nor pocket any of the proceeds of it." Bancroft, *History of B.C.*, p. 270.

[11] J. S. Helmcken, *Victoria Colonist*, Christmas Number, 1887.

[12] W. K. Lamb, "The Governorship of Richard Blanshard", *BCHQ*, Vol. XIV, January-April, 1950, p. 3.

[13] Douglas to Barclay, September 10, 1850. Letter-book in *PABC*. The "Oregon Territory" was still the general name for the Pacific Northwest.

[14] He had previously written one from Panama on December 26, 1849, announcing his arrival there on November 25, 1849.

[15] Blanshard, Despatch No. 2, April 8, 1850. *PABC*.

[16] Blanshard, Despatch No. 2. Grey, in a despatch dated July 16, 1850, agreed with Blanshard's decision.

[17] Between the writing of these two despatches, on May 13 he had presided over the first inquest ever held on Vancouver Island. See Lamb, *op. cit.*, p. 7.

[18] Blanshard, Despatch No. 3, June 15, 1850. *PABC*.

[19] Douglas to A. C. Anderson, March 18, 1850. Quoted in J. R. Anderson, "Notes and Comments", p. 133.

[20] Lamb, *op. cit.,* p. 10.

[21] He was appointed on June 22, 1850, and Blanshard informed Lord Grey to this effect on July 10, 1950. Grey approved the appointment in a despatch dated November 20, 1850.

[22] Blanshard, Despatch No. 4, July 10, 1850. *PABC.*

[23] Blanshard, Despatch No. 4, July 10, 1850. *PABC.*

[24] Blanshard, Despatch No. 5, August 18, 1850. *PABC.*

[25] Blanshard, Despatch No. 6, September 18, 1850. *PABC.*

[26] Blanshard, Despatch No. 7, October 19, 1850. *PABC.*

[27] The captain and officers of the *Daedalus* were perhaps the first on another occasion to glimpse the legendary "Cadborosaurus". See Anderson, "Notes and Comments", p. 182.

[28] On April 20, 1851, Lord Grey informed Blanshard that the Admiralty expected him to pay Capt. Wellesley £47.15.0 for giving him passage to Fort Rupert. Blanshard replied (Despatch No. 20, August 11, 1851) that he would transmit the request to the Governor and Directors of the HBC as he himself no longer had any available funds.

[29] It will be observed that the Indians were suggesting, as was their custom, a theory of collective responsibility, and that the whites, having first rejected it, then proceeded to a drastic application of it.

[30] On the 25th of February, 1851, he reported to Lord Grey that "Mr. Grant has returned to the Island and resumed possession of his farm at Soke". (Despatch No. 12).

[31] Helmcken, *Reminiscences,* III, 37-38. Blanshard took morphine for this complaint (*loc. cit.*).

[32] Blanshard, Despatch No. 9, November 18, 1850. *PABC.*

[33] *Hamlet,* V. ii.

[34] Blanshard, Despatch No. 10, February 3, 1851. *PABC.*

[35] See Sage, *Douglas,* p. 160; Helmcken, *Reminiscences,* III, 76; Leonard A. Wrinch, *Land Policy of the Colony of Vancouver Island, 1849-1866.* M.A. Thesis, UBC, October, 1932. *PABC,* pp. 23-4.

[36] It is surely significant that Blanshard in his despatches refrains as far as possible from mentioning Douglas by name.

[37] Blanshard, Despatch No. 11, February 12, 1851. *PABC.*

[38] Bancroft, *History of B.C.,* pp. 277-8.

[39] Blanshard, Despatch No. 12, February 25, 1851. *PABC.*

[40] Blanshard, Despatch No. 13, *PABC.*

[41] Blanshard, Despatch No. 14, *PABC.*

[42] Despatch No. 15, *PABC.* One wonders if the absence of a principal verb in this sentence is attributable to emotional stress.

[43] Despatch No. 16, June 10, 1851. The *Tory* actually arrived on May 14, and may have had more than 140 on board. Among them were Captain Cooper, Captain Langford and Cecilia Cameron, niece-by-marriage of

Douglas. See "The Diary of Martha Cheney Ella", *BCHQ*, Vol. XIII, No. 2, April, 1949, pp. 91-92.

44 Bancroft puts it more strongly: "Men, women and children were mercilessly cut down, persons innocent of any thought of wrong against their murderers, and their village again destroyed. Then the *Daphne* sailed away. Justice was satisfied . . . (*History of B.C.*, p. 275). Blanshard's account is in his Despatch No. 17, August 4, 1851.

45 A detailed account of these two farms may be found in L. B. Robinson, *Esquimalt, "Place of Shoaling Waters"*, Quality Press, Victoria, 1947, pp. 49-64.

46 Nearly all miners destined for the workings at Fort Rupert.

47 Born in 1824, he died in Victoria in 1920.

48 This included 3 bailiffs for Company farms, 74 laborers, 9 laborers' wives, and four children. The men were engaged for five years at £17 per annum, with free passage both ways and food, lodging and tools supplied by the Company. (Galbraith, *The Hudson's Bay Company as an Imperial Factor, 1821-1869*, p. 296.)

49 Sage, *Douglas*, pp. 168-9.
J. S. Helmcken thought that Blanshard himself either composed or revised this petition. (*Reminiscences*, III, p. 105).

50 He had been informed earlier in the month that the British Government had accepted the resignation which he had submitted in November, 1850 — nine months before.

51 A British warship took him from Victoria to San Francisco, and he was left to make his way from there to London as best he could.

52 Blanshard did, however, appear once more on the stage of history. A British parliamentary committee enquired into the affairs of the HBC in 1857. It sat for over 5 months (Gladstone was its most distinguished member) and questioned numerous witnesses, including Blanchard, Sir George Simpson and James Cooper. It recommended among other things that the relationship between the Company and Vancouver Island should be terminated, and the Colony should be extended to include parts of the mainland. See Bancroft, *History of B.C.*, pp. 376-381.

53 Bancroft, in a vivid phrase, declared "though backed by the greatest nation on earth, he was more helpless than the seventh wife of a savage." (*History of B.C.*, p. 277).

54 Dr. Helmcken assessed the situation after both principals were dead: "Of course in his time things had no shape, but he was Governor and wanted to act as such, but the power all lay in the hands of the Company at home and here — he did not like, to put it mildly, the Hudson's Bay Company in general and Douglas in particular, and so these two never pulled together — in fact it was generally believed and probably truly, that the Company wished Douglas to be Governor and so himself wished to be, and thus the Company have everything in their own hands. To add to the difficulty, Blanshard took sides with Langford, Skinner, and so forth who, of course, were or became averse to the Company likewise, but really I never see that under the condition of things and their agreement, they had much to justly complain of." (*Reminiscences*, III, 73).

[55] An Indian had brought a canoe-load of coal to the Fort as early as the spring of 1850 (Sage, *Douglas*, p. 172). As early as 1835 it was known there were coal deposits in the northern part of the Island. (Bancroft, *History of B.C.*, pp. 186-188).

[56] Joseph Despard Pemberton and his assistant, B. W. Pearse, arrived in May, 1851. Pemberton later wrote an interesting book, *Facts and figures relating to Vancouver Island and British Columbia*, (London, Longman, Green, 1860). He was elected a member of the first House of Assembly of Vancouver Island (1856). There is an article about Pemberton by his daughter, Harriet Susan Sampson, in the *BCHQ* for 1944 (Vol. VIII).

[57] Hemcken declared many years later that "he was a very intelligent and affable man". (*Colonist,* Christmas Number, 1887). Captain Grant wrote some years later: "His loss was very much to be regretted, as he was a gentleman in every way qualified to fulfil the duties of his position with credit to himself, and with prosperous results to the country." (*London Geographical Journal*, XXVII, p. 320; quoted in Bancroft, *History of B.C.*, p. 282).

[58] As late as 1877 a well in front of the *Colonist* office was known as Governor Blanshard's well, having been dug for him. (*Colonist,* August 8, 1877).

[59] W. K. Lamb, "The Governorship of Richard Blanshard", *BCHQ,* Vol. XIV, January-April, 1950, p. 39).

CHAPTER FIVE

Governor and Chief Factor Douglas

These little picketed enclosures appearing at intervals of two or three hundred miles, like secluded foxholes in boundless prairies, — what are they? To the unenlightened vision of the thoughtless red man they are magazines of celestial comforts, arms which give the possessor superhuman power in war and in the chase; containing implements of iron and steel whose cunning causes even nature to blush; woven wool which wards off cold, disease, and death; glittering trinkets whose wealth raises wrinkled imbecility above the attractions of youth and talents; and above all, tobacco and that blessed drink of heaven which, indeed, can minister to a mind diseased, while placing the body for a time beyond the reach of pain. To their builders, and to the white race everywhere, these solitary and contracted pens have a far different signification. They are depots of compressed power, dominating the land and all that is therein; they are germs of the highest human type, which shall shortly spring up and overspread the wilderness, causing it to wither beneath its fatal shade.[1]

On September 1, 1851, James Douglas assumed direction of the destinies of Vancouver Island as its second governor.[2] He brought to the task a lifetime of service in posts of steadily increasing responsibility; moreover, he enjoyed the complete confidence of his superiors both in the Hudson's Bay Company and the Imperial Government. As in addition to these favorable factors he was a man of uncommon ability and energy, the stage was set for a period of steady progress in the affairs of the colony, still not a decade old, and with a population well short of 500 souls.

Despite these promising omens, it was apparent that the new Governor was not without his problems. There were those bound up with the fact that he held two quite distinct positions—Governor of the Colony and Chief Factor of the Company—and was in duty bound to promote the interests of each—even, apparently, when they opposed each other.[3] There were those arising out of the inevitable transition from an exclusively fur-trading economy to one dependent on a wide variety of activities; there were those connected with the fact that no vestige of democracy yet existed in the settlement, in a century and a world that were witnessing an irresistible movement in that direction; and there were those springing out of the paradox that Victoria, like all the northern half of the continent, was dependent on Britain for its history and America for its geography, and seemed unable to make a final choice between them.[4] All these problems—except the last, which, continuing to give the city much of its distinctive flavor, is doubtless best unsolved,[5]—were faced and dealt with (according to his lights) by Douglas in the next few years.

Almost every area of public life saw an expansion from the most elementary beginnings to a stage of development in which at least the outlines of the city of the future could be discerned. In its provision for self-defence, there was a rapid expansion from a palisaded fort dependent on "blunderbusses, cutlasses, etc"[6] to an important naval base, giving protection to, and being protected by, the Royal Navy. In its sources of wealth, the fur trade was maintained and farming developed, while the foundations were laid of mining and lumbering. The indispensable organs of modern civilization such as schools, hospitals, roads, bridges and courts made their appearance, while the first steps were taken in the direction of parliamentary democracy. Immigration increased while some of those characteristics of Vancouver Island society which continue to be a source of pride to its inhabitants and amusement to untutored outsiders would, by the end of the period, be distinguishable. These changes could, of course, each be considered separately, but since in practice they were continually intermingling, it is likely better to recount the events of this period as they occurred and thus present the fabric, rather than the separate threads of the colony's day-to-day life.

The remaining months of 1851 saw few events of importance, other than the departure of the unhappy Blanshard in early September, and the arrival of Douglas's commission as Governor in November.

Seedtime and harvest, however, are independent of high politics, and the development of the natural resources of the colony, which had begun immediately the Fort was constructed in 1843, continued without interruption. It was while Blanshard was still governor that Colwood Farm had been established by the Company and placed in charge of Captain E. E. Langford.[7] Although Langford was prodigal of the Company's money—he was perhaps the first British Columbian to grasp the possibilities of the "expense account"—an increasing amount of grain and livestock was produced, the former being exported to the Russian colony of Alaska.[8]

Moreover, what the farm lacked in economic efficiency it made up for as a centre for the diffusion of the social graces. A man who keeps open house and also has five attractive daughters and the only piano in the district may expect to attract visitors, and before long there was a steady stream of young naval officers in the direction of the Farm.

The sale of land to private individuals was also getting under way. Captain Grant had temporarily leased his property to another settler and was elsewhere in search of El Dorado; but as employees of the Company retired from its service they often settled down in the country, which in those days meant almost everything outside the walls of the Fort. A society independent of the Company was thus slowly forming, though it was to be a few years yet before it was conscious of itself as such.

It was, naturally, colonization that eventually brought this about, and this continued at a slow but steady pace. The *Tory* had brought about 130 new arrivals in May 1851, and the *Norman Morison*,[9] making her second trip to these waters, about 35 more in October.[10]

Meanwhile, the education of the young was continuing under the direction of the Rev. Staines and his wife. By a piece of good fortune, we have a detailed account of Victoria's first school[11] by one of its earliest pupils. James R. Anderson was born in 1841, and came to Victoria with his sister from Fort Langley, being paddled across the straits from the mainland by Indians. Although he felt sure at the time that he would not survive the journey, he was to live on till 1930,[12] and in the evening of his days set down his recollections of his schooldays with a remarkable vividness of style and eye for the striking detail. His memoirs survive as a manuscript in the Provincial Archives, and make fascinating reading.

The school was located in the upper storey of one of the Fort buildings, and was decidedly spartan:

> The sole means of heating the school was a box stove in the room wherein we had our meals and lessons and devilish cold it was for those, who on account of their youth, were jostled to one side by the bigger ones.[13]

There were, however, compensations:

> One of our greatest joys was feasting our eyes on the sumptuous suppers enjoyed by the bachelors who had quarters immediately under our dormitory. By dint of raising up a board in the flooring and which formed the ceiling of the room below, we were enabled to view the mild orgies of the bachelors; oysters, sherry, port and brandy in abundance.[14]

If the pleasures of watching other people eat oysters should pall, there were always alternative diversions, such as slaughtering "the numerous rats which infested the building."

> One bold marauder got into my bed and was purloining a crust of bread which I had secreted when I discovered his presence and with a quick movement I pinned him to the side of the bed with my blanket covered arm. A bounty of a shilling a dozen was offered by Mr. Staines, but with our inadequate means of catching rats, having to manufacture our own traps, we did not earn many shillings.[15]

Other aspects of life under the Staines were still vivid 75 years later:

> Sunday at the Staines school is to this day a day of terror

Sir James Douglas

Lady Douglas — née Amelia Connolly

James Yates Sr. — 1848

Captain Edward Langford

to me. After morning prayers we had breakfast such as it was, bread and treacle and tea without milk. Church at 11 in the mess hall to which we were summoned by the ringing of the Fort bell, then dinner, potatoes and meat, sometimes fish, then a dreary afternoon learning the Collects; how I hated them. Frequently in spite of the hard wooden benches, I used to fall asleep and woe betide me if I were caught; one could not help it on a hot drowsy summer afternoon or perhaps lying full length thinking of the beautiful country . . .[16]

Indeed, it was the countryside that provided the happier memories, and under its influence even the sometimes cross-tempered schoolmaster would mellow. On one occasion, for example:

Determined to explore all the unknown parts near the fort, Mr. Staines hired a large canoe with a full crew of Indians in which he and all the boys of the school embarked and proceeded up the Arm through the Gorge which was at that time spanned by two logs furnishing a foot bridge, past what is now Craigflower, to the head of the Arm. Not a vestige of civilization beyond the rude bridge across the Gorge, not a boat or canoe to be seen, not a sound but the measured beat of the paddles accompanied by the wild canoe song of the native disturbed the stillness of the primeval forest which fringed the shores and we drank in the beauties of nature in wonderment.

. . . The dark night, the half-naked crew with painted faces, the boiling waters of the Gorge all thrown into relief by the bright fire which had been lit and the wild song all combined to make a lasting impression on my mind. Mr. Staines was a curious mixture of violent temper and good fellowship. When he was out with the school boys on such occasions as I mention, he was the soul of good humour, imparting instruction in natural history and otherwise making much of the boys, sometimes starting a song and getting the boys to join in the chorus.[17]

By and large, one gets the impression that the merits of Victoria's first school (if such it was) rather outweighed its defects, since Anderson concedes that:

Mr. Staines, of rather uncertain temper, and disposed at times to be unduly severe in administering corporal punishment, was nevertheless a good student and teacher in Natural

History, and, personally, I can conscientiously say I was never cruelly or even severely chastised, as in all truthfulness, I must admit some of the boys were.[18]

Even Douglas, though not unreservedly favorable to Staines, was willing to concede, at least in the early years of the school, that progress was being made:

The children have greatly improved in their personal appearance and one thing I particularly love in Staines is the attention he bestows on their religious training. Had I a selection to make, he is not exactly the man I would choose, but it must be admitted we might find a man worse qualified for the charge of the school.[19]

So, assisted by his loyal and efficient wife (who was, perhaps, the real "push" behind the school),[20] Staines labored to teach his charges the mysteries of "hic, haec, hoc".[21] They in their turn made good any deficiencies in his curriculum. ("Our amusements consisted of marbles, cricket, rounders, shinny, horse riding, fighting Indian boys, worrying Indian dogs, some surreptitious shooting with our antiquated flint lock muskets, besides any occasional mischief as boys alone are capable of conceiving").[22] And 1851 in due course became 1852.

This perhaps was the year that saw the faint beginnings of the city of the future, as streets were first laid out. The settlement was at that time bounded on the west by the harbor, on the east by what is now Government street, on the south by the Fort, and on the north by what is now Johnson street. Almost the only works of man beyond these small confines were the farm buildings and cultivated fields upon which the settlement depended for its sustenance.

This year also saw the arrival in May at Esquimalt of H.M.S. *Thetis*, a frigate of 36 guns and 1450 tons,[23] commanded by Captain Augustus Kuper.[24] His gunnery lieutenant was John Moresby (son of Rear Admiral Moresby, Commander-in-chief, Pacific Station, from 1850 to 1853), who himself later became an admiral, and who in his book *Two Admirals* has given us some vivid pictures of the early days of the port.

Two features of the colony immediately impressed him forcibly:

the harbor where they anchored and the Governor who greeted them. Of the former, Moresby wrote:

> Trees, trees everywhere, many of them 200 feet high, laced with undergrowth, hoary with lichen. That was my first impression—that and the majestic silence and loneliness of the place. Suddenly, with a crash like the rocketing of a hundred cock-pheasants, a mighty stag rose almost at our feet (where now stand the workshops of a first-class naval dockyard), and ere our startled brains and guns could adjust themselves, he was off and away through the forest. No dreaming after that! Here was reality, and every crack of a dry twig, every whisper of a leaf, gave a thrill of excitement.[25]

Of the dominant figure on this little stage, Moresby gives a vivid portrait, which includes yet another version of the distant events of 1828:

> The Governor greeted us in stately fashion . . . It was easy to see that here indeed was a *man,* middle-aged, tall and well-knit, with keen features, alert and kindly. I recognized the type that has broken out of our island-home in all centuries to colonise and civilise—the born pioneer. His influence over the surrounding tribes was unbounded, and the more so because of his perfect acquaintance with their dialects, and the fact that his wife was herself an Indian princess, and his saviour from death at the hands of her people. Here lay his romance. By stratagem her tribe had seized Fort James (*sic*) in the Rockies, and Douglas (then in command), the centre of a horde of maddened Indians, was at his last struggle, when, like Pocahontas herself, an Indian girl, the daughter of a chief, tore her way to his side, held back the savages, and pleaded his cause with such passion that the red man granted his life to her entreaties. She lived to share his honours, and to become Lady Douglas, wife of the Governor and Commander-in-chief of British Columbia.[26]

The first result of this visit was not perhaps the most important. On May 29, the crew of the vessel took part in the first cricket match ever played on Vancouver Island, and soundly trounced the locals.[27]

Emboldened, perhaps, by this success, they next turned their attention to road-building.

It did not take us long to realize that in bad weather communication with the Fort was risky by water, for an officer and two men lost their lives in a rough sea and the floating kelp which entangles swimmers along the shore. It was, therefore, resolved to break a road through the forest, and the novel task was tackled with enthusiasm. Axes sent their echoes ringing down the glades; mighty trees fell. We macadamised the track after a fashion, and from henceforth by this road (now traversed by electric cars) we had easy access to Victoria.[28]

In the meantime, Douglas continued to fill the two roles of Governor and Chief Factor. In the former position, his duties were not, perhaps, yet burdensome. His house was in a small stockaded fort of its own, about two hundred feet north of the main fort. "There, with Mr. Golledge[29] as his secretary, he carried on the affairs of state. Needless to say, these were not of an onerous nature, no parliament, no courts, nothing to bother."[30]

More of his time, perhaps, was devoted to the affairs of the Company whose servant he had been for so much longer. When, for example, Captain James Cooper, a former ship's captain now employed by the Company, attempted to introduce private enterprise into the economic life of the colony by buying cranberries from the Indians and re-selling them in San Francisco, Douglas promptly ordered all available supplies of these commodities to be bought up, and thus forced Cooper out of business. The Company had been granted exclusive trading privileges with the Indians, and while Douglas was Chief Factor this right would be jealously upheld.[31]

Similarly, the strict control of liquor was vigilantly maintained. When, on one occasion, the men of the Fort got hold of a barrel of spirits, Douglas had it smashed to pieces before their eyes. One eye-witness still recalled many years later

 . . . the disappointed and intoxicated men on their hands and knees taking a last draught as the liquor ran out, not even taking the trouble to use their hands to scoop it up.[32]

Despite the stranglehold that the Company held on it, the economic life of the Colony was, however, expanding. The mines at Nanaimo were producing considerable quantities of coal, and a fort was built by James McKay to defend the settlement there. Sooke, too, was becoming a busy centre; as early as 1850 Captain Grant had built a sawmill there; now the Muir family[33] began shipping piles from the area to California.[34]

Douglas himself at this time, in addition to his duties as Governor and Chief Factor, essayed a career as a businessman. In December 1851 the "Vancouver's Island Steam Saw Mill Company" was formed, with Douglas, Pemberton, Finlayson, Work, and W. H. McNeill as share-holders. Machinery for the mill arrived on the *Norman Morison* in January 1853, but the venture was unsuccessful from the start. The mill was later sold to James Duncan, and burned down in 1859.[35]

Captain Cooper, his venture into cranberries thwarted, joined in this promising new industry. With a partner, Thomas Blinkhorn, he bought land near Metchosin, built a small schooner, the *Alice*,[36] and, amongst other activities, began shipping timber to San Francisco, then in the midst of its gold rush.[37]

For a brief moment, indeed, the possibility appeared of a gold rush nearer home. Small amounts of ore with free gold were found in the Queen Charlotte Islands, and in June the *Thetis* was sent north to investigate. That gold existed was easily verified ("Our business was to report on the gold prospects, and there it was, running in quartz veins through the granite rocks overhanging the deep inlet."),[38] but the veins were not large enough to be profitably worked. The ship traded with the natives, and Moresby noted what was to become in the years ahead, despite all the efforts of Douglas to stop it, a melancholy motif in the relations of whites and Indians:

> It is sad to think that these fine people, degraded by contact with so-called civilization, have almost disappeared. Indeed, the beginnings could be seen on our own quarter-deck as they exchanged their furs for "fire-water" and drank it greedily.[39]

A more hopeful portent was the modest progress made in road-building. On the 8th of May, Douglas was able to make a report to the Secretary of the Company:

> I am exceedingly gratified to learn that the Governor and

Committee approve of making the road from this place to Soke
. . . The surface of the road requires levelling and to be otherwise improved, but even in its present state it is passable for
horsemen, and exceedingly useful in driving cattle . . . The
expence on the road does not, so far, exceed the sum of
thirty pounds and I am of opinion that a further sum of about
seventy pounds, making in all one hundred pounds, will make
the road sufficiently accessible for the present wants of the
settlers, seeing that it is not immediately required for wheeled
carriages, bulky produce being transported by water; but
simply as a cattle road. In improving it further for the passage
of wheeled carriages, it will be necessary to construct three
bridges at different points of the road, which would lead to a
considerably larger outlay than that above mentioned, but it is
difficult for Mr. Pemberton to give a correct estimate of the
actual probable expense, as that depends so much on the price
of labour which is at present high say: Mechanics from 2½
to 3 dollars a day; Labourers 1¼ to 2 dollars a day, and
besides that difficulty, there is another of greater weight
that there are no Mechanics in the Colony capable of executing
or disposed to undertake such contracts . . .[40]

Later that summer, Douglas reported that Pemberton was working on a survey of the Sooke and Metchosin districts.[41]

Education was also receiving attention, and Douglas reported:

I observe with much satisfaction that the Governor and
Committee approve of the establishment of schools for the
children of labourers and smaller settlers and I shall lose
no time in selecting sites for the school houses and grounds,
and taking the other preparatory steps toward that object . . .[42]

Acting on this declaration of policy, early in 1852 Douglas
opened the first common school in Victoria, with Charles Bailey
(or Baillie) as master. Some time the next year, the first school
house was built,[43] and Mr. Barr installed as master. A school was
opened in 1853 in Nanaimo, though there was as yet no schoolhouse
there.[44]

In the meantime, romance was finding that it, too, had a part
to play in the life of the young colony. The Fort doctor, J. S.
Helmcken, had found his soul-mate in the person of the Governor's
daughter Cecilia. Over forty years later, in his *Reminiscences,* he
could still recall the blossoming of his affections:

. . . the room of Mr. Douglas, partly an office and partly domestic, stood open, and there I saw Cecilia his eldest daughter flitting about, active as a little squirrel, and one of the prettiest objects I had ever seen; rather short but with a very pretty graceful figure of dark complexion and lovely black eyes—petite and nice. She assisted her father in clerical work, correspondence and so forth—in fact a private secretary.

I was more or less captivated.[45]

Before long, the young doctor and the even younger Cecilia (he was born in 1824, she in 1834) decided to become man and wife, and Helmcken set about providing a house—no easy matter, in view of the great shortage of both labor and materials.

There being no lumber, it had to be built with logs squared on two sides and six inches thick. The sills and uprights were very heavy and morticed—the supports of the floor likewise— the logs had to be let into grooves in the uprights.

Well, the timber had to be taken from the forest—squared there and brought down by water. All this had to be contracted for by French Canadians, then when brought to the beach I had big oxen of the company to haul it to the site. Then other Canadians took the job of putting the building up as far as the logs were concerned—and then shingling—the Indians at this time made shingles—all split. All this was very heavy, very expensive and very slow work, for the men were by no means in a hurry . . .[46]

It was intended that the marriage should take place early in 1853, but an unforeseen event now intervened to alter this plan.

At this time the Company had a sheep farm at Lake Hill (also known as "Christmas Hill"). Two shepherds, Peter Brown and James Skea, looked after the flocks. On the morning of November 5, 1852, Skea came upon the body of Brown, who had been shot in the chest. When this alarming news was brought to the Fort, Douglas, knowing that to let crime go unpunished was merely to invite further trouble, immediately set about discovering the identity of the murderer.

Before long, no doubt through information given by more law-abiding natives, he learned that there had been two murderers, both Indians, one a Cowichan and the other the son of a Nanaimo chief.

Assembling a force of vigorous French-Canadian half-breeds from the Company's employees, Douglas went north in H.M.S. *Thetis*. First, however, he asked his prospective son-in-law to advance the date of his marriage, so that in case he himself was killed in the course of the expedition, his daughter would have someone to depend on.[47] Helmcken agreed, and the rites were duly solemnized by the Rev. Staines on December 27, 1852.

A week later, Douglas left in the *Beaver* for Esquimalt, where the HBC ship *Recovery* was picked up. Then with Captain Kuper of the *Thetis* and his two lieutenants, Arthur Sansum and John Moresby, together with about 130 sailors and marines,[48] the little flotilla proceeded first to Saanich (where a false report had suggested that the fugitives were hiding) and then to the mouth of the Cowichan River, arriving there on January 6, 1853. To Lieut. Moresby, the sombre mission they had come upon seemed almost less impressive than the still unspoiled scenery of the area;

> Our speed was, perhaps two miles an hour; but who could grumble at delay admidst such scenery as opened to our astonished eyes?—a maze of islets transfigured with snow, plumed with pines, sparkling with a fairy glitter of frost and sunshine, and all around enchanting bays and islets, and the blue channels of the interlacing sea, brooded over by the eternal silence of the Rockies.[49]

Douglas and his party went ashore, and "a small tent was pitched for the Governor, where were deposited presents for the tribe, besides his pistols and cutlass, the use of either to depend on circumstances".[50] A tense scene resulted, as the whites were confronted by "over 200 tall warriors, their height exaggerated with head-plumes, faces terrifically painted with red ochre, decked with loin-ropes of shells which met their deer-skin leggings and clattered with every movement as they leaped from the canoes."[51] The latter were not at first disposed to surrender the culprit, considering that according to the custom of their tribe, a payment in goods would be sufficient. After a parley of two hours, Douglas succeeded in persuading them to surrender one of the culprits.[52]

The ships then proceeded to Nanaimo, where the other murderer was relentlessly hunted through the forests where he had sought refuge:

> The track led to a large stream and was lost, to be regained on the snow-covered boulders higher up, and then came a stretch of deep water, which it was agreed that the fugitive must have crossed by swimming. Reaching the shallow water, they struck the trail once more, and at last in an open glade they ran him to earth, hidden under the roots of a fallen tree, and so brought him, bound and wearied, to the stockade.

> It was pitiful enough to see the splendid wild man captive among his own people. What they felt I know not. What they evinced was the stoical indifference of their tradition. Not a sound was uttered, not a look showed pity or anger as we closed round our prisoner and set off on the return march.[53]

There remained only the last act of the drama that had begun at Lake Hill two months previously. A jury was empanelled on the *Beaver* (the first ever to be assembled on Vancouver Island) and since the prisoners admitted their guilt, a verdict was soon reached.

> Death, of course, was the sentence. That afternoon a gallows was erected on the island at the entrance of Protection Bay, and here they met their death with steady fortitude, in the fashion of brave men all the world over—a fashion varying with neither race nor time.[54]

Only a last poignant scene remained:

> The piteous sequence came when the old mother, tottering to her dead son's feet, kissed and clung to them, and implored that the fatal rope might be given to her. So small a mercy! And when her prayer was granted, she put it round her neck and pressed it to her lips, whilst her tears ran in torrents, and some of our own eyes were not dry.[55]

The same month that witnessed these sombre events also saw new arrivals in the Colony. The *Norman Morison,* making her third voyage from England to Vancouver Island, brought some 200 settlers,[56] including four figures deserving attention. These were Kenneth McKenzie, Thomas Skinner, Robert Melrose and James Deans.

Kenneth McKenzie had been selected as bailiff or overseer for the new Company[57] farm which he named "Craigflower".[58] Arriving with his wife and five children (three more were born on the farm), with the help of carpenters, blacksmiths and laborers who had come on the same ship a large farm house was soon erected. Modern equipment was lacking and beams had to be hewn by hand and nails made in the forge—but so well was the work done that the building still stands today, and the modern tourist, arriving at the crossroads where Admirals Road, Craigflower Road and the Island Highway meet, may see the thick front door, built to withstand the arrows of hostile Indians.

From this farm, which comprised 900 acres,[59] and had its own carpenter's and blacksmith's shop, saw-mill, flour-mill, brick-kiln and slaughter-house, produce was sent down the Gorge to the Fort. Douglas himself often visited the Farm, and high naval officers would be found around the great fireplace, discussing the news of the great world outside. The outbreak of the Crimean War in 1854 increased the importance of Esquimalt, and the farm supplied bread and meat to visiting British warships. McKenzie himself was appointed a justice of the peace in that year, and did his best despite his limited knowledge of the law, to maintain order in the little community.

Constance Cove Farm was two miles away, near where the Graving Dock is today. Thomas Skinner had been engaged as bailiff; he too arrived in the colony with a wife and five children (another child was born within a month of his arrival). Little had been done to prepare for the new colonists, and the Skinner family was crowded for a time into a small shack on Kanaka Row[60] (now called Humboldt Street). So disillusioned was one of the maids in the party that she returned aboard the *Norman Morison* and sailed back to England. The rest of the group, however, stuck it out, and with the help of Indian labor a farm-house was built overlooking what was later called "Skinner's Cove", now the site of the Dominion Graving Dock.[61] They called their new home "Oaklands", after the great oaks in the district, some of which still stand. Good crops of wheat and potatoes were soon being harvested, and in 1854 a primitive census listed 18 adults and 16 children on the Farm.

Skinner, like McKenzie, was appointed a justice of the peace in 1854, and later became the member for Esquimalt in the first legislative assembly of Vancouver Island.

By an interesting stroke of fortune, we have an artless but illuminating account of day-to-day happenings in those distant days.[62] Robert Melrose, one of those arriving with his wife on the *Norman Morison* to work on Craigflower Farm, kept a diary in which he noted any event he considered important. His criterion of selectivity seems sometimes obscure, but this detracts little from the interest of his entries. Birth, marriage and death, seed-time and harvest, the erection of new buildings, the slaughter of livestock, losing encounters with the bottle, both by himself and his fellow-workers—all are grist to his mill. One minute we are told of: "Victoria races celebrated on Beacon Hill. Holiday given." A few lines lower we have: "The Author ¼ Drunk."

Considerable attention is paid, indeed, to the fraction of inebriety assigned by Melrose to himself or to others—the entries vary from "½ drunk" through "¾ drunk" to "whole drunk"—but these are interspersed with notes of philosophical lectures given by a variety of speakers at the Farm.[63] These were on uniformly lofty subjects, varying from "The Nobility of Man", "The duty and advantage of prayer", and "the Resurrection of the Body" to one given by Melrose himself on "the Earth's Diameter, Circumference, Revolution, etc". There is some tendency, however, for these excursions into metaphysics to fade into the light of common day, and we are repeatedly brought back to earth by such entries as:

Jan 1/55. New Year's Day celebrated in a glorious Bacchanalian manner.
Jan 24/55 James Deans bought an Indian woman.
Jan 29/55 James Deans divorced his Indian woman.

These last two entries suggest that we look for a moment at their subject, so clearly a man of decision. Deans had also come out on the *Norman Morison,* and was at first employed in the Company store. Later he was sent to Craigflower Farm where he worked for two and a half years; the last part of his five-year term was spent at Lake Hill Sheep Station, where there were a few years later

1700 sheep. For these services he received £17 a year plus his board, with the privilege (denied, we recall, to Governor Blanshard) of buying anything he wanted in the store at half-price. At the end of this period he was granted 25 acres of land.

None of this, however, endeared the Company to him; in his view, it was not merely a monopoly but almost a tyranny, hostile to colonization and determined to make the most out of those in its power. As he declared in his memoirs:[64]

> The charter of the Hudson Bay Coy from the British Government to colonize the Island turned out a complete failure, the interest of the company as fur-traders rendering it necessary for them to do all in their power (sub rosa) to discourage immigration, altho in accordance with the terms of said charter they were bound to foster it and afford every assistance to settlers.
> The "truck system" i.e. the paying for labor &c in goods in lieu of coin was also a source of discontent & annoyance & rendered settlers subservient to a humiliating degree upon the Hudson Bay Company. It is not astounding that the Colonization of the Island failed to prove a success.

Apart from Deans' accusations (which are confirmed both by those with first-hand experience of Vancouver Island in this period and by subsequent writers with access to details of Company policy), his memoirs give us much useful information regarding the early days of the Colony. There is, for example, the most detailed description of the fort buildings and their location that we have:

> The site of the fort was an oak opening. The ground to the extent of an acre was cleared, and inclosed by a palisade, forming a square, on the north and south corners was a tower, containing 6 or 8 peices of Ordinance each, the north one served as a prison, the south one for firing saluts, when ever the governor visited any place officerly. In the centre of the east and west sides were maine gate ways, each had a little door, to let people out or in after hours. On the right entering by the front or south gate, was a cottage, in which was the post office, it was kept by an officer of the Company a Captain Sangster. Next in order was the smithy. Next and first on the south side was

a large store house, in which fish oil &c were stowed away. Next came the Carpenter's shop. Close to this was a large room provided with bunks for the Company's men to sleep in. Next, and last on that side, was a large building, a sort of barrack for new arrivals. Between this corner and the East gate was the Chaple and Chaplin's house. On the other side of this gate was a large building which served as a dineing room for the office adjoining this was the cook house and pantry. On the 4th side were a double row of buildings for storing furs, previous to shipment to England, and goods before taking their place in the trading store. Behind these stores was a fireproof building used as a magazine for storing gunpowder. On the lower corner was another cottage in which lived Mr Finlayson and family, who was then Chief Factor. On the other side at the front or west gate, was the flag staff and bellfry. The central part of the enclosure was open, and always kept clean. Through this inclosure ran the main road leading from the 2 gates. On one side of this road was a well . . . To this well the miners came for their supplies of water, which was hauled up with a rope & bucket.[65]

If the colony gained some interesting new figures in 1853, it also lost one. Captain Grant, Vancouver Island's first independent settler, having failed to find success there as either a farmer or a surveyor, or in Oregon as a prospector, now quitted North America forever.[66] He does not disappear entirely from history, however; he took part with distinction but a certain individualism[67] in the Crimean War, he read a paper on Vancouver Island in 1857 to the Royal Geographical Society in London, Richard Blanshard being one of the audience; and four years later died in India.

Meanwhile, other parts of the Island continued to develop. On December 3, 1852, Douglas was able to give his superiors in the Company "the highly satisfactory intelligence that our mining operations at Nanaimo have been crowned with success."[68] The Nanaimo bastion (still standing today) was finished in the spring of 1853, and by the end of the year, 2000 tons of coal had been shipped to San Francisco.

The question as to whether the area belonged to the white or the red man also received attention, and in May Douglas disclosed the policy he intended to pursue:

I observe the request of the Governor and Committee, that I should take an early opportunity of extinguishing the Indian claim in the coal District, and I shall attend to their instructions, as soon as I think it safe, and prudent to renew the question of Indian rights, which always gives rise to troublesome excitements, and has on every occasion been productive of serious disturbances."[69]

Douglas visited the area in the *Otter*[70] in August, examining the workings with close attention, and making a full report on the settlement to his superiors in the Company:

Twelve dwelling houses, a Forge, 1 Lumber Store, and a Bastion are finished, or in progress, but we have still a great deal to accomplish before house accomodations are provided for the expected re-inforcement of Miners from England, but everything in our power shall be done, to make them comfortable, when they arrive in this country . . .

While at Nanaimo, I had much conversation with the Miners, and other married servants of the Company, on the subject of opening an elementary school, for their children, who have been much neglected, and are growing up in ignorance of their duties as Christians and as men. Seeing that they all expressed an ardent wish to have the means of educating their children, I transferred Mr. Baillie, who has for some time been employed as Teacher of the Victoria Day School, but who is not now required here, to the Establishment of Nanaimo where he has since opened School . . .

I will also take the liberty of suggesting to the Governor and Committee the propriety of sending out a Clergyman for Nanaimo. The expense of that appointment will be richly repaid by its influence in improving the morals of the people, and the saving in police charges, while in many other respects it will redound to the honour and advantage of the Company.

The party selected for that office should be a member of the Free Kirk of Scotland, the Miners being generally of that persuasion, and not disposed to receive instructions from the Clergy of any other denomination.[71]

Nanaimo was not the only area whose religious needs engaged Douglas. In May, writing to HBC headquarters, he gave some account of the difficulties facing him in this regard:

That there is no church as yet built in the Colony is a fact which I admit, and sincerely regret, as the want is felt by the public at large; although there is no building devoted exclusively to religious purposes, divine service is regularly performed every Sunday in the Fort hall, which is sufficiently large to accomodate the congregation, which commonly meets there. I much regret that it has been out of my power to build a church, as no mechanic in the Colony will undertake the work at a reasonable price, and I was of opinion that it was advisable to delay the construction of such costly buildings until the Colony is better provided with mechanical labour, and the public money can be laid out to more advantage.[72]

Later that summer, Douglas was able to report some progress:

The instructions concerning the erection of a Church at this place shall receive immediate attention, the Mason being in fact at this moment preparing materials for laying a stone foundation. The body of the Church will be constructed of wood, and I shall have the timber hewn as soon as workmen can be done to undertake the job.[73]

Relations with the natives since the apprehension and punishment of the Lake Hill murderers were uneventful, and Douglas reported that in his judgment they would remain so:

Alarms have occasionally been got up among the timid about an Indian invasion but I do not think there is the slightest cause to apprehend such a calamity on a large scale, individual crimes, may and will be committed by Indians in defiance of the greatest watchfulness, but I have no fear of any general inroad of the natives. War was carried to their own doors last winter and they are sensible that we can at any moment repeat the experiment, and march a force into any part of their country and that it is in our power to harass and annoy them in a thousand ways, should they attack the Colony.[74]

In the meantime, Douglas and his Council grappled with the problems arising from the slow but steady emergence of such fundamental instruments of civilization as roads, bridges and schools. The financial burdens these imposed were by modern standards ludicrously light, but even so, seemed heavier than the Colony could meet. Proceeds from the sale of land had been scanty, mainly because genuine colonists had proved so scarce. Some other source of revenue was essential; such modern devices as the income tax and the sales tax were unknown; and, then as now, whoever was asked to provide the necessary revenue would be certain to feel outraged. Pondering this problem, a perennial one with legislators, Douglas arrived at the conclusion (not subsequently rejected in the century since) that the liquor traffic might prove a convenient source of social benefits.[75] Accordingly, on March 29, 1853, he proposed that liquor vendors should be licensed. After a whole day's debate, this policy was agreed to by the Council (Tod, Finlayson and Cooper).[76] The Company took out a wholesale licence and James Yates, proprietor of a busy tavern, was forced to acquire a retail licence. Thus at the cost of the ill-will of Yates and his customers, the government's financial problem was, for the time being, solved. Douglas reported his actions to the headquarters of the Company:

> We have also imposed a heavy Licence Duty on Inns, Beer and Ale Houses, a measure fiercely opposed by the whole body of publicans and other blood suckers, who are preying upon the vitals of the Colony, exhausting its wealth and making a return of poisonous drinks, ruinous to the morals of the people, and the prolific source of poverty and crime. Two classes of Licences for the sale of spirituous drinks are to be issued, Wholesale and Retail Licences, the Duty to be levied on the former is fixed as £100, on the latter at £120 per annum. This is not too high when it is considered that there are no customs nor excise duties nor any public burdens whatever borne by the people of this Colony. I do not suppose that the duty will put a stop to drunkeness, but it will at least take from the tippler a part of the means devoted to intemperance, and that part will be applied to the substantial improvement of the Country and to counteract in some measure the influence of his evil example.[77]

Later that year, Douglas reaffirmed his belief in the correctness of his policy, declaring that it

> ... has been attended with many salutary results there being now only one licensed ale house at this place and that conducted in a very orderly manner. The consumption of spirits is greatly reduced, and the scandalous scenes of

Yates Street of gold rush days

Wharf Street — 1863

Mayor Thomas Harris

Governor Arthur Edward Kennedy

drunkenness and excess which were the disgrace of Victoria, before the passage of the License Act, are now never seen.[78]

Education also received considerable attention from Douglas. As early as October 8, 1851, only a month after becoming Governor, he had written to Archibald Barclay, secretary of the Company:

> ... recommending the establishment of one or two elementary schools in the Colony to give a proper moral and religious training to the children of settlers who are at present growing up in ignorance, and the utter neglect of all their duties to God and to Society.[79] That remark applies with peculiar force to the children of Protestant Parents; the Roman Catholic children in this country having had until lately a very able and zealous teacher in the Revd. Mr. Lampfrit, a French Priest of the Society des Oblats, who is now living with the Indians in the Cowitchen Valley.
>
> One school at Victoria, and one at Esquimalt will provide for the present wants of the settlements, and a fixed salary of £50 a year to be paid by the Colony with an annual payment by the Parents of a certain sum not to exceed thirty shillings for each child with a free house and garden is the plan and amount of remuneration I would propose to the Committee. In regard to the character of the Teachers, I would venture to recommend a middle aged married couple for each school of strictly religious principles and unblemished character capable of giving a good sound English education and nothing more, these schools being intended for the children of the labouring and poorer classes, and children of promising talents, or whom their parents may wish to educate further, may pursue their studies and acquire the other branches of knowledge at the Company's school conducted by the Revd. Mr. Staines. I would also recommend that a good supply of School Books from the alphabet upwards, with slates and pencils be sent out with the Teachers, as there are very few in this country.[80]

By March of 1852 he had opened a common day school for boys in Victoria and also a girls' day school at Colwood Farm.

On March 29, 1853, the Council decided to open two more schools—one at Maple Point (as the Craigflower area was then known) and one in Victoria about a mile from the Fort. £500 was

appropriated for these purposes.[81] Some time during 1853 afternoon classes began at Craigflower, even though the schoolhouse
(still standing, and the oldest such building in Western Canada)
was not to be opened till the spring of 1855.[82]

By the fall of 1853 Douglas was able to report with some
satisfaction that:

> "The town of Victoria contains 87 dwellings and Store
> Houses and many other buildings are in progress. A public
> school house has been erected this season, and we are now
> building a Church capable of containing a congregation of
> 300 persons."[83]

It was in this year, also, that the public and private life of
the Governor crossed each other for a moment. He had always
kept in touch with his sister Cecilia; her marriage had now foun-
dered, her husband having disappeared. She therefore married
David Cameron, a cloth merchant of Perth, who was employed in
Demerara, and in 1853 they emigrated to Victoria.[84] (It will be
recalled that Cecilia's daughter by her first marriage, also named
Cecilia, had arrived three years before).[85] Douglas was able to
arrange a position for Cameron connected with the coal mines in
Nanaimo, and the family circle was thus pleasantly enlarged.

As it happened, Douglas had for some time been uneasy as
to the quality of justice dispensed by his newly appointed magistrates.[86] He therefore thought it prudent to set up a court of
appeal from their vagaries, and chose Cameron as the colony's
first judge. This was to occasion a considerable amount of resentment, which had perhaps three main origins. There were those who
felt (with some reason) that Cameron was unqualified for the
position; there were those who objected to the Governor appointing his brother-in-law to a key position, which might make possible
a "family compact" form of government (Douglas' son-in-law,
Dr. Helmcken, was the fort doctor, and at one time had been a
magistrate); and there were those opposed to Douglas (or at least
to the Company he represented) and who now felt that they had
been handed an ideal issue over which to dispute his authority
and perhaps discredit him with the Imperial Government.

Earlier in the year a petition had been drawn up and circulated in the colony. It complained of the high price of land and the lack of a democratic form of government or reliable courts of justice, requested that the Island be put under the rule of a governor independent of the Company, and demanded that a majority of the executive council should be elected. It also urged that a House of Assembly, elected on a wide franchise, should be established. It was signed not only by the Rev. Staines but even by such old associates of Douglas as Tod, Tolmie and Finlayson.[87] With the appointment of Douglas's brother-in-law as Judge of the newly created Supreme Court, the agitation was renewed, and a second petition, protesting this action of Douglas, was drawn up for transmission to the authorities in London. Such men as Cooper, Langford, Skinner and Yates supported it,[88] and it was decided that the Rev. Staines should personally convey the petition to the Home Government.

Staines was by this time in much disfavour with the Governor. In some respects he had been a satisfactory employee—he had performed numerous marriages, notably those of John Work, Roderick Finlayson, W. F. Tolmie and J. S. Helmcken; his duties had taken him as far afield as Sooke, Metchosin, Fort Langley and Nisqually. However, in other ways he had fallen short: he devoted much of his time to raising pigs and was involved in a law-suit about them; he was suspected of having composed an anonymous letter to the authorities in London objecting to Douglas' management of affairs; numerous parents had complained of the quality of his teaching; worst of all, perhaps, his constant hostility to the Company had had "the effect of rendering the labouring classes dissatisfied and suspicious". So, at least, declared a petition[89] signed by many parents and presented to the Board of Management of the Western Department of the Company.

Douglas in a letter to Barclay[90] had spoken of the schoolmaster's "disagreeable manner and unyielding temper" and had suggested getting rid of him. In a letter to the Duke of Newcastle[91] Douglas took note of the fact that Staines had not yet paid for the 400 acres he was occupying at Metchosin, and reported his suspicions that the clergyman hoped eventually to get them for nothing. In another letter to Barclay Douglas declared flatly: "The Rev.

Mr. Staines is a fomentor of mischief and I believe a preacher of sedition."[92]

The Company had agreed that Staines should be replaced, at least as schoolmaster, and he had been officially informed on the first of February, 1854, that in this respect his services would be terminated as of June 1, 1854.

He was still, however, the Fort Chaplain; but abruptly abandoning this post, he set sail with the petitions from Sooke for San Francisco. As it happened, he got no farther than Cape Flattery; the ship (the *Duchess of San Lorenzo*) was destroyed in a storm, and Staines was drowned.[93]

This did not however prevent the surviving malcontents from continuing their efforts. New copies of the petitions were drawn up and forwarded to London.[94] Not much attention was paid to them there; the authorities had confidence in Douglas, and the British parliament soon found itself facing a crisis more serious than an obscure dispute in one of the smallest and remotest colonies: on March 27, 1854, the Crimean War had begun.[95]

It might have seemed at first that this conflict, which was in any case merely a "limited war" of the kind that prevailed in the period between the religious wars of the seventeenth century and the ideological wars of the twentieth century, would have little effect on a part of the world so far from the battlefields of Inkerman and Balaclava as Vancouver Island. Indeed, if Alaska had not still been a Russian possession,[96] this might well have proved the case. As it was, the war was responsible for the emergence of Esquimalt as a major outpost of British naval power in the Pacific, a development which in the century since has given the Victoria area so much of its distinctive atmosphere.

A circular letter from the Imperial authorities, written on February 23, 1854, warning that war was expected, had reached Douglas in May, some weeks after it had actually broken out. In June, he received news of the outbreak of hostilities three months previously. His despatches to his superiors in the British Government and the Company, which not long before had reported "a state of profound tranquility",[97] immediately took on a more serious tone. On May 16, even before he had been notified of the declaration of war, he wrote to the Duke of Newcastle, the Colonial Secretary, suggesting an attack on Alaska; it would require, he estimated, about 500 soldiers.[98]

Problems of defence as well as attack were considered by Douglas. On the 15th of June he wrote to Barclay:

> We have just heard of the declaration of war with Russia, and I am rather surprised that no measures have been taken for our protection. No vessel of war has yet arrived on the coast, and there is no military force at my disposal, and I cannot raise a military force in the country for want of means. I would moreover observe that a labourer taken from the plough is not to be trusted in circumstances of danger, without some previous training.
>
> . . . a naval force ought hereafter to be permanently stationed here for the security of the settlement.[99]

On July 12, the Council[100] after appropriating £500 for roads and bridges, £500 for a court-house, and £500 towards finishing the church, "proceeded to consider the state of the country, and the means of defending it against the Queen's enemies in the case of invasion." It discussed at some length a proposal by Douglas for the creation of a mixed white and Indian force to defend the colony.[101] The Governor was unable, however, to convince his colleagues that Indians could safely be trusted with weapons. It was decided, though, that the crew of the *Otter* (numbering about 30) should be armed, and with this far from numerous body of defenders Douglas had to be content.[102]

Actually, the danger to Vancouver Island was never so great as Douglas for a time believed. His superiors in the Company, sensing the approach of war, had prudently concluded an agreement with its Russian counterpart, by which each promised not to molest the trading outposts of the other.[103] Douglas, however, was not made aware of this for a considerable time—a reminder to us, perhaps, that though he bulked large in his own small world, there were higher reaches of policy-making from which he was excluded.[104]

Russian warships and military outposts were, however, fair game, and in the first summer of the war a combined Franco-

British attack was made on the Russian fortress of Petropaulovsk on the coast of Kamchatka. The attack was not successful, and numerous casualties resulted.[105] As no hospital facilities existed on Vancouver Island, the wounded had to be taken to San Francisco. The difficulty of this situation was apparent, and in February 1855 the new commander-in-chief of the Pacific Station,[106] Rear-Admiral Bruce, wrote to Douglas, expressing the hope that hospital facilities would be available in case casualties resulted from new forays against the Russians. Douglas took prompt action, and three wooden huts were built at a cost of slightly under £1000.[107] They were 30' by 50', with large windows and 12-foot ceilings, and were designed to accommodate 100 patients.[108]

As it happened, when the Allied squadron again reached the coast of Kamchatka in June 1855, they found that the Russian garrison had prudently withdrawn, and no bloodshed resulted. Only one patient was admitted to the new Esquimalt hospital—an engineer who had scurvy.[109] Nevertheless, a definite beginning had been made in converting Esquimalt into a major British naval base, and though Douglas' three huts may seem paltry compared with the elaborate installations of today, the former are the seed from which the latter have sprung.[110]

The war also gave a considerable economic impulse to the Colony; Admiral Bruce had given Douglas some idea of what his requirements might be:

> He has sent an order for 1000 tons of coal for the use of the Steam Fleet, which will please God be in readiness by that time; and also for a large supply of Vegetables and fresh provisions; the latter may be procured at Nisqually,[111] but it will be impossible at that Season of the year to get Vegetables in sufficient quantities for so large a force, but we will do our best.[112]

Money was also collected for relatives of men serving in the forces; Douglas appointed a committee, consisting of the Rev. Edward Cridge (successor to the Rev. Staines as Fort Chaplain), Robert Barr, a schoolmaster, and James Yates the saloonkeeper,[113] to supervise this activity, and £60 was collected. (In 1856 there was also a "Nightingale Fund".)[114]

The war did not, however, retard the general development of such essential organs of civilization as roads, bridges, schools and churches. On the 24th of August 1854, Douglas reported to Barclay:

> The road to Soke is progressing favourably by means of Indian labourers, conducted by two white overseers, the labourers being paid at the rate of 8 dollars a month.
>
> White labourers cannot be procured under the rate of 2 and 2½ dollars a day, so that we cannot afford to employ them on the public works. Carpenters and other tradesmen are still more unreasonable, as they charge from 4 to 6 dollars for a day's work . . .
>
> The Jail is finished, and a Court House must soon be erected for the convenience of the public.[115]

The same month, the Council passed an act prohibiting "the Gift or Sale of Spirituous Liquors to Indians".

Douglas was clearly not unaware of the delicate causal connection between government spending and the creation of good will toward the spenders:

> A few thousand pounds judiciously laid out in improvements would diffuse a general feeling of satisfaction, and have the effect of attaching the people to the colony.[116]

The same year, £1000 was appropriated by the Council toward a hospital, £500 for the court-house, and £500 each for roads and bridges.

On the 21st of June 1855 the first Colonial militia was set up (more for protection against Indians than Russians). It consisted of eight privates, who received $30 a month and their rations, one corporal who got a dollar more a month, and one sergeant who received $33 a month. (On February 27, 1856, this force was expanded to 30, consisting of one lieutenant, one sergeant, two corporals and 26 privates).[117]

Education was always a subject in which Douglas took a keen interest, and in the fall of 1854 the framework was erected of Craigflower School (which was officially opened in the following spring, with Charles Clark as the first teacher).[118]

Immigration continued, though at a far from rapid rate. A group of coal miners and their families, after a rough journey on the *Princess Royal*[119] arrived in Nanaimo[120] on November 27, 1854, where they saw the octagonal bastion familiar to us today, then recently built by French-Canadian axe-men.

It is interesting to note that Douglas was the first to realize the commercial possibilities of the area's off-shore oil resources. Writing to Lord Russell, Secretary of State for the Colonies, on the 21st of August, 1855, he gave him some details of this promising source of wealth:

> The oil exported from this colony is procured from the native tribes inhabiting the west coast of Vancouver's Island, and is manufactured by them from the Whale and Dogfish. It is of excellent quality, and has a high character in California where it brings from 2 to 3 dollars a gallon in consequence of retaining its fluidness, and burning freely in the coldest weather. It is estimated that a quantity equal to ten thousand gallons was purchased from the natives of the west coast last year, and considering the imperfect means they possess for taking the fish and bringing out the oil, it is not unreasonable to suppose that with the use of proper means, the returns of oil would be very greatly increased. The oil trade is carried on by a few enterprising individuals who live among the Indians and collect the article as it is manufactured by the natives.

This year (1854) also saw the birth of the Douglas' last child, Martha.[121]

Meanwhile, at Craigflower Farm, its open-hearted proprietor was experiencing his troubles. The Company saw the Farm as a necessary economic venture pure and simple; Captain Langford, on the other hand, inclined to the view that his primary duty was to exemplify the traditional role of the English country gentleman. Admittedly, he gave some attention to the land; by the end of 1854, 190 acres of heavily wooded ground had been cleared (all by hand labor),[122] and crops as diverse as wheat and wool were being gathered; while livestock on the farm included 13 horses, 9 cows, 523 sheep, 97 swine and 80 fowls.[123] Meanwhile his sister came out from England and successfully operated an "Academy for young ladies", in which two of the Governor's daughters were pupils.

What the Company eventually took exception to, however, was the lavish scale on which the genial captain dispensed hospitality to his many visitors, notably officers from ships in port.[124] In 1853 he drew on the Company for purely social functions a sum almost eight times his annual salary;[125] this included the price 70 gallons of spirits. His employers were "not amused", reprimanded him severely, and envisioned his dismissal. Under the weight of their disapproval, the Captain made some amendment in his ways.[126]

A newcomer to Victoria in this period, whose fame would increase with the years, was the Rev. Edward Cridge, who, succeeding the Rev. Staines as Fort Chaplain, arrived with his wife on the *Marquis of Bute* on April 1, 1855.[127] His wife opened the first Sunday School in the colony, and he himself was appointed Vancouver Island's first inspector of schools in February 1856. His first report to the Governor was made on November 30 of that year.[128]

It was still a small world, however, in which Vancouver Islanders lived. Some idea of this may be gained by considering figures of income and expenditure for the year ending November 1, 1855. Income from land sales was £334.17.6, and from the duty on "licensed premises", £340; total expenditures were £4,107.2.3., which included the following:

Government premises	£ 7	15	10
Surveying department	683	18	1
Roads and Bridges	1388	5	5
Parsonage and chaplain	1362	7	5
Public schools	320	4	11
Poor rates	10	10	3
Administration of justice	100	—	—
Expenses of jail	30	9	2
Militia	81	8	8[129]

More than passing interest attaches to the first census ever taken on Vancouver Island.[130] It gives a remarkably complete picture as of December 31, 1854, of its inhabitants, classified by age and sex, as well as of the amount of its animal and vegetable produce. It found 774 persons on the Island, of whom 232 lived in Victoria[131] and 151 in Nanaimo. It showed that nearly half the population of the Island was under 20 years of age, but that apparently only 15 people were over 50, and no one at all over 60!

There was still only one church on the Island,[132] but there were six saw-mills and three flour mills and 39 stores and shops. There were three schools: one in Victoria with 26 pupils, one at Maple Point (Craigflower) with 26, and one at Nanaimo with 29.

Altogether it was still a very small community over which Douglas presided—even though this had little effect on the conduct of the Governor, who maintained at all times an attitude of inflexible dignity.[133]

1856 was a year which saw a few only moderately important events, and one highly significant one. Among the former we should note the construction of an Anglican church on land granted to the Church by the HBC; The Rev. Cridge, as noted above, began his vigilant supervision of Vancouver Island's school system, a Rifle Company was formed, consisting of one lieutenant, one sergeant, two corporals, and 26 privates;[134] the Crimean War came to an end on the 30th of March;[135] the HBC began allowing settlers to purchase land on the instalment plan, and a commission was set up to attempt to determine the exact boundary with the U.S.A. in the waters around the Island.[136] On the more personal side, the Governor's son James, whose fourth birthday had been celebrated the previous year by a big picnic held in Esquimalt, reached the age of five.[137]

But more important than all these was the giant step taken toward democratic self-government. The first move in this direction had been when Governor Blanshard had been ordered to appoint a council to assist him in his duties, an order which he had implemented in the last few days of his term of office. Now the authorities in London had decided that British subjects could not be kept permanently under the authority of a government which they had no part in selecting. Accordingly, Douglas was informed by Henry Labouchère, Secretary of State for the Colonies, in a despatch dated February 28, 1856, of the drastic reorganization of the colony's political life which he was instructed to inaugurate: he was to proceed without delay to set in motion the machinery for the election of an Assembly. The number of electoral districts and the qualifications for voting or for offices were to be left to the discretion of the Governor, who was to reserve the right to veto any measure passed by the new body.[138]

The Secretary of State was evidently aware that all this would come as something of a shock to Douglas, for in the closing words of his despatch he did what he could to soften the blow:

> I am aware that Her Majesty's Government are imposing on you a task of some difficulty as well as responsibility in giving you these instructions, especially as they have to be carried into execution with so small an amount of assistance as the present circumstances of your settlement afford. But I have every reason to rely on your abilities and public spirit; and you may, on your part, rely on the continuance of such assistance and support as Her Majesty's Government can render you, and on their making full allowance for the peculiarities of your position.[139]

Douglas' feelings on receiving these unexpected instructions are evident from his reply:

> It is, I confess, not without a feeling of dismay that I contemplate the nature and amount of labour and responsibility which will be imposed upon me, in the process of carrying out the instructions conveyed in your despatch. Possessing a very slender knowledge of Legislation, without legal advice or intelligent assistance of any kind, I approach the subject with diffidence; feeling, however, all the encouragement which the kindly-promised assistance and support of Her Majesty's Government is calculated to inspire.
>
> Under these circumstances I beg to assure you that every exertion on my part shall be made, to give effect to your said instructions, at as early a period as possible . . .
>
> I am utterly averse to universal suffrage, or making population the basis of representation; but I think it expedient to extend the franchise to all persons holding a fixed property stake, whether houses or lands in the Colony; the whole of that class having interests to serve, and a distinct motive for seeking to improve the moral and material condition of the Colony.[140]

Douglas laid the Home Government's despatch before the Council, and after considerable discussion rules were laid down for the necessary election. The ownership of £300 worth of property would qualify a man for office, and the ownership of twenty acres of land for the franchise. Four electoral districts were set up: Victoria, Esquimalt-Metchosin, Nanaimo and Sooke. Victoria was to have three members, Esquimalt-Metchosin two, Nanaimo and Sooke one each. The first popular election on Vancouver Island was duly held,[141] and the members returned were as follows: Victoria, J. D. Pemberton, James Yates and E. E. Langford; Esquimalt-Metchosin, Dr. Helmcken and Thomas Skinner; Sooke, John Muir; and Nanaimo, John F. Kennedy.

On the 12th of August the new House of Assembly convened. After electing Dr. Helmcken as speaker, it engaged in some dispute over the validity of some of the election results. Eventually Langford agreed to resign, and J. W. MacKay was chosen in his place.

The House had been opened with a speech from Governor Douglas which beneath its layers of florid Victorian pomposity revealed an intelligent awareness of the problems facing the newly formed legislature and the colony on whose behalf it would act:

Gentlemen of the Legislative Council, and of the House of Assembly:

I congratulate you most sincerely on this memorable occasion; the meeting in full convention of the General Assembly of Vancouver's Island, an event fraught with consequences of the utmost importance to its present and future inhabitants; and remarkable as the first instance of representative institutions being granted in the infancy of a British colony.

The history and actual position of this colony are marked by many other remarkable circumstances. Called into existence by an Act of the Supreme Government, immediately after the discovery of gold in California, it has maintained an arduous and incessant struggle with the disorganizing effects on labour of that discovery. Remote from every other British settlement, with its commerce trammelled, and met by restrictive duties on every side, its trade and resources remain undeveloped.

Self-supporting, and defraying all the expenses of its own Government, it presents a striking contrast to every other colony in the British empire, and like the native pines of its storm-beaten promontories, it has acquired a slow but hardy growth.

Its future progress must, under Providence, in a great measure depend, on the intelligence, industry and enterprise of its inhabitants, and upon the legislative wisdom of this Assembly.

Gentlemen, I look forward with confidence and satisfaction to the aid and support which the executive power may in future expect to derive from your local experience and knowledge of the wishes of the people, and the wants of the country. I feel assured that, as public men, holding a solemn and momentous trust, you will, as a governing principle, strive with one accord to promote the true and substantial interests of the country; and that our legislative labours will be distinguished alike by prudence, temperance, and justice to all classes.

Gentlemen, I am happy to inform you, that Her Majesty's Government continue to express the most lively interest in the progress and welfare of this colony.

Negociations are now pending with the Government of the United States, which may probably terminate in an extension of the reciprocity treaty to Vancouver's Island. To show the commercial advantages connected with that treaty, I will just mention that an import duty of 30 l. is levied on every 100 l's worth of British produce which is now sent to San Francisco, or to any other American port; or, in other words, the British proprietor pays as a tax to the United States, nearly the value of every third cargo of fish, timber, or coal, which he sends to any American port. The reciprocity treaty utterly abolishes those fearful imposts, and establishes a system of free trade in the produce of British colonies.

The effects of that measure, in developing the trade and natural resources of the colony, can, therefore, hardly be overestimated.

The coal, timber, and the productive fisheries of Vancouver's Island, will assume a value before unknown; while every branch of trade will start into activity, and become the means of pouring wealth in the country.

So unbounded is the reliance which I place in the enterprise and intelligence possessed by the people of this colony, and in the advantages of their geographical position, that, with equal rights and a fair field, I think they may enter into successful competition with the people of any other country.

The extension of the reciprocity treaty to this island once

gained, the interests of the colony will become inseparably connected with the principles of free trade, a system which, I think, it will be sound policy on our part to encourage.

Gentlemen, the colony has been again visited this year by a large party of northern Indians, and their presence has excited in our minds a not unreasonable degree of alarm.

Through the blessing of God, they have been kept from committing acts of open violence, and been quiet and orderly in their deportment; yet the presence of large bodies of armed savages, who have never felt the restraining influences of moral and religious training, and who are accustomed to follow the impulses of their own evil natures, more than the dictates of reason and justice, gives rise to a feeling of insecurity, which must exist as long as the colony remains without military protection.

Her Majesty's Government, ever alive to the dangers which beset the colony, have arranged with the Lords Commissioners of the Admiralty, that the *President* frigate should be sent to Vancouver's Island; and that measure will, I have no doubt, be carried into effect without delay.

I shall, nevertheless, continue to conciliate the good will of the native Indian tribes, by treating them with justice and forbearance, and by rigidly protecting their civil and agrarian rights; many cogent reasons of humanity and sound policy recommend that course to our attention, and I shall therefore rely upon your support in carrying such measures into effect.

We know, from our own experience, that the friendship of the natives is at all times useful, while it is no less certain that their emnity may become more disastrous than any other calamity to which the colony is directly exposed.

Gentlemen of the House of Assembly, according to con-stitutional usage, with you must originate all Money Bills; it is, therefore, your special province to consider the ways and means of defraying the ordinary expenses of the Government, either by levying a Customs duty on imports, or by a system of direct taxation.

The poverty of the country and the limited means of a population struggling against the pressure of numberless priva-tions, must necessarily restrict the amount of taxation; it should, therefore, be our constant study to regulate the public expenditure according to the means of the country, and to live strictly within our income.

The common error of running into speculative improvements, entailing debts upon the colony, for a very uncertain advantage, should be carefully avoided.

The demands upon the public revenue will at present chiefly arise from the improvement of the internal communications of the country, and providing for the education of the young, the erection of places for public worship, the defence of the country, and the administration of justice.

Gentlemen, I feel, in all its force, the responsibility now resting upon us. The interests and well-being of thousands yet unborn may be affected by our decisions, and they will reverence or condemn our acts according as they are found to influence for good or for evil the events of the future.

Gentlemen of the House of Assembly, I have appointed Chief Justice Cameron to administer the oath of allegiance to the Members of your House, and to receive your declarations of qualification; you may then proceed to choose a speaker, and to appoint the officers necessary for the proper conduct of the business of the House.[142]

When it recovered from the Governor's oratory,[143] the House proceeded to consider the question of ways and means. The available revenue was that from "licensed premises"; in 1855 it had amounted to only £340.[144] The first supply bill (December 18, 1856) was for the modest sum of £130. This, it was believed, would be sufficient to cover lighting, heating and furnishing the House, stationery, copying documents, and the salaries of a clerk, sergeant-at-arms, and messenger. It was duly passed, and the Island settled down under its new dispensation.

So 1856 passed into 1857. Life in the hamlet of Victoria—it held perhaps three hundred souls[145]—proceeded uneventfully. The appurtenances of civilization were slowly multiplying—the first theatre was opened at this time.[146] Yet the palisades were still standing; the possibility of trouble with the Indians[147] had not altogether vanished. Outside the stockade lay the nearest of the Company farms; what is now the City's business district held waving fields of wheat. Along one side of the Fort was the forerunner of Government Street; from its northern end one could reach the rough roads that led to Esquimalt, Saanich and Sooke. A lane ran eastward from the main Fort gate through swamp and meadow; some day it would be known as Fort Street.

Yet beyond these scratches in the soil of the almost unexplored island—what? A minute settlement at Nanaimo, others at Metchosin and Sooke, a few venturesome souls in the Saanich hinterland, the crumbling ruins of Nootka and Fort Rupert. For the rest, only the dark woods held by the fierce Cowichans, and the villages on the open Pacific where the resourceful Nootka battled the monsters of the deep.

Even with the centres of civilization, the link was tenuous. Occasional ships made the long journey to London, the Sandwich Islands or San Francisco. By land, there were neither roads nor railways; to the east lay the fastnesses of New Caledonia, the impassable barrier of the Rockies, and the vast area known as Rupert's Land. To reach the first city east of Victoria under the British flag, one would have to trudge at least two thousand miles.

R. C. Mayne[148] commented on the growth of the settlement:

> Upon my first visit to Victoria in 1849, a small dairy at the head of James Bay was the only building standing outside the fort pickets, which are now demolished.[149] But shortly after, upon Mr. Douglas' arrival, he built himself a house on the south side of James Bay;[150] and Mr. Work, another chief factor of the company, arriving a little later, erected another in Rock Bay, above the bridge. These formed the nucleus of a little group of buildings, which rose about and between them so slowly that even in 1857 there was but a small wharf on the harbour's edge.[151]

Yet these disabilities and others like them were softened by the setting. Across the Straits, the Olympics breathed serenity; then as now, greenery abounded, and spring came early and stayed long. Comfortable farm houses held blazing fire-places; holidays gave excuses for gay picnics. The colonists, even the humblest, ate better fare than the compatriots they had left behind, while English flowers outside their cottages helped dull the ache of homesickness. English papers in the Fort library kept the intellectually-inclined abreast of the state of the world six months previously; while visiting ships of the Royal Navy gave a lift to the hearts of old sailors and young maidens. The tiny assembly attempted to clothe its deliberations in all the dignity of Westminster, and its decisions and those of the courts provided material for gossip or debate.

r. John Sebastian Helmcken

Bishop Cridge

Honourable Amor de Cosmos

Sister Mary Providence, pioneer
educator and philanthropist

No ceremony was known in those pleasant times. All the half-dozen houses that made up the town were open to us. In fine weather, riding-parties of the gentlemen and ladies of the place were formed, and we returned generally to a high tea or tea-dinner at Mr. Douglas's or Mr. Work's, winding up the pleasant evening with dance and song. We thought nothing then of starting off to Victoria in sea-boots, carrying others in our pockets, just to enjoy a pleasant evening by a good log-fire. And we cared as little for the weary tramp home to Esquimalt in the dark, although it happened sometimes that men lost their way, and had to sleep in the bush all night.[152]

Shakespeare, one felt, must have had this spot in mind:

> This other Eden, demi-paradise,
> This fortress built by Nature for herself
> Against infection and the hand of war,
> This happy breed of men, this little world,
> This precious stone set in the silver sea,
> Which serves it in the office of a wall,
> Or as a moat defensive to a house
> Against the envy of less happier lands . . .[153]

Yet no moat or fortress can withstand forever "the wreckful siege of battering days".[154] Already, events in the history of the Island to this point had proved this fact repeatedly. For long centuries, only the red man had hunted its forests and fished its waters; yet once the tribes of Western Europe made their great leap from their narrow peninsula into the unknown world beyond it, it was inevitable that in the course of time, they would touch and overflow these distant shores, and that the culture which had forged the means to conquer the oceans would slowly but surely prevail against those modes of life not armed with such potent weapons. So, too, it had proved in the realm of political development; when Douglas had landed at Clover Point in 1843, never once could he have envisioned reading his speech from the throne of 1856 to the miniature assembly; yet the logic of events—the steady broadening of nineteenth century democracy in the homeland—had made it inevitable that similar institutions must be extended to Englishmen beyond the seas; inevitable, too, in an age of free trade and free enterprise, that the feudal and monopolistic concepts of life and government still held by the Hudson's Bay Company must some day be swept away.

So now; for some centuries man, having found in North America "something commensurate to his capacity for wonder",[155] had been engaged in looting, or, as some said, developing it; from the very beginning he had believed that there was a richer if less certain source of wealth than fish or furs, but till the nineteenth century El Dorado—the City of Gold—had eluded him. Then, almost over night, men had arrived from the ends of the earth to search for it in California, where it had apparently been found. The leisurely way of life taken over from the old regime of Spain had been swept away; in its place was a swarming, struggling mass of humanity, all feverishly seeking the precious nuggets that meant riches.

Now this scene was to be repeated in New Caledonia, as the mainland of British Columbia was still called. While Douglas was addressing his seven-man legislature as if he had been in the Palace of Westminster itself, and John McLoughlin, his one-time superior, was dying in Oregon City, and far away in London a parliamentary committee, looking into the affairs of the Hudson's Bay Company, was hearing hostile testimony from Richard Blanshard and James Cooper,[156] up and down the creeks and rivers of the Interior patient, hopeful, persevering men were searching for the gleam in the bottom of their goldpans which might mean that long months of toil and discouragement had been crowned at last with success.

And now, at least for some of them, this came to pass. The exact date of the first truly big strike is lost, but it was likely in 1856 or 1857. A prospector, James Huston, was perhaps the first to find gold at Tranquille Creek near Kamloops[157] in sufficient quantity to excite interest.

News moved slowly in those days, but quickly enough for Douglas to write to the Colonial Office in 1856, informing them of the discovery:

Victoria, April 16, 1856.

To Rt. Hon. Henry Labouchère, M.P.:

I hasten to communicate for the information of Her

Majesty's Government a discovery of much importance, made known to me by Mr. Angus McDonald, Clerk in charge of Fort Colvile, one of the Hudson's Bay Company's Trading Posts on the Upper Columbia District.

That gentleman reports, in a letter dated on the 1st of March last, that gold has been found in considerable quantities within the British territory, in the Upper Columbia, and that he is moreover of opinion that valuable deposits of gold will be found in many other parts of that country; he also states that the *daily earnings* of persons then employed in digging gold were ranging from 21 to 81 for each man. Such is the substance of his report on that subject, and I have requested him to continue his communications in respect to any further discoveries made.

. . . Several interesting experiments in gold washing have been lately made in this colony, with a degree of success that will no doubt lead to further attempts for the discovery of the precious metal. The quantity of gold found is sufficient to prove the existence of the metal, and the parties engaged in the enterprise entertain sanguine hopes of discovering rich and productive beds.[158]

More reports filtered down from the Interior to the Governor in the months that followed, and his superiors were duly informed.

I have heard through other almost equally reliable sources of information, that the number of persons engaged in gold digging is yet extremely limited, in consequence of the threatening attitude of the native tribes, who being hostile to the Americans, have uniformly opposed the entrance of American citizens into their country . . .

It is reported that gold is found in considerable quantities, and that several persons have accumulated large sums by their labour and traffic, but I cannot vouch for the accuracy of those reports; though, on the other hand, there is no reason to discredit them, as about 220 ounces of gold dust has been brought to Vancouver's Island direct from the Upper Columbia, a proof that the country is at least auriferous.

From the successful result of experiments made in washing gold from the sands of the tributary streams of Fraser's River there is reason to suppose that the gold region is extensive, and I entertain sanguine hopes that future researches will develope stores of wealth, perhaps equal to the gold fields of California.[159]

Late in 1857 the future began casting its shadow more plainly across the present:

> . . . I have received further intelligence from my correspondents in that quarter.
>
> It appears from their reports that the auriferous character of the country is becoming daily more extensively developed, through the exertions of the native Indian tribes, who, having tasted the sweets of gold finding, are devoting much of their time and attention to that pursuit . . .
>
> The reputed wealth of the Couteau[160] mines is causing much excitement among the population of the United States territories of Washington and Oregon, and I have no doubt that a great number of people from those territories will be attracted thither with the return of the fine weather in spring.[161]

It was evident, then, to Douglas, that the discoveries would certainly attract prospectors; his concept of their numbers, however, would fall far short of the eventual reality. That the discoveries meant the end of the world he had known and whole-heartedly believed in, does not seem to have occurred to him at all.

But so it was to be. The winter of 1857 was the last before a motley and leaderless army would scramble ashore where Douglas with a few companions had landed in 1843 to found a trading post. Then, the wood for the palisades had been bought from the Indians in exchange for blankets; now, in a single season, the fort and its cannons would become only a quaint reminder of an already legendary past, a mere hindrance to the unconscious forward trampling of events.

The Company, too, would pass through a transformation as great. It still held undisputed sway over not merely Vancouver Island but a huge area of the central part of the continent; while the Canadian Confederation by contrast was only a subject for debate by the more farsighted editorial writers.[162] It was organized on almost feudal lines; in its own way, it had its lords and vassals, knights and men-at-arms, and orders which must be obeyed were passed down the chain of command from the ultimate authority of the Governor and Committee in London. The Company had found it convenient to tolerate agriculture, but to the two greatest forces of change in 19th century life, industrialism and democracy, it was either indifferent or hostile. All this, too, was about to change, and the metamorphosis from a chain of fur-trading posts to a chain of department stores would soon be under way.

Many years later, Dr. Helmcken remembered how the future made itself felt as the silent but disturbing presence in the old Fort dining-hall:

> About 1857 Governor Douglas at the mess table shewed us a few grains of scale gold—not more than a drachm—which had been sent him from the North Thompson. This was the first gold I saw and probably the first that arrived here. The Governor attached great importance to it and thought it meant a great change and busy time. He spoke of Victoria rising to be a great city . . .[163]

The remaining years of the century would prove the truth of these predictions; and even the next twelve months would witness a giant stride toward fulfilling them. Already, squatting by their campfires in the California hills, disappointed miners were hearing rumors of easy riches to be had a thousand miles to the north. In the spring of 1858, first in their hundreds and then in their thousands, they would be arriving at Fort Victoria. All they would want there would be the tools and supplies to press on to the Interior; but even when the feverish excitement abated and the flood of humanity had subsided, the gold rush would have left its indelible mark. Gone would be the sleepy hamlet, gone the monopoly of the all-powerful Company, gone the attempted miniature recreation of England on the shores of the Pacific. In their place would be the rude beginnings of the bustling, competing, cosmopolitan capital of today. Man's age-old quest for gold had been the cause of many deeds, from murder to self-sacrifice; to Victoria it would bring something more constructive than either: the birth of the city, the end of the palisades.

FOOTNOTES

[1] Bancroft, *History of British Columbia*, p. 53.

[2] His salary was £800 per annum (later considerably increased), in addition to his recompense by the Company for his duties as Chief Factor.

[3] In 1838, writing to the Governor and Committee of the Company, one of its employees (speaking of the Willamette River settlers) had declared: "The interests of the Colony and Fur Trade will never harmonize, the former can flourish, only, through the protection of equal laws, the influence of free trade, the accession of respectable inhabitants; in short, by establishing a new order of things, while the Fur Trade must suffer by each innovation." The employee was James Douglas. (Quoted in J. S. Galbraith, *The Hudson's Bay Company as an Imperial Factor, 1821-1869*, U. of Toronto Press, 1957, p. 12).

[4] John S. Galbraith maintains that "British Columbia became British rather than American or Russian largely because of the work of a small number of fur-traders and of the capitalists they represented." (Galbraith, *op. cit.*, p. 174).

[5] In all political systems, there are relationships which it is wiser to leave undefined." — De Maistre.

[6] R. Finlayson, *Biography*, Victoria, 1891, p. 11.

[7] An interesting account of Langford's ways and works is found in "The Trials and Tribulations of Edward Edwards Langford" by S. W. Pettit, (*BCHQ*, Vol. 17, January-April, 1953, pp. 5-40).

[8] See Scholefield and Howay, *British Columbia from the earliest times to the present*, 4 volumes, Vancouver, 1914, I, 476; also Finlayson, *History of Vancouver Island and the Northwest Coast*, MS in *PABC*, n.d., p. 22.

[9] Built of teak at Moulmein, Burma. See A. N. Mouat, "Notes on the *Norman Morison*", BCHQ, III, 3, July, 1939, p. 23.

[10] Up to April, 1852, the Company had brought out 271 men, 80 women, and 84 children; it had sold 147½ acres of land to 11 people, and 19 more had applied for 2355 acres. (Galbraith, *op. cit.*, p. 298).

[11] This claim has been disputed. Douglas, writing to Archibald Barclay, Secretary of the HBC, on October 8, 1851, speaks of "the Roman Catholic families in this country having had until lately a very able and zealous teacher in the Rev. Mr. Lampfrit, a French Priest of the Society des Oblats, who is now living with the Indians in the Cowichan Valley." See D. L. MacLaurin, "Education before the gold rush", *BCHQ*, October, 1938, pp. 247-263.

[12] He was struck by a motor-car at the corner of Transit and Newport, Oak Bay, on the evening of April 9, 1930, and died instantly. See *Colonist* of April 10 for an account of his career, which included a period as B.C.'s first Deputy Minister of Agriculture. Some idea of how few generations it takes to comprise the whole of B.C.'s history may be gained from the fact that Anderson had once known at Fort Vancouver an old Kanaka "who used to tell us with a great deal of pride of the part he took in the despatching of Captain Cook and of his having participated in the subsequent feast". (Anderson, *Notes and Comments on early days and events in British Columbia, Washington and Oregon*, MS in *PABC*, 1925, pp. 209-210).

[13] *Ibid.*, p. 161.

[14] *loc. cit.*

[15] Anderson, *op. cit.*, p. 166.

[16] *Ibid.*, p. 160.

[17] Anderson, *op. cit.*, p. 178.

[18] *Ibid.*, p. 158.

[19] Anderson, *op. cit.*, p. 159.

[20] "Mrs. Staines was a much more energetic person, she it was who really kept the school going and in spite of many undoubtedly adverse circumstances managed comparatively most creditably. I can see her now in my mind's eye, with a row of curls down each side of her angular face; by no means unprepossessing however, spare figure, clad in black, a lady undoubtedly, and when walking out holding up her skirts on each side and ordering the girls to follow her example." (*Ibid.*, p. 159). Mrs. Staines was not, however, incapable of error. On one occasion in preparing the salad for a dinner party, she inadvertently substituted castor oil for salad oil, with predictable results. (Helmcken, *Reminiscences,* III., 99).

[21] Latin was long a compulsory subject in the schools of Vancouver Island.

[22] Anderson, *op. cit.*, pp. 166-167.

[23] Walbran, *British Columbia Coast Names,* Ottawa, 1909, p. 348.

[24] Port Kuper, Queen Charlotte Islands, is named after him.

[25] Admiral John Moresby, *Two Admirals,* London, John Murray, 1909, p. 121.

[26] *Ibid.*, p. 122.

[27] Walbran, *British Columbia Coast Names,* Ottawa, 1909, pp. 342-3.

[28] Moresby, *Two Admirals,* pp. 122-3. Before the road was built, sailors often carried their boats between Thetis Cove and Portage Inlet. Hence the name of the latter. (Robinson, *Esquimalt, Place of Shoaling Waters,* Quality Press, Victoria, 1947, p. 78).

[29] Golledge's career was to prove a checkered one. When gold was discovered at Leechtown, near Victoria, he became a Gold Commissioner there. However, "He took to heavy drinking, and became in a few years a hopeless derelict. In 1884 he was convicted of stealing an Indian canoe and the *Colonist* said 'it is hoped that Golledge will rid the province of his presence, which has become distasteful to respectable people'." (B. Ramsey, *Ghost Towns of British Columbia,* Mitchell Press, Vancouver, 1963, pp. 202-204).

[30] Anderson, *Notes and Comments,* p. 156.

[31] See Sage, *Douglas,* pp. 185-6, and Bancroft, *History of British Columbia,* p. 256. This incident made Cooper a life-long enemy of the Company. He testified against it before the House of Commons in the Enquiry of 1857. See his *Maritime Matters,* MS in *PABC.*

[32] Anderson, *Notes and Comments,* p. 180.
Dr. Helmcken, no doubt after an inner struggle between his duties as a physician and his duties to the Company, thoughtfully sprinkled tartar emetic on the whisky, which made the men violently sick. (Helmcken, *Reminiscences,* III, 24).

[33] "Mr. Muir used to say that the advice given him by Mr. Douglas when he went to Sooke was this: 'Never break your word to an Indian, even if

it is a promise to give him a licking'—advice which he strictly followed with the best of results, as he lived in amity with the natives in spite of the fact that he was comparatively quite isolated. Mr. Muir is credited and, I believe, rightly, with having introduced the broom to this country, certain it is that there was none before his arrival." (Anderson, *Notes and Comments,* p. 186).

[34] Ormsby, *British Columbia: A History,* Macmillan, 1958, p. 117.

[35] W. K. Lamb, "Early Lumbering on Vancouver Island, Part I, 1844-1855," *BCHQ,* Vol. II, No. 1, January, 1938, pp. 42-46.

[36] This was not of course the first ship built on Vancouver Island. We must not forget Nootka.

[37] Ormsby, *British Columbia,* p. 117.

[38] Moresby, *Two Admirals,* p. 126.

[39] *Loc. cit.*

[40] Douglas to Barclay, 8 May, 1852. *PABC.*

[41] Douglas to Barclay, 11 July, 1852. *PABC.*

[42] Douglas to Barclay, 8 May, 1852. *PABC.*

[43] This was, it will be observed, two years before Craigflower school was opened.

[44] D. L. Maclaurin, *The History of Education in the Crown Colonies of Vancouver Island and British Columbia and in the Province of British Columbia.* Ph.D. Thesis, U. of Washington, 1936, p. 22.

[45] Helmcken, *Reminiscences,* II, 85-86. *PABC.*

[46] Helmcken, *Reminiscences,* III, pp. 57-58.
Helmcken's house still stands and is open to inspection by the public. It is the second oldest in the Victoria area, the oldest being John Tod's house, built in 1851, (now 2564 Heron Street, Oak Bay).

[47] Helmcken, *Reminiscences,* III, 64. *PABC.*

[48] The ships also carried 16 gallons of cognac, 8 gallons of sherry, 8 gallons of port wine, 48 gallons of gin and 500 Havana cigars. (B. A. McKelvie and W. E. Ireland, "The Victoria Voltigeurs", *BCHQ,* Vol. XX, July-October, 1956, p. 229.)

[49] Moresby, *Two Admirals,* p. 128.

[50] *Ibid.,* p. 126.

[51] *Ibid.,* p. 130.

[52] "The surrender of a criminal, as in the case of the Cowegin murderer, without bloodshed, by the most numerous and warlike tribe on Vancouver's Island, at the requisition of the civil power, may be considered as an epoch in the history of our Indian relations which augurs well for the future peace and prosperity of the Colony. (Douglas to Barclay, 20 January, 1853, *PABC*).

[53] Moresby, *op. cit.,* pp. 134-135.

[54] *Ibid.,* p. 135. The site of the execution, after being called for a short time "Execution Point" has ever since been known as "Gallows Point".

55 Moresby, *Two Admirals*, p. 135.

56 Bancroft, *History of British Columbia*, p. 258.

57 The "Company" was technically the "Puget Sound Agricultural Company", but this was a subsidiary of the HBC, set up to forestall charges that the latter company was engaged in more than merely trading furs with the Indians.

58 A detailed description of the farm is given in Robinson, *Esquimalt*, pp. 77-83.

59 The Company still owned parts of it as late as 1934, when it reverted to the municipality for unpaid taxes. (Robinson, *Esquimalt*, p. 83).

60 The Kanakas (who came from the Sandwich Islands) at one time were fairly numerous in Victoria, but Kanaka Bay in Esquimalt is now the only reminder of them. Their ultimate fate remains obscure, but a clue is given by the existence of a "Kanaka Bar" on the Fraser River, a relic of the gold-rush days which began in that area in 1858.

61 The farm warehouses were torn down when the Dock was built. (Robinson, *Esquimalt*, p. 71).)

62 In the Provincial Archives. See also *BCHQ*, Vol. 7, issues of April, July and October, 1943.

63 These were, perhaps, Victoria's first "non-credit courses".

64 James Deans, *The Settlement of Vancouver Island*, Victoria, 1878. MS in *PABC*.

65 Deans, *Settlement*, pp. 6-7.

66 He left behind him two things not always associated: a number of small debts (W. E. Ireland, "Captain Walter Colquhoun Grant, Vancouver Island's first independent settler", *BCHQ*, Vol. 17, January-April, 1953, p. 112) and a reputation as "a splendid fellow, and every inch an officer and a gentleman". (Helmcken, *Victoria Colonist*, Holiday Number, Christmas, 1887, p. 3). Governor Simpson, writing to Douglas, had commented as early as 1850 that " . . . he must either be very plausible, or else possesses a peculiar talent for getting into the pockets of his friends . . . " (Simpson to Douglas, August 30, 1850, *PABC*). Possibly, Grant was a gentleman in the worst sense of the term.

67 "Many stories are told of his eccentricities. Among them one to the effect that his horse being shot under him, he deliberately removed the saddle and bridle under a smart fire and retired from the field unhurt with his property." (Anderson, *Notes and Comments*, p. 158).

68 Douglas to Barclay, 3 December, 1862. *PABC*.

69 Douglas to Barclay, 16 May, 1853. *PABC*.

70 Built in 1852 in London, the *Otter*, 144 tons, was 122 feet long, and arrived on this coast in June, 1853. (Walbran, *British Columbia Coast Names*, pp. 367-8).

71 Douglas to Barclay, 3 September, 1853. *PABC*.

72 Douglas to Barclay, 27 May, 1853. *PABC*.

73 Douglas to Barclay, 12 July, 1853. *PABC*.

74 Douglas to Barclay, 21 March, 1853. *PABC*.

75 The Roman Emperor Vespasian, criticized for deriving part of the government revenues from public lavatories, replied "Pecunia non olet" —
"money has no smell". These institutions are still referred to in France
as "Vespasiennes"; devious are the routes to immortality.

76 Cooper took considerable persuasion; he was still no doubt aggrieved by
Douglas' part in his cranberry venture, and had been further vexed by a
Council ruling that no Council member could engage in the liquor trade.

77 Douglas to Barclay, 8 April, 1853. *PABC*. The tax on liquor dealers
brought in £220 in 1853, £460 in 1854, and £340 in 1855. (Bancroft,
History of British Columbia, p. 339).

78 Douglas to Barclay, 4 November, 1853. *PABC*.

79 Douglas on several occasions expressed his concern regarding the duties
owed by the lower orders of society to the upper. References to the
corresponding duties of the "best people" toward those beneath them
seem more difficult to locate.

80 Douglas to Barclay, 8 October, 1851. *PABC*.

81 D. L. MacLaurin, "Education before the gold rush", *BCHQ*, October,
1958, p. 251. See also his Ph.D. thesis (University of Washington, 1936),
*The History of Education in the Crown Colonies of Vancouver Island
and British Columbia and in the Province of British Columbia.*

82 The census taken by Douglas in 1855 revealed a total of 81 school
children, distributed between Victoria, Craigflower and Nanaimo. (Mac-
Laurin, "Education Before the Gold Rush", p. 255.)

83 Douglas to Barclay, 10 October, 1853.

84 W. K. Lamb, "Some Notes on the Douglas Family", *BCHQ*, Vol. XVII,
Nos. 1 and 2, January-April, 1953, p. 46.
"She bore a great resemblance to him—a tall stout—dignified—rather
muscular (with a little fat) lady, with the West Indian manners—very
polite and nice, but she differed from her brother in that she liked a
joke and laughed rather pleasantly." (J. S. Helmcken, *Reminiscences,
PABC*, IV, p. 32).

85 Young Cecilia married William Young in 1858. He soon became Colonial
Secretary of Vancouver Island (and later of British Columbia), and
eventually Governor of the Gold Coast. (Lamb, *op cit.*, p. 47).

86 "They, however, unfortunately wandered beyond their depth, in trying a
case for illegal detention of property wherein the damages claimed were
about ten thousand dollars, and displayed an ignorance of the law which
causes me much uneasiness." (Douglas to Barclay, 4 November, 1853.
PABC).

87 Douglas predictably declared that they "should have had more sense and
good feeling for the service than to take part in any proceeding affecting
the Company's rights or character." (Douglas to Barclay, 16 August,
1853. *PABC*).

88 Tod, Work, Finlayson, Tolmie and Pemberton, however, supported the
appointment of Cameron, and a letter signed by over 40 citizens was
sent to Douglas informing him to this effect. It is quoted in Scholefield
and Howay, *British Columbia*, I. 549.

89 In the HBC archives, London. See "Rev. Robert John Staines: Pioneer Priest, Pedagogue, & Political Agitator", *BCHQ*, Vol. XIV, No. 4, October, 1950, p. 217.

90 Douglas to Barclay, 27 May, 1853. *PABC*.

91 28 July, 1853. *PABC*.

92 In HBC archives. Quoted in Slater, *op. cit.*, p. 216.

93 "When intelligence of this came there was a general pity—he was praised or blamed—a martyr or a fool as the case may be, but all nevertheless regretted his end." Helmcken, *Reminiscences*, III, 97.
Staines Point on the south end of Trial Island near Victoria is named after him.

94 They were presented in the House of Commons on March 9, 1854.

95 This was no doubt one factor in the decision to extend the grant of Vancouver Island to the HBC for another five years.

96 It was purchased by the United States in 1867.

97 Douglas to Barclay, 4 November, 1853. *PABC*.

98 Douglas to Newcastle, 16 May, 1854. *PABC*.

99 Douglas to Barclay, 15 June, 1854. *PABC*.

100 It consisted in 1853 of Tod, Finlayson and Cooper; in 1854 John Work replaced Cooper.

101 An outline of its deliberations may be found in *Minutes of the Council of Vancouver Island*, King's Printer, Victoria, 1918.

102 "On the night of Pearl Harbour, Japanese naval forces were off Alaska, a task force actually bound for Kiska was believed to be heading for Vancouver Island. Vancouver and Victoria were blacked out and the pathetic little air force at Patricia Bay prepared to commit suicide against overpowering odds." (Bruce Hutchison, *The Incredible Canadian*, Longmans Green, Toronto, 1952, p. 302).

103 The whole subject of this agreement, which had been given the approval of both governments, is gone into in Galbraith's, *The Hudson's Bay Company as an Imperial Factor, 1821-1869*, U. of Toronto Press, 1957, pp. 163-169.

104 Douglas knew of the neutrality agreement by the fall of 1854, but was only officially informed of it in September, 1855. ("The war scare of 1854: the Pacific Coast and the Crimean War," Donald C. Davidson, *BCHQ*, October, 1941, Vol. V, No. 4, p. 251).

105 We might reckon among them Rear-Admiral David Price, who committed suicide just before the attack.

106 Organized in 1837 with headquarters at Valparaiso, Chile.

107 Douglas to William G. Smith, 10 October, 1855. *PABC*.

108 *Loc. cit.*

109 Donald C. Davidson, "The War Scare of 1954: the Pacific Coast and the Crimean War," *BCHQ*, Vol. V, No. 4, October, 1941, p. 250.

110 Correspondence regarding the base may be found in *BCHQ*, Vol. VI, No. 4, October, 1942, pp. 279-296.

[111] Nisqually House at the mouth of the Nisqually River was the first settlement of white men on Puget Sound in what is now the State of Washington. It was a trading post of the Hudson's Bay Company till the fall of 1841, when it was turned over to the Puget Sound Agricultural Company.

[112] Douglas to Barclay, 25 April, 1855. *PABC.*

[113] As representatives, presumably, of soul, mind and body.

[114] Davidson, *op. cit.,* p. 251.

[115] Douglas to Barclay, 24 August, 1854. *PABC.*

[116] Douglas to Barclay, 13 September, 1854. *PABC.*

[117] See *Minutes of the Council of Vancouver Island,* King's Printer, Victoria, 1918, under these dates.

[118] For a time church services were also held there by the Rev. Cridge.

[119] One baby who died was thrown overboard "and no more Notice taken of it then as if it had been a ded Cat". See the article by Barrie Goult, "First and Last Days of the Princess Royal", *BCHQ,* Vol. III, No. 1, January, 1939, p. 19. The log of the first mate, Charles Gale, from which the above quotation is taken, is in the HBC Archives in London.

[120] At one time called Colvile.

[121] She was to live on till 1933, by which time her sister Amelia had been dead for over a century.

[122] Robinson, *Esquimalt,* p. 61.

[123] *Loc. cit.*

[124] He may have considered this as to some extent an investment; two of his daughters eventually chose naval officers as husbands; one of them, Captain Bull, died after a few months of marriage, and is buried in Pioneer Square. (Robinson, *op. cit.,* p. 62).

[125] Ormsby, *British Columbia: A History,* Macmillan, 1958, p. 103.

[126] An interesting picture of farm life in this period is given in "The Diary of Martha Cheney Ella" (*BCHQ,* Vol. XIII, No. 2, April, 1949). She was a teen-age girl when she arrived on the *Tory* in 1851, lived with Thomas Blinkhorn and his wife at Metchosin, married Henry Ella on July 19, 1855, had seven children, and died in 1911.

[127] In August, 1856, he officiated at the opening of the first church in Victoria, and the same year at the first session of the Legislative Assembly. On December 5, 1872, he protested at the close of Sunday Service in the Cathedral against the introduction of "ritualistic practices" into the Service. He was convicted of "brawling in church" and deprived of his license to preach. He then (with most of his congregation, including Douglas), formed the "Church of Our Lord", which, erected at the corner of Humboldt and Blanshard Streets, still stands and flourishes. Cridge was born December 17, 1817, and died on May 6, 1913. A full account of this affair is given in *"Edward Cridge and George Hills: doctrinal conflict 1872-1874, and the founding of Church of Our Lord in Victoria, British Columbia, 1875"* (M.A. thesis, U. of Victoria, by Susan Dickinson). Miss Dickinson makes it clear that although differences of personalities were involved, the roots of this controversy lay in corres-

ponding divisions and developments in the religious life of the Mother-country.

[128] Details of it are given in Donald Maclaurin, *The History of Education in the Crown Colonies of Vancouver Island and British Columbia and in the Province of British Columbia.* Ph.D. thesis, U. of Washington, 1936, pp. 25-29.

[129] Bancroft, *History of British Columbia,* p. 339.

[130] Reproduced in *BCHQ,* Vol. IV, No. 1, January, 1940, pp. 51-58.

[131] Douglas had previously told Barclay (October 10, 1853) that there were by his reckoning 254 people in Victoria in 1853: Victoria had thus actually decreased in population.

[132] For information about Victoria's early churches, see Edgar Fawcett, *Some Reminiscences of Old Victoria,* Toronto, William Briggs, 1912, pp. 149-151.

[133] Matthew Macfie in his *Vancouver Island and British Columbia* (London, 1865) has much to say on this matter. He tells us that Douglas was always followed by a uniformed bodyguard, and that "his efforts to appear grand, and even august, were ludicrously out of proportion to the insignificant population he governed, numbering less than the inhabitants of many a country town in England. When he spoke to anyone within the precincts of the Government House, his Quixotic notions of his office, which he evidently thought splendid, prompted him to make choice of the sesquipedalian diction he employed in his despatches . . . His manners always gave me the impression that to make up for early disadvantages he had religiously adjusted his whole bearing to the standard of Lord Chesterfield, and it is needless to say how amusing was the combination of his lordship and this dignified old fur trapper. His attitude toward the officials serving under his government was austere and distant. This he had acquired under the sort of military regime observed between the officers and servants of the Hudson's Bay Company. I have heard magistrates addressed by him in a pompous manner that no English gentleman would assume toward his porter." (pp. 394-5).

[134] See "The Victoria Voltigeurs" by B. A. McKelvie and W. E. Ireland, *BCHQ,* Vol. XX, July-Oct. 1956, p. 235.

[135] This did not prevent another "Russian scare" a few years later, and numerous gun emplacements were constructed along the coast to repel the Slavic invasion. As late as the 1950's if the elaborate paraphernalia of "civil defence" is any evidence, it was still being expected.

[136] The dispute appeared insoluble and was eventually settled by the arbitration of the Kaiser in 1872.

[137] Ormsby, *British Columbia: A History,* p. 126.

[138] The last royal veto in England had been by Queen Anne.

[139] Scholefield and Howay, *British Columbia,* p. 540.

[140] Scholefield and Howay, *British Columbia,* p. 540.

[141] "The affair passed off quietly, and did not appear to excite much interest among the lower orders"—Douglas, writing to the Colonial Secretary a few days later. (Scholefield and Howay, *British Columbia,* p. 542.)

Douglas was somewhat free with the term "the lower orders"; he himself, it may be recalled, was the illegitimate child of a woman whose name he either never knew or was disinclined to record. It is amusing in this connection to note that he himself was looked down on by the wives of some of the settlers as being, in one of his capacities at least, "engaged in trade". (Ormsby, *British Columbia,* p. 113).

142 *Miscellaneous Papers relating to Vancouver Island,* House of Commons, 1857.

143 That not all the HBC old-timers were enthusiastic about the development of democratic institutions in the colony is shown by a letter of John Work's written at this time. In it he says: "We have had an election lately of Members of a house of Assembly to assemble in a few days . . . I have always considered such a Colony & such a government where there are so few people to govern as little better than a farce and this last scene of a house of representatives the most absurd of the whole." (Work to Edward Ermatinger, 8 August 1856; Ermatinger letters, quoted in Scholefield and Howay, *British Columbia,* Vol. I, p. 555.)

Douglas himself was not an invariable supporter of the principle *vox populi vox dei.* In a letter written to his daughter (Mrs. A. G. Dallas) not long after his retirement from public life, he declared: "Garrotting is far too good for the stupid Assembly that passed the fatal unconditional Union Resolutions". (Sage, *Douglas,* p. 341.)

144 Scholefield and Howay, *British Columbia,* p. 546.

145 It would by this time have been considerably larger if there had not been a steady emigration of newly arrived laborers to the United States. Fortunately, as there were as yet no newspapers in Victoria, the public was spared agonized editorials on the "muscle drain".

146 Ormsby, *British Columbia,* p. 127.

147 They numbered perhaps 30,000 (Ormsby, *Loc. Cit.*). There were bitter Indian wars in Washington territory in this period. On one occasion Douglas gave some financial assistance to Governor I. I. Stevens.

148 Lt. Richard Charles Mayne entered the Navy in 1847, was in Victoria water as a midshipman in H.M.S. *Inconstant* in 1849, and became a lieutenant in 1856. He was on the surveying vessels *Plumper* (in these waters 1857-1860) and *Hecate* (here in 1861). He died in 1892. Mayne Island is named after him.

149 The last of the old fort buildings were taken down in 1864.

150 It stood approximately where the new Museum and Archives have been constructed.

151 R. C. Mayne, *Four Years in British Columbia and Vancouver Island,* London, John Murray, 1862, pp. 30-31.

152 Mayne, *Op. Cit.,* p. 31.

153 *Richard the Second,* II. 1.

154 Shakespeare, *Sonnet LXV.*

155 The phrase comes from the closing lines of F. Scott Fitzgerald's *"The Great Gatsby".*

[156] It eventually recommended that the Royal Grant of Vancouver Island to the HBC should be terminated in 1859, and that Canada should be permitted to acquire the vast prairie region known as Rupert's Land. This was equivalent to encouraging the formation of a dominion "from sea to sea".

[157] Bruce Hutchison, *The Fraser*, 1950. (Paper-back edition, Clarke Irwin, 1965, p. 48.)

[158] *Copies or extracts of correspondence relative to the discovery of gold in the Fraser's River District in British North America,* London, Queen's Printer, 1858, p. 5.

[159] *Op. Cit.*, p. 6. (Despatch dated October 29, 1856).

[160] This was the name of the Indian tribe of the region.

[161] *Op. Cit.*, p. 8 (Despatch dated December 29, 1857).

[162] "Since the British government was reluctant to exercise direct control, the Company remained the only representative of the British Empire in North America west of Canada. Consequently the policies of the Company created the conditions upon which British Statesmen were forced to act in diplomacy involving western North America. To a considerable extent, therefore, British foreign policy in this area was influenced by the decisions of the governor and committee and by the activities of their employees in North America." (Galbraith, *Op. Cit.*, p. 23.)

[163] Helmcken, *Reminiscences*, III. 119.

An artist's view of Victoria — 1862

First printing press in the Colony

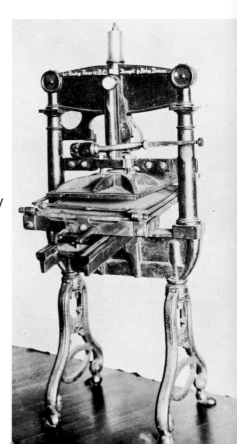

The Victoria Chamber of Commerce
advertised the Fraser-Cariboo gold
rush in San Francisco

CHAPTER SIX

The Treasure Seekers

The sermon had been preached, the last hymn sung, the blessing given; now the little congregation was decorously leaving the church. It was a Sunday morning in late April; winter still held sway over most of the northern part of the continent, but Vancouver Island, washed by warm tidal currents from the south Pacific, was already deep in spring. There was time, then, for the exchange of social greetings, to linger a few minutes in conversation, to regard, from the gently sloping hill on which Victoria's first church was built,[1] the harbor at its foot from which they had first glimpsed the palisaded settlement that was now their home.

It was fifteen years since that other spring day in 1843 when James Douglas had landed on the southern tip of the Island and set to work constructing "The Fort". At that time no city had been envisioned by even his keen eye, not even a thriving community; least of all did he suspect that some day he would be the governor of a newly-formed colony of which Victoria would be the capital. All that was intended by Douglas and his superiors in the Company was a well-constructed, properly fortified trading-post, where beads and blankets might profitably be exchanged with the natives in return for beaver and otter pelts.[2]

The Fort had risen; trade had duly prospered. One by one, new enterprises had been added; the wealth of the magnificent forests where trees, favored by the mild climate and wet winters, grew to enormous heights, was soon appreciated; sawmills had been built and lumber shipped as far as South America, and spars to distant England.[3] Farming had been encouraged, schools and some primitive roads constructed, and a few miles to the westward an important naval base established. Near Nanaimo, 75 miles to the north, coal in good quantities had been found, and a few shiploads of men had been brought out to work the mines.

Yet for all this, Victoria in the spring of 1858 was still essentially but one of the many far-flung outposts of the "Governor and Company of Adventurers of England Trading into Hudson's Bay". Moreover, aware that civilization would inevitably bring the end of the frontier and the fur-trade, the Company was content to see the little colony remain so. Nor was the Imperial Government, busy with a thousand greater tasks, much interested in the handful of Britons marooned at the far end of a tedious four to six months voyage from their native hearths. The glories of empire, by the end of the century axiomatic, were fifty years earlier still viewed with a languid eye by many in high places; to those who saw the planet not as the field of honor but a balance sheet, they were worse than a nuisance—an expense. Thus the growth of the settlement had hitherto been slight, its population that Sunday morning in 1858 was perhaps 300 souls, and no sizable addition to this number seemed in prospect.

True, the perceptive Douglas (who now combined in a single person the important offices of Governor and Chief Factor) had realized that the recent discoveries of gold on the Fraser and Thompson rivers might well betoken "A great change and busy time"; yet not even he foresaw fully what was to come.

Even less aware of what the next few months would hold were those who, fortified by thoughts of the sermon behind them and their Sunday dinners to come, stood for a few minutes and looked out over the placid scene that they had come to know as home—yet looked, though they did not know it then, their last upon this familiar, pleasant place.

For, at this very moment, only a few hundred yards away, the signal was being given for an astonishing new chapter in the story of Victoria. Piling ashore unceremoniously from the ship *Commodore*, just in from San Francisco, came a motley army of over four hundred men, drawn here by a dream, by a hope, by an urge beyond reason, by a single passion—gold. In an hour, the population of the settlement had been more than doubled, its composition changed forever. The modest requirements of the fur-trade, the class structure carefully modelled upon that of England,[4] the formalities and leisurely ways of an orderly society essentially directed from above — all these, if they were not to be obliterated, were about to feel the force of a hurricane; its gusts composed not of wind but of surges of humanity.

Since this is the story of a city, not a province, the tale of the discoveries themselves cannot be dwelt on. Suffice it to say that up and down the rivers and creeks of the interior for many years to come the search for gold would continue, attracting adventurers from the four corners of the earth. Some would be favored with a fortune, some with a pittance; while others, caught perhaps in a raging torrent or attacked by hostile natives, would find only an unmarked grave. Greed and treachery, heroism and endurance, would all play their part; blindly they would create first an industry, then a colony, then a province; eventually, it might be claimed, a nation. Yet regretfully the story of the goldfields, so full of interest, so far-reaching in its consequences, can merely be touched on here.[5] Instead, our attention must focus on the mouth of the funnel through which the tide of humanity now poured. Only yesterday it had been but an outpost of the fur trade; five years hence, it would bear the proud name of city; now, however, it was a chaotic, teeming confusion in between.

The best account of that first incredible summer is doubtless that given by Alfred Waddington. Born about 1801 near London of a well-connected family,[6] educated in both England and France, he had visited parts of the world as far apart as Brittany, Brazil and California. In the spring of 1858 he came to Victoria to open a branch of the wholesale grocery firm of Dulip and Waddington of San Francisco, and witnessed both the wild boom set off by the gold rush and the acute depression caused when it failed to measure up to expectations. To counteract the view, soon widely expressed by the disgruntled and disappointed, that Victoria was henceforth to have merely a promising past, in late 1858 he published *The Fraser Mines Vindicated*. Not only has this considerable historical interest as the first book ever printed in Victoria (or anywhere in what is now British Columbia),[7] but it gives an invaluable eye-witness description of perhaps its most colorful days.[8]

With an artist's eye for contrast, he first draws a quick sketch of the Fort as it would never be again:

> No noise, no bustle, no gamblers, no speculators or interested parties to preach up this or underrate that. A few quiet gentlemanly behaved inhabitants, chiefly Scotchmen, secluded as it were from the whole world . . . As to business there was none, the streets were grown over with grass, and there was not even a cart.[9]

Then came the virtually instantaneous transformation:

> This immigration was so sudden, that people had to spend their nights in the streets or bushes, according to choice, for there were no hotels sufficient to receive them.
>
> Victoria had at last been discovered, everybody was bound for Victoria, nobody could stop anywhere else, for there, and there alone, were fortunes, and large fortunes, to be made. And as the news of such a flourishing state of things soon found its way to California, it was not long before the steamers brought up fresh crowds.
>
> Never perhaps was there so large an immigration in so short a space of time into so small a place. Unlike California, where the distance from the Eastern States and Europe precluded the possibility of an immediate rush, the proximity of Victoria to San Francisco, on the contrary, afforded every facility, and converted the whole matter into a fifteen dollar trip. Steamers and sailing vessels were put in requisition, and old ships and tubs of every description actively employed in bringing passengers, something like to a fair.[10]

Inevitably, this eager army of treasure-seekers caused an economic convulsion:

> As to goods, the most exorbitant prices were asked and realized; for though the Company had a large assortment, their store in the Fort was literally besieged from morning to night; and when all were in such a hurry, it was not every one that cared to wait three or four hours, and sometimes half a day,

for his turn to get in. The consequence was, that the five or six stores that were first established did as they pleased.[11]

In the wake of the treasure-seekers came those who brought their treasure with them. These

> . . . might be seen coming on shore with certain heavy bags full of gold coin, which they were obliged to have carried. They had expected to get ground lots for nothing, and buy the whole city cheap, and were sadly disappointed to find they had come a little too late.[12]

Not everyone, however, was so easily convinced that he had "come a little too late":

> These "big bugs" were closely followed by another class, and Victoria was assailed by an indescribable array of Polish Jews, Italian fishermen, French cooks, jobbers, speculators of every kind, land agents, auctioneers, hangers on at auctions, bummers, bankrupts, and brokers of every description . . . To the above lists may be added a fair seasoning of gamblers, swindlers, thieves, drunkards, and jail birds, let loose by the Governor of California for the benefit of mankind, besides the halt, lame, blind and mad. In short, the outscourings of a population containing, like that of California, the outscourings of the world . . . When the older inhabitants beheld these varied specimens of humanity streaming down in motley crowds from the steamers and sailing vessels, and covering the wharves, as if they had come to take possession of the soil, they looked on in silent amazement, as if contemplating a second irruption of barbarians.[13]

The exact number who arrived in Victoria and Esquimalt that year will never be known with certainty. A reliable estimate placed it at 20,000,[14] and another eye-witness would tend to confirm it. Lieut. R. C. Mayne was an English naval officer sent out in H.M.S. *Plumper* to survey these coasts. He arrived in the area late in 1857,[15] and saw the startling changes which a few short months soon brought:

> The excitement in Victoria reached its climax, I think, in July. On the 27th of the previous month the *Republic* steamed into Esquimalt harbour from San Francisco with 800 passengers; on the 1st of July, the *Sierra Nevada* landed 1900 more; on the 8th of the same month, the *Orizaba* and the *Cortez*

together brought 2800; and they all reported that thousands wanted to follow.[16]

The Esquimalt Road, connecting the Fort with the naval base, was soon a busy thoroughfare:

> Only a few months before, we used to flounder through the mud without meeting a single soul; now it was covered with pedestrians toiling along, with the step and air of men whose minds are occupied with thoughts of business; crowded with well-laden carts and vans, with Wells Fargo's, or Freeman's "Expresses", and with strangers of every tongue and country, in every variety of attire. Day after day on they came to Victoria, on their way to the Fraser; the greater part of them with no property but the bundle they carried, and with "dollars, dollars, dollars!" stamped on every face.[17]

Regardless of the social status of the newcomers, however, the results of their arrival were soon abundantly evident:

> Shops, stores, and wooden shanties of every description, and in every direction, were now seen going up, and nothing was to be heard but the stroke of the chisel or hammer. In six weeks 225 buildings, of which nearly 200 were stores, and of these 59 belonging to jobbers or importers, had been added to a village of 800 inhabitants; and people seemed to think the number insufficient, for others were on foot. Besides which the whole country around the town was covered with tents, resembling the encampments of an army.[18]

Land prices soared. The Company, which had originally offered lots at $50 and then at $75, raised their price to $100. For once, however, buyers made more from the transactions than did the Company. Some of the lots

> . . . were resold a month afterwards at prices varying from fifteen hundred to three thousand dollars, and more. Amongst others, one half of a fifty dollar corner lot, the whole of which had been offered successively for 250, 500, 750, and 1000 dollars, and finally sold for 1100 dollars, was resold a fortnight afterwards, that is to say the half of it, for 5000 dollars. Old town lots, well situated, brought any prices, and frontages of 20 and 50 feet, by 60 feet deep, rented from 250 to 400 dollars per month.[19]

This rapid rise in prices was paralleled in other areas of the economy. Workmen got $10 to $15 a day,[20] while a British naval officer, Lt. C. W. Wilson, R.E., attached to the Commission determining the exact boundary with the U.S.A., reported:

> The prices are outrageous here, 1/6 lb. for mutton, 4/- lb. for butter, bread 5d a lb., beef 1/- lb. & washing 10/- for 12 pieces whether large or small.[21]

Despite high prices, there was in this period a noticeable increase in the amenities of life:

> The best teas at 1s and 1s 4d per lb. find their way, via Sandwich Islands, from China. Wines round the Horn and cigars from Manilla pay no duty. English fruits are grown, and those of the tropics imported. Grapes are 1s per pound. Every restaurant prints an elaborate bill of fare. There is no want of public baths. Saddle-horses can be hired, and vehicles to drive about in. The blacks make excellent cooks.[22]

Unfortunately, as usual in such cases, the "boom" had a darker side; the rise in land values was paralleled by a fall in moral standards. The results were most immediately noticeable in that section of society least able to cope with this bewildering series of events—the native Indians. The combination of easy money, liquor, and a horde of transient miners produced a rapid collapse of standards among the Songhees tribe, encamped just across the Inner Harbor from the Fort:

> Subsequently to the tide of immigration in '58, and until the removal of a bridge that formerly connected Victoria with the Indian encampment on the opposite side of the harbour, I have witnessed scenes after sunset calculated to shock even the bluntest sensibilities. The fires of Indian tents pitched upon the beach casting a lurid glare upon the water; the loud and discordant whoopings of the natives, several of whom were usually infuriated with bad liquor, the crowds of the more debased miners strewed in vicious concert with squaws on the public highway presented a spectacle diabolical in the extreme. Even now one cannot walk from the ferry up the Esquimalt Road by day or by night without encountering the sight of these Indian slaves[23] squatting in considerable numbers in the bush, for what purpose it is not difficult to imagine, and the extent to which the nefarious practices referred to are encouraged by the crews of Her Majesty's ships is a disgrace

to the service they represent, and a scandal to the country. Hundreds of dissipated white men, moreover, live in open concubinage with these wretched creatures. So unblushingly is this traffic carried on, that I have seen the husband and wife of a native family canvassing from one miner's shanty to another, with the view of making assignations for the *clootch-men* (squaws) in their possession.[24]

Meanwhile, at the eye of this hurricane, Douglas grappled with a score of problems. His tasks, in the face of this startling new situation, were basically three-fold: he had to uphold the economic rights of the Company and the political rights of the Imperial Government, to maintain law and order, and to make sure that Vancouver Island and the adjacent parts of the mainland, now inundated with largely American newcomers, remained under British control.

Moreover, he had to perform these tasks in the face of two formidable difficulties: he had virtually no physical force at his command, and communication with his superiors in London was so slow as to be almost useless. With respect to the former, he was dependent on the Colonial Militia (consisting of one lieutenant, one sergeant, seven corporals and twenty-six privates), the crew of the *Otter* (also numbering about thirty), and such assistance as British warships in the area might afford. Regarding requests for aid or advice from the Imperial Government, mail still required close to four months to make the round trip between Victoria and London. The crisis that confronted Douglas, however, admitted of neither weakness nor delay, and in this moment, so decisive for himself, the colony, and the future Dominion of Canada, he did not hesitate; speaking and acting as if forces to rival those of Xerxes were at his instant command, he threw into the breach his last resources: energy, decisiveness and character.[25]

Already, he had taken some preliminary moves on his own initiative. In December 1857 he had declared all gold mines in the Fraser and Thompson districts to be possessions of the Crown, and announced that after February 1, 1858, mining licences (fixed in January 1858 at $5 or 21s)[26] would have to be obtained from the authorities at Victoria.

The British Government, when it learned of Douglas' actions in

March 1858, were pleased that he had not merely waited for their instructions. They were disturbed, however, by the consideration that, at least in his capacity as Governor of Vancouver Island, he had apparently no legal authority over the mainland. It was while they were wrestling with this problem[27] that the gold rush burst in full force, and from this point we may trace Douglas' reactions to it in the despatches which he was soon sending in rapid succession to the Colonial Secretaries of the period.[28]

In a despatch to Lord Stanley, for example, he reported that the *Commodore* was again in port with four hundred new immigrants, and that ". . . the excitement about the Couteau gold mines is on the increase, and people are pushing from all quarters in that direction."[29]

He had already concluded that it was "utterly impossible, through any means within our power, to close the Gold Districts against the entrance of foreigners . . . "; nevertheless, he informed Lord Stanley, he proposed to maintain the rights of the Company, and to that end had issued a proclamation. Dated the 8th of May, 1858, not a hint of the precariousness of the situation is anywhere discernible in it:

> Whereas it is commonly reported that certain boats and other vessels have entered Fraser's River for trade; and whereas there is reason to apprehend that other persons are preparing and fitting out boats and vessels for the same purpose:
> Now, therefore, I have issued this my Proclamation, warning all persons that such acts are contrary to law, and infringements upon the rights of the Hudson's Bay Company, who are legally entitled to the trade with the Indians in the British Possessions on the north-west coast of America, to the exclusion of all other persons, whether British or Foreign.
> And also, that after fourteen days from the date of this my Proclamation, all ships, boats, and vessels, together with the goods laden on board, found in Fraser's River, or in any of the bays, rivers, or creeks of the said British Possessions on the north-west coast of America, not having a license from the Hudson's Bay Company, and a sufferance from the proper officer of the Customs at Victoria, shall be liable to forfeiture, and will be seized and condemned according to law.[30]

Nor was Douglas content to issue orders from his office in the little compound near the Fort. In the course of his career, when the situation required it, he had ranged as far afield as Alaska and California; now, when a stream of reports was being daily swept down "Fraser's River" to the sea, he would not merely sit at his desk and try, in the "rocker" of his mind, to separate fact from rumour; he would go and see for himself.

In his next despatch[31] he reported to Lord Stanley that, taking the indefatigable *Otter* and accompanied by H.M.S. *Satellite,* he had visited the diggings as far north as Fort Langley, thirty miles up the river. He had seized from some miners goods which he believed were to be used for operations contrary to the HBC monopoly of trade with the Indians; sixteen unlicensed canoes had also been charged five dollars each for a licence. From Fort Langley he had proceeded, in canoes manned by Indians, another 80 miles to Fort Hope; here he found men earning as much as $50 a day.[32] It was now apparent that the gold fields were very rich, and that they would prove an irresistible magnet to as yet unreckonable numbers.

> . . . the conviction is gradually forcing itself upon my mind, that not only Fraser's River, and its tributary streams, but also the whole country situated to the eastward of the Gulf of Georgia, as far north as Johnstone's Straits, is one continued bed of gold of incalculable value and extent."[33]

Douglas urged on his superiors the necessity of immediate guidance:

> ". . . the case is urgent, and calls for rapid and decisive measures in the outset, for in the course of a few months, there may be one hundred thousand people in the country."[34]

The right policy, he suggested, would be one of bowing but not yielding to the storm:

> I think it therefore a measure of obvious necessity that the whole country be immediately thrown open for settlement, and that the land be surveyed, and sold at a fixed rate not to exceed twenty shillings an acre.[35]

Within a week, Douglas had what appeared to be even graver news to report:

The recent defeat of Colonel Steptoe's detachments of United States troops, consisting of dragoons and infantry, by the Indians of Oregon territory, has greatly increased the natural audacity of the savages, and the difficulty of managing them. It will require, I fear, the nicest tact to avoid a disastrous Indian war.[36]

Fortunately, no such outbreak occurred (though from time to time for some years there would be occasional murders—perhaps in some cases justified—of miners by the Indians of the gold regions), and in his next despatch Douglas makes no reference to this danger.

A subsequent despatch perhaps marks the height of the gold fever:

Since I last had the honour of addressing you on the 19th instant, the excitement on the subject of the Fraser's River Gold Mines has been more than ever exhibited in the rush of people from all parts of the coast to this Colony.

The Custom-House books of this place show a return of 19 steam ships, 9 sailing ditto, 14 decked boats, which have entered at the port of Victoria since the 19th of May last, having 6,133 passengers on board, all either bound directly for Fraser's River, or proposing to settle at this place, with the view of entering into business connections with parties at the mines.

The ascertained number of persons who had actually sailed from the port of San Francisco, with the intention of going into the Fraser's River Mines, up to the 15th instant, was 10,573, and there was then no abatement in the demand for passages, every vessel being taken up as soon as advertised to sail for Vancouver's Island.

These statements give a proximate idea of the number of persons at and on the way to Fraser's River from California and other more distant countries, but do not present the increase of population derived from the United States territories of Washington and Oregon, through parties of adventurers who have entered the British Possessions by land. We are, therefore, led to the inference that this country and Fraser's River have gained an increase of 10,000 inhabitants within the last six weeks, and the tide of immigration continues to roll onward without any prospect of abatement.[37]

Douglas was still, however, acutely aware of how scanty were the forces at his command to cope with any serious challenge to the authority of either the Company or the British crown:

> With the exception of the aid received from Her Majesty's Ship *Satellite* operating on the sea coast, I have had no military forces whatever to employ in the interior of Fraser's River, which is now occupied by a population little short of 9,000 white miners, and hundreds of other persons are travelling towards the gold mines, and preparing to join them.[38]

Yet despite his isolated and exposed position as leader of a bare handful of Britons, destined perhaps to be swept away by a sudden surge of blind humanity, there was never a thought of retreat. Beyond the scale in which gain and loss, difficulty and danger might have been weighed by others, lay duty, and fortified with the belief that in serving this he served also the higher, unseen power behind events, there could be no turning back.

> The country, nevertheless, continues quiet, and, not withstanding our want of physical force, I have not scrupled in all cases to assert the rights of the Crown, and to enforce the laws of the land for the punishment of offences; and we have, thanks to the Almighty, encountered neither resistance nor opposition in the discharge of those sacred duties.[39]

The gold rush was now only a few months old; yet already Douglas had begun to look beyond it. A road to the interior was essential. In his despatch of July 26 he mentions that he would probably commence its construction that same summer; his next despatch (August 19) announces that it is already under way. Five hundred men are employed, and the prescient Governor declares:

> That route will be of the greatest advantage to the country, and, when opened, will form the commercial highway into the interior districts, there being little probability of the existence of any other practicable route from the sea coast.[40]

At the end of August he made his second trip to the River, and was pleased with both the progress of the gold mining industry and the comparative lack of violence throughout the area. He might well at this point have felt satisfied with his efforts, and it must therefore have come as a disagreeable shock to find himself, for almost the only time in his career, rebuked, even if indirectly, by the Imperial authorities.

A number of changes had been taking place which, though 8000 miles from Fort Victoria or the bars of the Fraser, were destined ere long to cast their shadow across them. Lord Stanley had resigned as Colonial Secretary and been succeeded by Sir Edward Bulwer Lytton.[41] Moreover, the far-flung enterprises of the Hudson's Bay Company were coming under ever severer scrutiny. Many, in an age that was witnessing the triumph of free trade, objected to this relic (as they saw it) of the days of protected monopoly; and its affairs had been the subject of a parliamentary investigation in 1857. Some who have already figured in these pages—Richard Blanshard and James Cooper,[42] for example— had testified concerning it in far from enthusiastic terms, and their hearers had, in the main, been impressed by their testimony. The days of the special position of the Company in British North America were in fact clearly numbered,[43] and this in turn raised doubts regarding the equivocal position of Douglas as both Governor and Chief Factor.[44] All this was reflected in Sir Edward's despatch of July 1, 1858:

> Her Majesty's Government, feeling the difficulties and the critical nature of your present circumstances, have not hesitated to place these considerable powers in your hands; but they rely on your forbearance, judgment, and conciliation to avoid all resort to military or naval force which may lead to conflict and loss of life, except under the pressure of extreme necessity. Still less need I impress upon you the importance of avoiding any act which directly or indirectly might be construed into an application of Imperial resources to the objects of the Hudson's Bay Company, in whose service you have so long been engaged.
>
> Even the suspicion of this, however unfounded, would be eminently prejudicial to the establishment of Civil Government in the country lying near the Fraser's River, and would multiply existing difficulties and dangers. All claims and interests must be subordinated to that policy which is to be found in the peopling and opening up of the new country, with

the intention of consolidating it as an integral and important part of the British Empire.[45]

Douglas' feelings on receiving this carefully worded communication will never be known with exactitude, but that he felt deeply hurt by it is surely a fair inference. His reply, however, is couched in the same dignified terms that, both in his despatches and his private conversation, he had long been accustomed to employ:

> Though so long and intimately connected with the Hudson's Bay Company, I have uniformly striven, during my administration of the Government of Vancouver's Island, to dispense equal justice to all its inhabitants, and to avoid even the suspicion, so allowable in the circumstances, of undue influence being used on my part in favouring the objects of the Hudson's Bay Company. I was cautious even about enforcing the laws in respect to the rights of that association, which has in fact exercised no right nor enjoyed any privilege of trade or otherwise in this Colony that was not equally shared by every freeholder in the country.
>
> Her Majesty's Government may also rely upon a proper and discreet use being made of the military and naval force at my disposal, and that it will not be called into action except in cases of extreme necessity, and also that all claims and interests will be rendered subordinate to the great object of peopling and opening up the new country, and consolidating it as an integral part of the British Empire.[46]

It seems likely, however, that the British Government was not so much rebuking Douglas as preparing him for what they now saw to be the inevitable parting of the ways between his two loyalties. On July 1, 1858, a bill had been introduced in the House of Commons creating the colony of "New Caledonia", to extend from the Rockies to the Pacific Ocean, and including the Queen Charlotte Islands but not Vancouver Island. There was already a French colony of this name, however, and a new name, personally selected by Queen Victoria, was chosen instead. On August 2, the act creating the colony of British Columbia was signed by the Queen. Two weeks after the bill had been introduced in the House of Commons, and Lytton had written his official implied rebuke to Douglas, he had written him a confidential despatch, intimating that, provided he would sever his connections with the Hudson's Bay Company, he might reasonably expect, while retaining his post as Governor of Vancouver Island, to be offered the additional position of Governor of British Columbia.[47] Douglas, apparently after some consideration of this offer, decided to accept it, and so wrote to Lytton on October 4.[48] Lytton, on his part, had been so sure that he would do so that on September 2, without waiting for Douglas' acceptance, he had sent him his commission.[49]

In November, Douglas travelled to the mainland for his inauguration as Governor of British Columbia. Even before this, on his two previous visits, he had begun the building of roads and planned the laying out of the townsites of Fort Hope and Fort Yale. Now he was to receive the legal authority for these and other actions. It was a cold wet fall day; in the main hall of the HBC at Fort Langley, before about a hundred people, Douglas administered the oath of office to Matthew Baillie Begbie as first judge of British Columbia,[50] Begbie in turn read the Queen's Commission appointing Douglas as Governor; and the new Governor then read a proclamation ending the Company's exclusive trading rights on the mainland. Thus on November 19, 1858, British Columbia officially came into existence.

One final action remained to set the seal of approval on what had led to this moment. In recognition of his services to the Empire in the past, and a sign that they had every confidence in his abilities in the future, the British Government soon afterward made the new Governor a Companion of the Order of the Bath (C.B.)

So ended one of the two careers of the man so justly termed "the father of British Columbia". From now on, till his retirement from public life in 1864, he would devote all his energies to the direction of the affairs of the two colonies, and his major achievements will find a place in these pages. For the moment, however, it seems proper to re-direct our attention to the local affairs of what was still called, though with increasing irrelevance, "The Fort". Here since spring ships had been dumping their cargoes of assorted humanity, then hastening away southward to reload.

Some of the newcomers brought only their hopes and the clothing on their backs; others, however, brought capital, and under its transforming influence the trading-post was soon submerged. In its place, though built in frantic haste, and with no regard for aesthetics, rose, day by banging, clattering day, a town.

Hitherto we have had to reconstruct the history of Victoria from memoirs and government documents. After mid-summer 1858, however, we can follow its fortunes more closely in the columns of the daily press. The first newspaper to make its appearance (June 25) was the *Victoria Gazette*.[51] Published within the Fort grounds by James W. Towne & Company of California, it was edited by H. C. Williston and C. Bartlett. Five days a week, for the price of 12½ c or "one bit", it presented a remarkable variety of news. The journal portrayed in detail the heady boom of early summer, the doubts and fears as it began to falter in the autumn; it followed local politics as the miniature House of Assembly grappled with the new needs of the burgeoning community: streets, bridges, lighting, hospitals, policemen, firemen, jails and parks; it kept its readers in close touch with the progress of the road being built from the coast into the Interior; it gave a fair picture of events beyond the seas, from the laying of the Atlantic cable and the Indian Mutiny to the domestic troubles of Charles Dickens,[52] and finally, sometimes no doubt unintentionally, it reflected the manners and mores of a time that was neither ours nor that of the days of 1843, but uniquely yet fleetingly its own. All this was combined in four pages remarkably free from typographical errors, interspersed with advertisements that in themselves almost tell the whole story of the period, and garnished, as befitted a journal of mixed auspices, with American spelling and British politics,[53]

July, it seems clear, was the high point of the boom that had only begun in April. (Lieut. Mayne, we recall, had declared that "the excitement in Victoria reached its climax, I think, in July".)[54] No fewer than forty-five vessels were reportedly on the way to Victoria; a list is given of their names.[55] The town itself was also given over to a species of shipbuilding, as boats capable (or so it was hoped) of carrying six or eight men across the Straits to the mainland were hurriedly being knocked together in the "French ravine" at the back of Johnson Street. The approved shape was that of a coffin,[56] and for as little as a hundred dollars those insensitive to questions of symbolism might purchase one; several scores were under construction at once, and soon the Straits between the Island and the mainland were dotted with them.

> Boats, canoes, and every species of small craft, are continually employed in pouring their cargoes of human beings into Fraser's River, and it is supposed that not less than one thousand whites are already at work and on the way to the gold districts.
>
> Many accidents have happened in the dangerous rapids of that river; a great number of canoes having been dashed to pieces and their cargoes swept away by the impetuous stream, while of the ill-fated adventurers who accompanied them, many have been swept into eternity.
>
> The others, nothing daunted by the spectacle of ruin, and buoyed up by the hope of amassing wealth, still keep pressing onwards towards the coveted goal of their most ardent wishes.[57]

The Governor was by no means inclined to discourage these latter-day Argonauts. In mid-July, when questioned by a group of would-be gold miners as to their chances of success, in an impromptu reply he declared:

> Now I know, men, what you wish me to tell you. You wish me to say there is lots of gold in Fraser's River, but that I will not say, because I am not certain of the fact myself. But this I will tell you as my own settled opinion, that I think the country is full of gold, and that east and north and south of Fraser's River, there is a gold field of incalculable value and extent.
>
> I have told our glorious Queen so; and I now tell you so; and if I mistake not, you are the very men who can prove by your courage and enterprise whether my opinion be right or wrong . . .
>
> The law of the land will do its work without fear and without favor. Therefore appeal to it in all cases; let it do justice between man and man; let it defend your rights and avenge your wrongs.
>
> Now my friends go on and prosper; there is hard work before you, and I hope you will be repaid with rich strikes and big nuggets.[58]

It is remarkable, all things considered, how peaceful the "invasion" was. Douglas had at first feared that a period of lawlessness might engulf the settlement. The miners had previously been represented to him as ". . . the very dregs, in fact, of society";[59] he was now happy to inform his superiors that

Their conduct while here would have led me to form a very different conclusion; as our little town, though crowded to excess with this sudden influx of people, and though there was a temporary scarcity of food, and dearth of house accommodation, the police few in numbers, and many temptations to excess in the way of drink, yet quiet and order prevailed, and there was not a single committal for rioting, drunkenness, or other offences, during their stay here.[60]

Another eye-witness observer, however — perhaps a more impressionable one — found the atmosphere somewhat livelier:

Vancouver Island itself is most beautiful, but turned quite upside down, by the gold discovery, a regular San Francisco in '49 you are hardly safe without arms & even with them, when you have to walk along paths, across which gentlemen with a brace of revolvers each, are settling their differences; the whiz of revolver bullets round you goes on all day & if any one gets shot of course it's his own fault, however I like the excitement very much & never felt better in my life.[61]

Without attempting to reconcile these two accounts, we may say that crime was not unknown in early Victoria—nor, for that matter, punishment.[62] An Indian caught breaking and entering was given twenty-four lashes in the Fort Yard by the Sheriff, and the editors of the *Gazette* recorded their approval:

Whatever may be urged against public whipping as a penalty for violations of law, there is little question of its efficacy in the prevention of crime, especially in a new country, and as applied to semi-civilized or barbarous delinquents.[36]

A few weeks later, a less serious offence drew a lighter penalty and a more jocular comment from the *Gazette:*

Alexander Fraser was arraigned before the Police Court yesterday, on a charge of having been drunk and disorderly, in riding his horse at a furious rate up and down Johnson Street, thereby endangering the lives of passers-by. The charge being sustained, the Court imposed a fine of $5.00 with costs, making a total of $13.50. This should be a warning to Alexander and all other wine-loving horsemen, to keep a tight rein not only upon their steeds, but upon their appetites.[64]

Lt. Wilson, we might note, played a modest part in suppressing the nearest thing to a riot that the settlement experienced in this period. This occurred on the night of July 31, 1858.

> Last night we were roused up by a message from the Governor to say that a riot had broken out at Victoria, & our presence was instantly required. The men were soon turned out & got on board the *Plumper* (one of our men of war here) which carried us round. It was very exciting when we came in sight of the town & the order was given to load & the ship's guns run out & cleared for action; we had to disembark in boats & if there had been any resistance there would have been very few of us not knocked over. Luckily however we found that after rescuing a prisoner & knocking over the sheriff the mob had dispersed, however our work was not all finished as we had to search some of the ships & get back the prisoner which we succeeded in doing with four of the ringleaders in the rescue without much resistance. After this the Governor gave us a good supper, & we then had a dreary march home at 3 in the morning, not blessing the authorities for calling us up during the night.[65]

Meanwhile, at a more mundane level, a network of land transportation was being either developed or envisioned. Locally, an express service was inaugurated between Victoria and Esquimalt;[66] it left once an hour, and charged the modest fare of a dollar a trip. Roads were being pushed northward into Saanich,[67] an area still sparsely settled by either Indians or whites.[68] On the mainland, a much more ambitious project was under way—the Lillooet-Harrison Road to the Upper Fraser.[69] Some idea of the importance which the Governor attached to it is shown by the fact that five hundred men were employed in its construction, and that by early October it was possible to report that "the Lillooet-Harrison route to the Upper Fraser may now be considered open, and so far as we are able to judge from information in our possession, will remain passable throughout the winter."[70]

Even larger visions were slowly moving into the realm of practical possibility. It was confidently claimed that a transcontinental railroad would exist "in a few years",[71] and a long article on the subject[72] explored the difficulties and advantages. Hopes were no doubt heightened by the successful laying during the summer of the transatlantic cable; Queen Victoria and President Buchanan had exchanged messages by means of it, and these were reprinted for the edification of Victoria residents.[73] An editorial in the *Gazette* even suggested that the logical next step was a "transpacific telegraph".[74]

Towns were meanwhile being laid out on the mainland, even before the new colony of British Columbia was officially in existence. In the prospective new community of Langley, lots were eagerly bid for; among the successful purchasers was a figure who had arrived in Victoria during the summer and who would soon become one of its best-known figures; although christened plain Bill Smith, he now rejoiced in the unusual name of Amor De Cosmos.[75]

In the meantime, while beyond the distant horizons the Indian Mutiny flared,[76] and rumblings below the border gave warning of the approaching American Civil War, Victorians were swept up by the excitement of the fantastic boom. Dwellings rose rapidly in all directions around the Fort. Some were far from substantial; in August the Commissioner of Police, A. F. Pemberton,[77] declared houses of cloth and wood to be a public nuisance.[78] By late September, however, the "second brick building in town" was nearly finished;[79] this was the Royal Hotel on Wharf Street, opened in October with a ball![80]

Inevitably, with the great increase in population, the need for civic improvements became urgent. The tiny House of Assembly (which at this time comprised Messrs. J. D. Pemberton,[81] J. Kennedy, T. J. Skinner, J. Yates, J. W. McKay, with J. S. Helmcken as Speaker), considered the need for a jail and hospital,[82] for fire-engines, for paving the streets and lighting them with gas,[83] and for building a bridge across the harbor at Point Ellice.[84]

Most of these needs made some progress toward realization. On July 31, a meeting was held to organize a volunteer fire department;[85] two fire engines, ordered by Governor Douglas, arrived from San Francisco. They cost $1600 and $1750, and proved in a public demonstration that they were "sufficiently powerful to throw a full stream of water over any building in the town with ease".[86]

A lively debate took place on the proper covering for the streets. The *Gazette* had its doubts about cobblestones; some advanced thinkers, it reported, favored "the method adopted by MacAdam";[87] yet planks, it averred, were cheaper and quicker.[88] At all events. "a really durable pavement is at present out of the question."[89] The House of Assembly, leaving technical details to the experts, appropriated £2000 for the repair of roads in the Victoria District and £600 for the improvement of the Esquimalt Road. To pay for these improvements, residents were spared the indignities of assessments and tax notices; the revenue was to be raised in the usual manner by taxes on public houses. By October, the *Gazette* was able to report that "Waddington Alley, running from Yates to Johnson Streets, is being planked in a substantial manner. This is the first street ever planked in Victoria."[90]

Nor did the aesthetic needs of Victorians, present and future, escape the editors of the *Gazette*. Disturbed at what seemed to them the onrush of urban sprawl, they hastened to avert its more unpleasant consequences. In a fine flash of prescience they pointed out that the creation of public parks would in time prove a stimulus to an industry not yet founded and a word uncoined: tourism.

> We simply make our suggestion as we have heretofore offered similar ones, on the broad principle that a large portion of the prosperity of a metropolis must come from its attractions as a place of residence or a point of resort. We have advantages in this respect possessed by few towns in their outset, and if we are wise we will develop them.[91]

Later in the year, the editors of the *Gazette* were happy to report yet further advances on the cultural front:

> Among the social needs of the approaching inclement season are a library and reading-room, and we are pleased to see that a movement is on foot which will result in the formation of the nucleus of the first and the actual establishment of the second.[92]

One new aspect of life in Victoria not to be overlooked was a change in the racial composition of the settlement. True, such names as Hibben (Staple and Fancy Stationery; diaries for 1859 and dictionaries of Chinook were also available), and Thomas Trounce (architect and builder) occur in the advertisements of the period,[93] but these are greatly outnumbered by non-Anglo-Saxon patronymics. Selim Franklin, E. S. Mendels, Ehrenbacher and Oppenheimer, Meiss and Adler (all auctioneers), Sporborg and Company (grocers and provision dealers), Licicero and Stahle (barbers and hairdressers), E. Pique (teacher of singing), Ghiradelli, Antonovich and Co. (commission merchants), Koshland and Bro. (clothing and dry goods), S. Elsasser (dealer in groceries), Haas and Rosenfeld (wholesale dealers in clothing), Rousset, Auger and Co. (who demonstrated their versatility by offering for sale cigars, quicksilver, beans and billiard tables)— these are merely a sampling of the newcomers to these shores. Nor was this new development to be devoid of influence on the future history of the colony; when, a decade later, there was talk of British Columbia throwing in its lot with the United States, and a petition to the President of the United States, supporting such a development, was circulated in Victoria, an analysis of its signers also shows a remarkably high proportion of non-Anglo-Saxons,[94] or, to put it another way, of those who had no particular reason to feel an instinctive loyalty to the Crown. In October 1858, indeed, several Victoria policemen had to resign their posts as they were unwilling to take an oath of allegiance to the Queen.[95]

Although exact figures are unavailable, it seems likely that French immigration to Victoria at this time was considerable. Political and economic troubles in France during the years 1848-1852 had caused a sizable exodus of Frenchmen to California, and in 1858 some of it moved on to Vancouver Island. It is interesting to note that in June 1858 Douglas appointed O. J. Travaillot to the post of "Revenue Officer for the District of Fort Dallas or Fork of Thompson's River". Here he issued licences to miners, was an assistant gold commissioner, and helped to lay out the townsite of Hope. Some of his reports to Douglas were written in French—a venture in biculturalism that would have been considered either daring or unthinkable a century later.[96] (The House of Assembly, however, was not so broadminded; on August 24 it rejected a petition laid before it in French "as the House could not receive petitions presented in a foreign language."[97] A month later, however, the House considered a petition in English "from certain restaurant-keepers (French) complaining of their not being allowed to sell wines (an indispensable commodity) to their customers";[98] late in 1858 W. F. Horre established Victoria's first library;[99] in March 1859 a Madame Pettibeau opened a Seminary for Young Ladies on Fort Street, giving lessons in French and music; Edward Mallandaine, also French, began a "Select School" in 1860.[100]

Jews were also well represented in Victoria after 1858. One of them, Lumley Franklin, later became mayor, while his brother Selim Franklin was for a time a member of the Legislative Assembly. David Belasco, who eventually became world-famous as a theatrical producer, was brought from San Francisco by his parents at the age of five, and lived in Victoria for some years.[101]

There was also at this time a considerable colored immigration to Vancouver Island. The first shipload of miners (on the *Commodore*, April 25, 1858) contained about 35 negroes.[102] The first large merchant house (after the HBC) to be established in Victoria was that of Lester and Gibbs, both negroes. Gibbs, indeed, had a rather distinguished career, as he was later elected to the Victoria City Council, and after his return to his native land became the first negro judge in the U.S.A., and later U.S. Consul to Madagascar.[103]

Douglas evidently thought well of his new subjects, as in a rather striking move he appointed some of them policemen in Victoria. However this experiment apparently proved unsatisfactory—possibly due to the presence of so many white Americans in the settlement[104] — and was later discontinued. For many years, though, the Negroes of Victoria had their own militia unit — the "African Rifles" — and a celebration was held annually on the first of August to mark the anniversary of the emancipation of slaves in the British West Indies.[105]

Other signs of a strong American influence were also detectable;

for example, when a controversy arose in connection with seating arrangements in the local church. Ushers at the services, apparently unconversant with the finer points of the American Way, had seated whites and blacks at random; a letter to the *Gazette* protested this procedure, urging that the church authorities ". . . give to the colored people a place by themselves, as is done in all respectable churches in the world . . ."[106] The next day, however, another reader pointed out in reply that the negroes in Victoria "came to escape the tyranny and oppression of Republican Democratic church-going California"; while the day following, the Rev. Cridge poured carefully ambiguous oil on the troubled waters, promising that "the expressed wishes of any individuals with regard to their own personal accomodation in the church shall receive the utmost attention, and their gratification be limited only by a due attention to the claims of others . . . ", and then modulating effortlessly, in the time-honoured fashion of the clergy, into hints of an approaching appeal for funds.[107]

Another sidelight on the place of religion in daily life is provided by the fact that when examinations were held at Craigflower School, Scripture was a compulsory subject[108] — a reminder that the day-to-day affairs of life were still assumed to be contained within the larger framework of the Christian view of the universe and history.

This year also saw the founding of St. Ann's Academy, an institution that was to grow steadily with the years, and still be a prominent and much respected part of Victoria life a century later. Four Roman Catholic nuns, leaving Montreal on April 14, arrived in Victoria two months later. Their journey had been an arduous one; first they had had to travel from Eastern Canada to Panama; then after traversing the Isthmus (part of it, after an inner struggle, on sweating black backs) they had come up the west coast of the continent in the American paddle-steamer *Seabird*. After touching at San Francisco, Portland and Bellingham, they had reached Victoria on the afternoon of Saturday June 5. Their first dwelling-place (still preserved) was a two-roomed shack, roughly divided in two. On one side of the partition they took up their abode, while on the other they opened for school on Monday morning. Pupils were soon enrolled, representing a wide social spectrum; the daughters of Governor Douglas sat side by side with those of his critic James Yates, while both mingled unselfconsciously with half-breed girls. The first superior of the school was Salomé Valois (Sister Mary of the Sacred Heart), who was to be succeeded the following year by Sister Mary Providence (McTucker). The latter, of Irish origin, was highly educated, her microscope and magnet being still on display in the Convent's little museum. Instruction was conscientious and thorough, but the lighter side of life was not neglected; it was soon a familiar sight to see the nuns and their pupils gathering driftwood on the beaches in preparation for picnics. By late in the year the school had been enlarged and a prospectus had been printed.[109]

Social life was also expanding in this period. Such ships as the *Satellite*,[110] *Plumper*,[111] and *Ganges*[112] were often at Esquimalt, and dances on board ship became a feature of Victoria life. For example, in early August, a British naval officer recorded in his journal:

> In the evening we all went to a ball given by the officers of the *Plumper,* where we met all the young ladies of Vancouver (*sic*), they only number about 30 & are not very great beauties, however I enjoyed myself very much, not having had a dance for such a time. Most of the young ladies are half breeds & have quite as many of the propensities of the savage as of the civilized being. Two of the Miss Douglas' the governor's daughters had their heads flattened whilst they were young but it is now scarcely visible. They had just had some hoops sent out to them & it was most amusing to see their attempts to appear at ease in their new costume.[113]

On a later occasion, Commander Hugh Talbot Burgoyne, who had recently become one of the first winners of the Victoria Cross, displayed his decoration to the admiring dancers,[114] while in December Lt. Wilson was able to record:

> We are quite gay here now, nothing but Balls, private Theatricals, etc: with the Flag ship & other ships there is quite a small fleet.[115]

It may be appropriate at this point to notice that despite the heterogenous nature of the settlement's population, there was also what a later generation would call a "vertical mosaic". A strong tendency existed for the key positions to be held by men with close personal and cultural ties to the upper middle class of the British Isles; these ties were strengthened by the presence of the Royal Navy. As a modern writer on early Victoria expresses it:

> The British governing clique held firmly to its position as the upper class in Victoria. Governor Douglas and the succeeding governors, their wives and families, entertained the high supporting officials of the colony, most of whom were resident in Victoria. High-ranking officers of the Royal Navy and the Royal Engineers were included in this circle, and junior officers of the Services provided suitable escorts for the young ladies of these families. High officials of the Hudson's Bay Company completed this ruling hierarchy. Only slightly below ranked the professional section of the population, consisting almost entirely of British doctors, lawyers and clergy.

> The bulk of the population formed what might be properly called a "healthy middle class", or proprietary group, led by American and Jewish merchants. With various German, negro and British shop-keepers, this group took a growing and active part in municipal affairs, political, economic and social. Supporting this middle class were the skilled tradesmen of nearly every nationality, although as a group they did not make their influence felt to any great extent.

> Caste division as it applied to the labouring population transcended the bounds of nationalities, and the opportunity to advance into the ranks of the merchant section grew. German, Italian, Negro, Indian, Chinese and Kanaka household servants formed the large proportion of this group of semi-skilled and unskilled labour at the bottom of the social scale.[116]

This social differentiation had a tendency to extend into the field of religion, as was noted by an eye-witness who arrived in Victoria in this period:

> . . . without doubting the sincerity of religious devotion on the part of the people concerned, we may assert that the religious sect was commonly determined by the extent of a man's business, or his position in one of the already mentioned occupational groups. The Methodist churches were

made up mostly of small retailers and mechanics, the lesser tradesmen. Presbyterian and Congregationalist churches included jobbers and storekeepers, while the Church of England, the "state church" as it was called by many, contained bankers, lawyers, wholesale dealers and the governing class. "Just as with their augmented resources the people erect comfortable houses", said a visitor, "so they seek to provide themselves with a church suited to their advanced social position".[117]

Much of the early history of Victoria is often illuminated by these social distinctions, and many of the political quarrels of the subsequent years, as we shall see, reflect a struggle between those on the inside and those on the outside of the charmed circle of power.

It was a circle, however, whose boundaries were far from rigid —in the last analysis, the right attitude counted more than the right background. Douglas himself, after all, was of uncertain origin, Lady Douglas part Indian, Dr. Helmcken, though born in London, wholly German by ancestry, and the Pembertons Irish; but none of this interfered with their common social outlook. It may, however, have given them a sixth sense which warned them that conditions appropriate to the British Isles could never be exactly duplicated in the new world, and that the path of prudence was to be found in bending rather than breaking before the rising storm of North American democracy—or, to put it another way, that it was always better to evacuate the last ditch than to be found dead in it.

Meanwhile, like stock-markets of a later time, from month to month the gold fever soared and plunged. On July 31, 45 boats had been reported as on the way to Victoria; yet on August 14 the *Gazette* was speaking of the "present reaction", though considering it but a passing phase:

> We have little sympathy for many real estate operators in Victoria, who are sufferers by the present "reaction". We denounced their intrigues at the outset, and feel no regret at their downfall. But we are anxious, for the sake of many who will hold on through the present gloom, that their reward shall come as speedily and certainly as possible.

By August 27, the *Gazette* had recovered its good spirits:

In fact, everything now appears to indicate the recommence-
ment of that season of prosperity which was so suddenly and
disastrously terminated by the rising of the Lower Fraser.
On September 10, it reiterated this view:

Unless present indications are altogether deceptive, we are
in the last stage of the depression that has prevailed in this
vicinity since the cessation of immigration hither from California. Before a fortnight passes away, we may have entered
upon another period of inflation and excitement similar to
that which preceded our present condition.

The *Gazette* also pointed out[118] that in the previous thirty days,
there had been 67 buildings erected in Victoria, with 27 more
under construction—a total since the 12th of June of 344. Yet
on September 21, its editors were forced to declare that:

The town bears a sombre aspect—and the day on which
these remarks are penned is emphatically a "blue Monday".

An editorial on September 27 is baldly headed "The Existing
Depression";[119] yet on October 16 another editorial speaks of "the
revival of confidence", and a heading on October 23 declared
"The Panic Over".

So, with the ebb and flow of the Fraser, and of the movement
of miners along its banks,[120] hopes and fears succeeded each other.
There was little doubt, however, that the pace had slackened; the
Gazette itself was forced in October to change to a tri-weekly,
giving as its reason that fact that the population had "materially
decreased".[121] Yet as the year drew to its close, it was possible to
strike some sort of balance sheet, and it was clear that the balance
was in favour of the Colony.

Certainly the permanent population had greatly increased.
When the year had opened, it had been perhaps 300; although
now much below its peak (estimated at 7,000),[122] it had still
registered a substantial gain for the year. A beginning had been
made in the development of those services essential to a modern
community, such as paved, well-lit streets, fire and police protection, and newspapers;[123] while it was evident that some thought
was being given to the preservation of the natural beauties of the

area. Roads were slowly pushing outward from the Fort, and on the mainland were starting to reach from the mouth of the Fraser in the direction of what is now eastern Canada. The isolation of Victoria, once almost total, was slowly giving way to membership in the larger communities of North America and ultimately "the great globe itself".

Nor had the sudden disruption of an orderly society in which everyone had "known his place" produced a catastrophe. The town had only a few months previously been almost totally British — or rather Scottish — with each man having a position in an almost feudal hierarchy; now it was overwhelmingly or at least statistically American, with every man for himself; yet already it showed signs of absorbing these divergent traditions into a greater whole. The *Gazette* analyzed the matter in an editorial which, some would say, the subsequent passage of a century has not entirely invalidated:

> Americans, who now comprise a majority of our residents (at least in Victoria), are more excitable than the English, but their impulses do not carry them away headlong like those of the French. Inferior to the English in careful calculation of chances and deliberate planning, they are far more active, ready in adaptation of means to ends, and quite as enduring. These latter are the qualities most needed in a new country, and when freed from the influence of the natural excitability to which we have alluded, are capable of combination in action with that foresight and certainty of action peculiar to the English in a manner which will produce wonderful and lasting results. American energy exerting its power with a British balance-wheel will, we have strong hopes, place this Colony ere many years where California should have been today.[124]

There was, therefore, despite temporary setbacks, abundant reason for faith in the young community, and on a later occasion, in an editorial headed "Grounds for Self-Gratulation", the *Gazette* listed some additional grounds for confidence:

> In the first place, the security of owners in their titles to real estate is a feature which will hereafter give the town a marked advantage over San Francisco, in her past history.

Secondly, the order that has been maintained here, under circumstances giving rise to grave forebodings, aggravated by the numerical weakness of those directly pledged to sustain the law, cannot but have a decided tendency to inspire that confidence upon which is dependent the character of our future population—causing it to comprise a large proportion of families. Thirdly, though little has been yet done toward permanent public improvements in the town, sufficient has been attempted to give an earnest of what will follow . . .[125]

So 1858, the astonishing year of the treasure-seekers, drew to its end in a mood of cautious optimism. Already the settlement had been transformed, yet the onward sweep of change had really only begun. The next five years would see three important developments: the town would officially become a city; the palisades, now but the symbols of an outworn age, would be dismantled and sold for firewood; and finally, the man who had founded the first settlement on this spot in 1843 and then guided it through difficult times would, full of years and honors, lay down his public burdens. It is to these deep notes of change, tolling as they do the passing of the old order, that we now must turn our attention.

FOOTNOTES

[1] The church was begun in 1853 and completed in 1856. It stood on the Burdett Street hill.

[2] As early as June 1846, however, HBC Governor Simpson had said that "Victoria promises to become a very important place". (Waddington, *The Fraser Mines Vindicated,* Victoria, 1858, p. 11.)

[3] "Another source of wealth and enterprise may be found in the magnificent ship spars produced on Vancouver Island, which in point of size and comparative strength are probably the most valuable in the world, and may be procured in any number even were the demand to include the supply of spars for the whole British Navy." (Douglas to Lord Russell, Secretary of State for the Colonies, 21 August 1855. PABC.)

[4] "The object of every sound system of colonization should be, not to re-organize Society on a new basis, which is simply absurd, but to transfer to the new country whatever is most valuable and most approved in the institutions of the old, so that society may, as far as possible, consist of the same classes, united together by the same ties and having the same relative duties to perform in one country as in the other." (Barclay to Douglas, Dec. 1849; quoted from *"Land Policy of the Colony of Vancouver Island, 1849-1866",* Leonard A. Wrinch, M.A. Thesis, UBC, October 1932, pp. 28-29.)

[5] A wealth of fascinating material is to be found in such books as Mayne, *Four Years in British Columbia and Vancouver Island*, London, 1862; Duthie, *A Bishop in the Rough*, London, 1909; S. W. Pettit, Matthew Baillie Begbie, *BCHQ*, Vol. XI, Nos. 1, 2, 3, 4 (1947)—also reprinted separately; Bruce Hutchison, *The Fraser*, Toronto, Clarke Irwin, 1950 (reprinted in paperback edition 1965); Begbie, *Journey into the Interior of British Columbia*, printed in *Papers Relative to the Affairs of British Columbia*, Part 3, London, Queen's Printer, 1860; F. W. Howay, *The Early History of the Fraser River Mines*, Victoria, 1926 (PABC Memoir No. 6); *The Work of the Royal Engineers in British Columbia, 1858 to 1863*, Victoria, 1910; Scholefield and Howay, *British Columbia from the Earliest Times to the Present*. Vancouver, 1914, 4 vols.

[6] One of his nephews was premier of France for a short time and later French ambassador to Great Britain; Waddington became a member of the Vancouver Island House of Assembly in 1861-2; in 1867 he published in Victoria a pamphlet called "Overland Communication by Land and Water through British North America", in which he advocated a Canadian transcontinental railway. In 1871 he was in Ottawa seeking a charter for such a railway. He died suddenly of smallpox on Feb. 27, 1872. Mount Waddington is named after him.

[7] This claim has been disputed. Some give the honour to David Cameron's *Rules of Practice* or to various government proclamations regarding the establishment of the Colony of British Columbia. See J. Forsyth, *BCHA 1st Annual Report*, 1923, pp. 22-28. Also Victoria *Gazette* for January 11, 1859.

[8] It was printed in a building on Wharf Street by Paul de Garro on a press lent him by the Roman Catholic Bishop Demers (1809-1871). De Garro himself, who may have been a French count with a romantic past (see *Colonist* for August 3, 1861), eventually left for the goldfields in 1861 and was killed by a boiler explosion on the ship *Cariboo*. The press, which also on December 11, 1858, printed the first edition of the *British Colonist* (later the *Colonist*), was taken to the Cariboo in 1866 (where it printed the first issue of the *Cariboo Sentinel*). In 1908, it was presented to the museum of St. Ann's Convent, Victoria, where it is still a treasured exhibit. For a photograph of the press and more information about it, see the introduction to a private reprint of Waddington's work made in Vancouver in 1949 by Robert Reid.

[9] Waddington, *The Fraser Mines Vindicated*, Victoria, 1858, p. 15.

[10] *Ibid.*, pp. 16-17.

[11] Waddington, *op. cit.*, pp. 16-17.

[12] *Loc. cit.*

[13] *Op. cit.*, pp. 17-18.

[14] Macfie, *Vancouver Island and British Columbia*, London, 1865, p. 65.

[15] By a curious coincidence, he had visited Fort Victoria in 1849. See Mayne, *Four Years in British Columbia and Vancouver Island*, London, 1862, pp. 25 and 30.

[16] *Ibid.*, p. 46.

[17] *Ibid.*, p. 45.

[18] Waddington, *op. cit.,* p. 18.

[19] *Ibid.,* p. 19. Some land was also bought in Saanich and Cowichan from the colonial government, but transactions were hampered by the fact that twenty acres was the minimum amount sold to any one purchaser. (Ormsby, *British Columbia: A History,* Macmillan, Vancouver, 1958, p. 141).

[20] K. Cornwallis, *The New El Dorado,* London, 1858, p. 274.

[21] *Journal of Service of Lt. C. W. Wilson, R.E., PABC.* Entry for July 13, 1858.

[22] J. D. Pemberton, *Facts and Figures Relating to Vancouver Island and British Columbia,* London, 1860, p. 130.

[23] I.e., women captured in battle with other tribes.

[24] Macfie, *op. cit.,* p. 471.

[25] "One person with a belief is a social power equal to 99 who have only interest." — Mill.
"Hitherto, I had watched in silence. I now asked, 'What other reserves have we?' 'There are none,' said Air Vice-Marshal Park. In an account which he wrote about it afterwards, he said that at this I 'looked grave'. Well I might . . . The odds were great; our margins small; the stakes infinite." — W. Churchill, *Their Finest Hour,* Houghton Mifflin, Boston, 1949, pp. 335-6.

[26] Vancouver Island finally committed itself to decimal currency on December 12, 1862. (Peter Palmer, *A Fiscal History of British Columbia in the Colonial Period.* Ph.D. Thesis, Stanford, 1932, p. 178).

[27] Some tentative solutions to it considered by the British Government are detailed in Ormsby, *British Columbia: A History,* Macmillan, 1958, pp. 148-9.

[28] Douglas' despatches, and the replies of the various Colonial Secretaries to them, are collected in *Papers Relative to the Affairs of British Columbia, Parts 1-4,* London, Queen's Printer, 1859-1862. Stanley had succeeded Henry Labouchere, Colonial Secretary in Palmerston's ministry, which fell in February, 1858.

[29] Douglas to Stanley, Despatch No. 1. Sent May 19, 1858. Received July 13. Answered July 16.

[30] *Papers Relative to the Affairs of British Columbia, Part I,* p. 12. (Enclosed in Despatch No. 1).

[31] Douglas to Stanley, Despatch No. 2. Sent June 10, 1858. Received August 9. Answered August 14.

[32] *Ibid.*

[33] *Ibid.*

[34] Douglas to Stanley, Despatch No. 2.

[35] *Ibid.*

[36] Douglas to Stanley, Despatch No. 4. Sent June 15. Received August 9. Answered August 14. (Despatch No. 3. Sent June 15. Had concerned a a petition signed by James Yates and some others, protesting the "monopolizing policy of the Hudson's Bay Company").

[37] Douglas to Stanley, Despatch No. 6. Sent July 1. Received August 9. Answered August 14.

38 Douglas to Stanley, Despatch No. 7. Sent July 26. Received September 10. Answered September 16.

39 *Ibid.*

40 Douglas to Stanley, Despatch No. 8. Sent August 19. Received October 11. Answered October 16.

41 The town of Lytton was later named after him. He was also the successful author of *The Last Days of Pompeii.* Several British statesmen have achieved some celebrity as authors; Disraeli was a prolific novelist, and (some might add) in our own day the Earl of Avon has also tried his hand at fiction.

42 Cooper used the occasion to expound once more his grievances against Douglas regarding his cranberry venture of several years before. For his testimony see *Report from the Select Committee on the Hudson's Bay Company,* London, Queen's Printer, 1857, 3558-4037, and for Blanshard's, 5097-5357. Cooper later returned to Vancouver Island and on January 13, 1859, was chosen by the Imperial Government to serve under Douglas as Harbour-Master of British Columbia. It is interesting to speculate on the degree of enthusiasm with which the Governor welcomed the appointment.

43 It is worth noting that in the Eastern Hemisphere what might be called the "parallel organization" — the East India Company — was also about to have its monopolistic position ended by authority of the British parliament. The Indian Mutiny of 1857 was a factor in hastening the process.

44 These were reinforced by Douglas' proclamation of May 8, 1858, threatening to confiscate goods imported without a licence from the Company and a permit from the Victoria customs-house. These regulations were either relaxed or cancelled later in the year, but not before giving the authorities at the Colonial Office the impression that Douglas was basically interested in keeping the mainland as a private preserve of the Company. (See Ormsby, *op. cit.,* pp. 152-3).

45 Lytton to Douglas, July 1, 1858, Despatch No. 1 (confidential). *Papers Relative to the Affairs of British Columbia, Part I,* London, Queen's Printer, 1859.

46 Douglas to Lytton, Despatch No. 12. Sent September 29, 1858. Received November 29.

47 Lytton to Douglas (confidential,) Despatch No. 3: *Papers Relative to the Affairs of British Columbia, Part 1,* 16 July, 1858.
Affairs of British Columbia, Part 1, 16 July, 1858.

48 Douglas to Lytton, Despatch No. 1: *Papers Relative to the Affairs of British Columbia, Part 2,* 1859. Received December 10. Answered December 16. Douglas suggested that his salary be advanced to £5000 for his combined offices. Lytton in his reply (Lytton to Douglas (Private), Despatch No. 1, December 16, 1858: *Papers Relative to the Affairs of British Columbia, Part 2*) clearly thought this rather steep, and suggested £1800.

49 Lytton to Douglas, *Papers Relative to the Affairs of British Columbia,* 1859, Despatch No. 11.

50 Begbie (1819-1894) had arrived in Victoria on November 16, 1858. See S. W. Pettit, "Matthew Baillie Begbie", *BCHQ,* Vol. XI, 1947, Nos. 1, 2, 3, 4. (Also collected and printed in a separate pamphlet).

[51] Its editors originally thought of calling it "The Anglo-American". (E. Fawcett, *Some Reminiscences of Old Victoria,* Toronto, 1912, p. 73). For an account of other Victoria newspapers of the period, see J. Forsyth, *BCHA 1st Annual Report,* pp. 22-28.

[52] The commentators of the *Gazette* showed greater shrewdness in interpreting the "Dickens case" than many who knew the principals. See issues of September 11, 22, 24 and 25, and also read in this connection Ada Nisbet, *Dickens and Ellen Ternan,* U. of California Press, Berkeley, 1952.

[53] The *Gazette* eventually adopted "pro-American" policies, and its resulting drop in circulation was mainly responsible for its ceasing publication in November, 1859. See W. E. Ireland, "British Columbia's American Heritage", *Canadian Historical Association, Annual Report for 1948,* p. 68.

[54] Mayne, *Four Years in British Columbia and Vancouver Island,* London, 1862, p. 46.

[55] *Gazette,* July 31, 1858.

[56] J. S. Helmcken, *Reminiscences,* III, p. 122.

[57] Douglas to Labouchère, May 8, 1858. *Correspondence Relative to the Discovery of Gold in the Fraser's River District, London,* Queen's Printer, 1858.

[58] *Victoria Gazette,* July 28, 1858.

[59] Douglas to Labouchère, May 8, 1858, *Correspondence Relative to the Discovery of Gold . . . London,* 1858.

[60] *Ibid.*

[61] *Journal of Service of Lt. C. W. Wilson, R.E.* Entry for 13 July, 1858.

[62] What was apparently Victoria's first duel (which ended fatally) grew out of "a difficulty at the cricket ground on Beacon Hill". See *Gazette* for 14 September, 1858.

[63] *Gazette,* 12 August, 1858.

[64] *Gazette,* 2 September, 1858.

[65] *Journal of Service of Lt. C. W. Wilson, R.E.* Entry for 31 July, 1858. *PABC.*

[66] *Gazette,* 30 July, 1858.

[67] *Gazette,* 10 August, 1858. The first home in Saanich was established on the slopes of Mount Newton by William and Margaret Thomson on April 8, 1858. They later gave the land for St. Stephen's, the first church in Saanich. Their son, Alexander, was the first white child born in Saanich (March 14, 1859). It is possible that Angus MacPhail preceded the Thomsons in Saanich. (See *BCHQ,* XII, No. 3, July, 1948, pp. 248-255; also N. Lugrin and J. Hosie, *The Pioneer Women of Vancouver Island, 1843-1866,* Victoria, 1928, pp. 90-96.

[68] At this time there were probably only 200 Indians in Saanich; this low figure was due to a massacre by other tribes some twenty years before (*Gazette,* August 18, 1858). As a result of this disaster, the Indians now lived in "lodges surrounded by palisades some twenty feet high" (*loc. cit.*).

[69] Despatches by correspondents on the spot may be found in numerous issues of the *Gazette.*

[70] *Gazette,* October 7, 1858.

[71] *Gazette,* August 31, 1858.

[72] *Gazette,* November 16, 1858.

[73] *Gazette,* September 27, 1858.

[74] *Gazette,* September 22, 1858. Victorians in this period had no hesitation in "thinking big". An article in the September 29 issue of the *Gazette* discusses the possibility (raised in the British House of Commons) of a canal through the Rockies, to connect the Atlantic and Pacific Oceans.

[75] *Gazette,* November 30, 1858. For an account of his life to this point, see Roland Wild, *Amor De Cosmos,* Ryerson Press, 1958; W. G. Shelton (ed.), *British Columbia and Confederation,* Victoria, Morriss Printers, 1967, pp. 67-96; Margaret Ross, *Amor De Cosmos: A British Columbia Reformer,* M.A. Thesis, UBC, April, 1931.

[76] Captain Grant, Vancouver Island's first independent settler, took part in its suppression. See Chapter 5.

[77] Born in Ireland about 1808, he arrived in Victoria in December, 1855, and died in 1891. He was the uncle of J. D. Pemberton. See Ormsby, "Some Irish Figures in Colonial Days", *BCHQ,* XIV, January-April, 1950, pp. 61-82.

[78] *Gazette,* August 19, 1858.

[79] *Gazette,* September 30, 1858. The first brick building was the "Victoria Hotel".

[80] *Gazette,* October 13, 1858.

[81] Born in Ireland in 1821 and educated at Trinity College, Dublin. He was the first white man to visit Cowichan Lake in 1852. From 1853 to 1855 he surveyed the Island from Sooke to Nanaimo with great accuracy. He also designed and erected the Race Rocks and Fisgard Lighthouses. From 1856 to 1859 he was a member of the first Legislative Assembly of Vancouver Island, and from 1859 to 1864 Surveyor-General of Vancouver Island. In 1887 he founded the firm of Pemberton and Son. He died in 1893. See Ormsby, *op. cit.*

[82] *Minutes of the House of Assembly of Vancouver Island, 1856-1858,* *PABC* Memoir No. 3, Victoria, King's Printer, 1918. Entries for July, 27, August 5, August 17, 1858.

[83] *Minutes of the House of Assembly,* entries for July 27 and August 5. Also *Gazette* for August 20, 1858.

[84] *Minutes of the House of Assembly,* August 24, 1858.
Point Ellice was named after the Rt. Hon. Edward Ellice (1781-1863), a leading figure in the North West Company; he helped to bring about its amalgamation with the HBC, of which he was Deputy Governor from 1858 to 1863.

[85] *Gazette,* August 3, 1858.

[86] *Gazette,* July 29, 1858. Douglas had originally planned a fire brigade under the jurisdiction of the police, but public sentiment insisted on volunteer brigades. There was no civic-paid fire department till 1886. See F. W. Laing and W. K. Lamb, "The Fire Companies of Old Victoria", *BCHQ,* Vol. X, No. 1, January, 1946, pp. 43-75. This article contains pictures of some of Victoria's earliest fire-engines.

87 *Gazette,* October 5, 1858.

88 *Gazette,* September 24, 1858.

89 *Gazette,* September 24, 1858.

90 *Gazette,* October 12, 1858. The streets still, however, left much to be desired. Lt. Wilson wrote in his journal a few weeks later: "In the town of Victoria, the mud is so deep that it comes up to the horses' girths & foot passengers can only cross on planks laid across, indeed it is so bad that a story is told of a merchant who wished to carry on a conversation with a person on the other side of the street, hiring an Indian to shoot letters over with his bow & arrows." — *Journal of Service of Lt. C. W. Wilson,* entry for December 23, 1858. *PABC.*

91 *Gazette,* August 5, 1858.

92 *Gazette,* November 4, 1858.

93 The impressive assurances of some of these advertisements may be contrasted with the shriller injunctions of a century later. A patent medicine, for example, was extolled in these terms: "It stands alone; it is a panacea; and to give more certificates of cures were useless; for only the very ignorant skeptic can doubt, after the many respectable names already offered, of cures effected by it." (December 30, 1858).
San Francisco firms also took space in the *Gazette.* Remedies for seasickness figured prominently in their notices.

94 See W. E. Ireland, "The Annexation Petition of 1869", *BCHQ,* 1940, Vol. IV, No. 4, pp. 267-287; W. N. Sage, "The Annexationist Movement in British Columbia", *Transactions of the Royal Society of Canada, 3rd Series,* XXI, sec. ii, 1927, pp. 97-110; H. L. Keenlyside, "British Columbia — Annexation or Confederation", *Canadian Historical Association Report for 1928,* pp. 34-40.

95 *Gazette,* October 22, 1858.

96 See W. E. Ireland, "The French in British Columbia", *BCHQ,* Vol. XIII, No. 2, April, 1949, pp. 67-89.
Douglas himself was perfectly bilingual.

97 *Minutes of the House of Assembly of Vancouver Island 1856-1858,* p. 70.

98 *Ibid.,* p. 71.

99 F. E. Walden, *The Social History of Victoria, 1858-1871,* B.A. Thesis, UBC, 1951, p. 129.

100 *Ibid.,* p. 27. He also issued Victoria's first City Directory in 1860, a most useful work.

101 For further details of Victoria's Jewish community in this period, read David Rome, *The First Two Years,* H. M. Caiserman, Montreal, 1942.

102 Douglas to Labouchère, May 8, 1858. *Correspondence Relative to the Discovery of Gold* . . . London, Queen's Printer, 1858.

103 Gibbs later wrote an interesting autobiography — *"Shadow and Light"* (Washington, 1902). Regarding his Victoria experiences, he says "We received a warm welcome from the Governor and other officials of the colony, which was cheering . . . I cannot describe with what joy we hailed the opportunity to enjoy that liberty under the "British Lion" denied us beneath the pinions of the American eagle." (p. 63).

104 "The newly appointed police of the place were negroes, and consequently

heartily despised by the Americans." (K. Cornwallis, *The New El Dorado,* London, 1858, p. 274).

[105] See J. W. Pilton, *Negro Settlement in British Columbia, 1858-1871,* M.A. Thesis, UBC, 1951, p. 53.

[106] *Gazette,* August 24, 1858.

[107] *Gazette,* August 26, 1858.

[108] *Gazette,* August 4, 1858.

[109] See Lugrin and Hosie, *The Pioneer Women of Vancouver Island, 1843-1866,* Victoria, 1928, pp. 136-145.
Two more nuns arrived in 1859, and a further eight in 1863.

[110] H.M. Screw Corvette *Satellite,* 1462 tons, carried 21 guns. Stationed at Esquimalt 1857-1860. Captain, James C. Prevost. (Walbran, *British Columbia Coast Names,* p. 442).

[111] The *Plumper* was an auxiliary steam sloop of 484 tons. It arrived at Esquimalt November 9, 1857, and remained here till January, 1861. It was commanded by Captain Richards and R. C. Mayne was his Second Lieutenant. (Walbran, *op. cit.,* pp. 383-4).

[112] H.M.S. *Ganges* was stationed at Esquimalt 1857-1860. (Walbran, p. 198).

[113] *Journal of Lt. Wilson, R.E.,* entry for August 2, 1858. *PABC.*

[114] *Gazette,* October 30, 1858.

[115] Wilson, *op. cit.,* entry for December 2, 1858.

[116] F. E. Walden, *Social History of Victoria, 1858-1871,* B.A. Thesis, UBC, 1951, pp. 35-6.

[117] Matthew Macfie, *Vancouver Island and British Columbia,* London, 1865, p. 417.

[118] *Gazette,* September 16, 1858.

[119] On this same day, however, the House of Assembly passed a bill of supply totalling $14,610. Of this, $12,660 was for roads. (Palmer, *Fiscal History of British Columbia in the Colonial Period,* Ph.D. Thesis, Stanford, July, 1932, p. 178).

[120] The *Gazette* estimated on November 20 that of 24,153 who had left California for the Fraser River by sea, 8,200 had returned.

[121] *Gazette,* October 26, 1858.

[122] *Gazette,* December 25, 1858.

[123] The *Vancouver Island Gazette* had had a brief career in mid-summer; a French journal, *Le Courrier de la Nouvelle Caledonie,* had done the same a little later; and on December 11, 1858, the first issue of the *Colonist* (originally called the *British Colonist*) had appeared.

[124] *Gazette,* August 28, 1858.

[125] *Gazette,* November 2, 1858.

CHAPTER SEVEN

The Birth
of
The City

Of the fifteen years since the founding of the Fort, by far the most remarkable had been 1858. Like a tidal wave, the torrent of the treasure-seekers had swept through the quiet settlement, and for a time nearly every established landmark seemed obliterated. As 1859 began, however, the waters had somewhat subsided, and it was possible to estimate how much, if anything, had survived the unexpected flood.

One thing was plain: that the sleepy hamlet at the world's end where a handful of Britons, ever conscious of their exact position in the well-ordered hierarchy of power, went about their daily, not-greatly-changing tasks, and knew that as surely as Victoria was queen, fur was king, was now but a memory. For better or worse, the 19th century had come to "Vancouver's Island"; its engines of relentless change were driven by twin pistons — the steady transition of the fundamental source of wealth from farm and forest to the factory, and the development, both in theory and practice, of social and political equality. Already they had transformed large areas of the globe; now they battered against the little fort, and though the palisades still stood, their foundations were irrevocably weakened. True, the vigorous Governor still held the reins of office, and comported himself at all times with the bearing of one who knows himself the proconsul and visible representative of no mean empire; yet as early as 1856, on instruc-tions from his superiors, he had been obliged to set up a rudimentary House of Assembly, with whose popularly elected members he now shared his no longer undisputed power. More-over, since December 11, 1858, he had had to bear with the steady fire of criticism levelled at him by the eccentric editor of the newly founded *British Colonist,* Amor De Cosmos.

These were two respects in which it was clear that the little world of "the Company" was ending; but they were not the only two. On all sides, signs of a new age multiplied.

One, for example, was the drastically changed composition of the settlement. Once almost exclusively of British stock, it now had large representations of nearly every race and nation upon earth. Not many of these were likely to feel an instinctive reverence for the traditional ways and institutions of the colony, or loyalty to the distant government in London, and this was particularly true of the large American contingent—which, indeed, after mid-summer 1858 comprised the great majority of the inhabitants of the area. It was clear that profound social changes would almost certainly result from their presence; the only question, perhaps, was whether the "establishment" would bend or collapse before them.

One major feature of the "establishment", indeed, had already had sentence of death pronounced upon it. The monopolistic position of the Hudson's Bay Company had for some time aroused the resentment both of the independent colonists on the Island and of important political figures in the United Kingdom. Accord-ingly, it had been decided that its exclusive rights of trading with the Indians in the Far West should be abolished, and a prom-inent feature of the Victoria *Gazette* for New Year's Day 1859 was the printing of a proclamation, signed by Queen Victoria, announcing the cancellation of the Crown Grant of 1838.

In other respects, too, a new economic order was at hand. Once fur had been almost the sole export of the colony, and the source of nearly all employment. Then farming, followed by lumbering, had been added. Now, however, a score of occupations made their first appearance, as a bustling crowd of independent tradesmen opened stores and busily hawked their wares. Luxuries as well as necessities were available to those with the price, and rapidly, silently in men's minds the conception of the Fort was altered. No longer a fur-trading depot, it was now a market-place; yet not content with this, it already reached out blindly for the glittering crown of cityhood.

Such were some of the changes that came in the wake of the treasure-seekers, and those who lived through them may well have wondered as the new year dawned what further developments lay ahead.

Not all saw a future of unclouded skies. The *Gazette* in its issue of January 1, 1859 described the previous twelve months, somewhat strangely, as "a year, in great part, made up of disaster, defeat and depression", and certainly there was some slackening of economic activity in 1859. Dr. Helmcken in his memoirs recorded that "the failure of the mines and exodus of so many miners, produced great depression in Victoria . . . "[1] and added some details:

> The value of real estate fell in Victoria. I was offered part of my property back for less than I sold it for, but declined to buy and the same happened to others—everyone was depressed and gloomy, the reaction had come with a vengeance. Many of those who had speculated could not pay their assessments or due bills and were virtually ruined—everything looked blue and remained so.[2]

Matthew Macfie, who arrived in Victoria in September 1859, confirmed this picture of the economic setback:

> Many stores were closed and shanties empty. There was little business doing, and no great prospect ahead. This stagnant condition continued with but little abatement till the close of 1860 . . .[3]

Despite this testimony, however, there were soon in fact numerous signs that the settlement would surmount its temporary difficulties. At no time did economic growth come to a standstill, and during the year more and more of the customary features of civilization made their appearance in Victoria. The winter of 1858-1859 saw the erection of the Royal Hotel, described as "a fine two-storey brick building on Wharf Street", three large frame hotels (the Orleans, Colonial and Metropolitan),[4] a police barracks, the fire-proof warehouse of Messrs. Langley on Yates Street, the Custom House and Post Office on Government Street and a new Catholic church on Humboldt Street. Yates Street was paved with stone between Wharf and Government Streets, and parts of Johnson, Wharf and Government Streets were also paved. Many plank sidewalks were put down. In this year, too, the steamer *Governor Douglas* was built and put into operation.[5]

The first steps toward the proper illumination of the town were also taken in this year. The streets had hitherto been in almost total darkness at night, which inevitably was conducive to crime. On October 19 a group of men, most of them remarkably young, petitioned the Assembly for the right to incorporate a company to supply Victoria with gas. They asked for a fourteen-year monopoly or franchise, something to which De Cosmos, too doctrinaire to realize the difference between the vast HBC trading monopoly and an unavoidable local franchise, violently objected.[6] After the question had been widely and often acrimoniously discussed, the sponsors of the plan reduced the desired term to five years. In this revised form their plan was presented to the Legislature in October 1860. In November, the "Victoria Gas Company" was incorporated, and on December 19, 1860, the "Victoria Gas Company Act" was passed. A piece of land on Rock Bay was then bought and the construction of a plant begun; it was not, however, until 1862 that their plans reached fruition and the first streets in Victoria were lit by gas.[7]

Precautions against fire were also much improved. We have noted earlier that two fire engines were purchased in 1858. In April 1859, contracts were let for the construction of two cisterns in which to store water.[8] One was on Store Street and one on Government, and much of the work was done by convict labor— the famous "chain gang", long a familiar sight in the community.[9] The first cistern was finished in June, and filled with 25,000 gallons of water. A serious fire in October caused increased agitation for a properly organized fire protection service. Curiously enough, the idea that this was a normal function of government was apparently not considered.[10] Instead, money was collected by means of a public appeal, and additional equipment was ordered from San Francisco. In November, tenders were invited for the construction of an engine-house and meeting hall (the cost not to exceed $1500), which were soon erected at the corner of Bastion and Wharf streets. In this same month the Union Hook and Ladder Company was formally organized, and the apparatus ordered from San Francisco arrived early in 1860.[11]

Law and order was maintained with remarkable success, under the vigilant supervision of Augustus Pemberton and his 14 constables.[12] In April three men were charged with "furious driving on the streets and on the Esquimalt Bridge" and each fined $5.[13] A more serious crime was uncovered in June when C. A. Angelo, clerk of the Victoria Custom House, was found to have embezzled £2000.[14] The sudden appearance in the Harbor in March of 70 canoes containing over six hundred Indians resulted in some uneasiness but passed off uneventfully, and the arrival of numbers of Chinese en route for the Fraser River was also devoid of incident.

The question of appropriate costume for barristers aroused controversy at this time, when some of them made their appearance in court dressed in the English style, "full robed and rigged". The editors of the *Gazette* on June 2 ridiculed this as mere affectation, suggesting, as more appropriate to the milieu, "a blue or red blanket profusely studded with beads and buttons, and for the wig, substitute a gay feather." They maintained—how correctly, they received no opportunities to discover—that this would be "not near so likely to startle or astonish the common people." De Cosmos, however, in an editorial on June 1, somewhat surprisingly supported the traditional garb.

The needs of the sick were also taken in hand. The earliest hospital in Victoria had perhaps been the parsonage of the Rev. Mr. Cridge. Later a small hospital was established in "a cottage kindly loaned rent free by Mr. Blinkhorn on the corner of Yates and Broad streets". This, however, soon proved inadequate, and a committee was set up by Governor Douglas, consisting of A. G. Dallas, a director of the HBC, A. F. Pemberton, Magistrate and

Commissioner of Police, and the Rev. Mr. Cridge. This group devoted its efforts to raising funds and generating publicity for the cause. February 13, 1859 was proclaimed "Hospital Sunday", and collections at the two services at the Anglican Church provided $149. The House of Assembly voted the sum of $1100.[15] With the funds provided, the Committee "took possession of a piece of land on the Songhees Indian Reserve and erected a wooden building on the site later to be occupied by the Marine Hospital." The first medical officer in charge was Dr. James Trimble,[16] and the first item in the sundry account book was fundamental enough— "6 bars of soap, 1/6".[17]

Banks, too, made their appearance at this time. Alexander Macdonald established a private bank under the name of Macdonald & Co., while later in 1859 a branch of the Bank of North America opened in Victoria.[18]

The construction of a better bridge across the harbor was also a lively subject of discussion. The one in existence, which ran from the vicinity of the Fort to the nearest point of the Indian encampment, hampered the full use of the harbor, as well as facilitating contacts between the two races injurious to both. One beginning at Point Ellice seemed to many more desirable, and the matter was several times discussed by the tiny House of Assembly.

Even the stockade, once the sure shield against unimaginable terrors, was now regarded with incipient scepticism. On April 16 the *Gazette* declared it "an eyesore to our people and a serious hindrance to the prosperity of the south end of the town, by cutting off communication between the upper and lower portions, and we shall be but too glad to chronicle its demolition."

Indeed, it appeared that the defences which the fiercest Indian warrior could not surmount were now to be brushed aside by a more effective weapon: the hoop-skirt. A letter in the *Gazette* for April 21 showed which way the wind was blowing:

> Do you receive letters from ladies? If so I beg to tell you that we are delighted to hear by your last paper, that the frightful Stockade around the Fort is to be removed, and a handsome row of brick buildings on Wharf Street substituted for it. It will then be quite a pleasure to go there

shopping; now it is merely a duty. The small wickets do not suit our expanding dresses; to be sure we might ask the shivering porter to open the big gate, but the poor fellow does not seem to understand the use of language . . . We believe this very unpopular construction to have arisen from a conspiracy of papas, uncles and rich relatives, to prevent us from too often infringing upon their shop accounts . . .

That despite temporary setbacks a growing community was envisioned by many is shown by the attention given to the question of moving the Quadra Street Cemetery to some more secluded location. The phrases in which this matter was broached by the editors of the *Gazette* must, however, be admitted to strike strangely on a modern ear. A new cemetery, they declared, would be

. . . a place where our children and children's children, as they wander through the winding avenues of that "City of the Dead", or sit within the shade of some secluded dell, and as they look upon the mossy locks hanging from the ancient and venerable trees, will call to remembrance the early dead, and contemplate upon the mighty past."[19]

(We might note in this connection that the language of the time was already beginning to envelop itself in Victorian sesquipedalianism. An anonymous commentator in the *Colonist* for April 30 remarked acidly: "The age is becoming more refined. 'Root hog or die' is now rendered as follows: 'Penetrate the subsoil, my porcine friend, or expect an obituary notice on your untimely end.'")

Perhaps the most clear-cut evidence, however, that, at least in high places, there were no faint hearts, was given by the construction of the famous "birdcages", designed to accommodate the House of Assembly and other organs of the rapidly expanding government service. Previous to this, the representatives of the people had met in decidedly rustic surroundings:

The House of Assembly was a room about 20 feet in length and about a dozen in breadth, lined with upright planks, unpainted, unadorned, save perhaps with a few cedar mats to cover fissures. On each side were two doors leading to as many dormitories. In the centre stood a large dilapidated rectangular stove, its sides made of sheet iron, beautifully and picturesquely bulging.

At the end was a wooden home-manufactured table upon which stood a hundred page ledger, but without a mace, pen-knife or postage stamps, although the latter at that time existed for foreign purposes . . . Around the Speaker's table stood half-a-dozen ordinary chairs for the use of the members and at a respectable distance a couple of benches without backs for the audience . . .

At the end of the year the accounts indicated that this august body had cost about twenty-five dollars . . .[20]

Now, however, it was decided that a more dignified setting was required for the legislature and other departments of the government. In a message to the House, Douglas made known his intention of erecting not merely several new buildings on the southern shore of James Bay, but a bridge, eight hundred feet long, to connect them with the main business district of the town.

At first the House of Assembly was disinclined to endorse the project, considering it beyond the resources of the colony, and passed a resolution to this effect. The *Colonist* joined in the chorus, declaring on April 30:

The projected bridge across James Bay is 800 feet long, without approaches, and will cost $6000. When completed $8000 will be spent for what we could well afford to do without at present — and have the use of funds for more necessary improvements. But as the colonial offices are all to be moved out of town to improve the value of somebody's town lots, the Colony must be bled to build this bridge to reach them.

On May 16, De Cosmos returned to the attack:

. . . if it was allowed that the Executive could spend one dollar without consent of the Assembly, he could spend a million, or if he had authority to obstruct one part of the harbor, on the same principle he could dam up the mouth of the harbor, and stop all egress or ingress.

Douglas, however, was not abashed, and pointed out in a message to the House that the new bridge and buildings would be built at the expense of the Hudson's Bay Company, and that the

House "was not called upon to defray the cost".[21] He added some-what acidly that:

> . . . the support and maintenance of places for public worship, of the Colonial Schools, the salaries of the clergy-men and teachers, the construction of roads, the erection of the police courts, of the custom house, and other public edifices, the establishment of a police force, the administra-tion of justice, and all other measures providing for the public safety and convenience, have been thrown entirely upon my hands, without any pecuniary aid or assistance whatever from the House of Assembly.[22]

Douglas pointed out that the expanding needs of the settlements required a considerable variety of buildings:

> A Treasury with fire-proof vault; a Barrack for the military Guard; a Land Office; an Office for the Registrar of Deeds and Conveyances; an Office for the Colonial Secretary; a House for the Legislative Assembly; a Supreme Court; an Official Residence for the Governor; and other buildings of inferior importance.[23]

He also informed the House that the bridge had already been contracted for at a price of $3500 or £800.[24]

The House, thus firmly put in its place, thanked Douglas for "Your Excellency's courteous and candid reply"[25] and the work was soon well under way.

The main building, when completed, came as something of a surprise to the townsfolk. Erected at a cost that may have been as high as $100,000, it combined a wild agglomeration of styles. The *Colonist* of August 26, 1859 described it as "something between a Dutch Toy and a Chinese Pagoda", though the *Gazette* ventured the opinion that "the style of architecture is that of the Elizabethan period".[26] Others saw resemblances to a sheep corral, a pigeon roost, and a Chinese washhouse; all, however, agreed that it was "fancifully painted in various shades of red".[27]

Parts of it were of brick brought by sailing ships around the Horn; and the cost of the buildings was defrayed partly by the HBC and partly by selling lots in what is now the main business district of Victoria. The new structures were officially opened on March 1, 1860, and served as a home for the Legislature (except for the years 1866-1868, when the capital was at New Westminster), until the closing years of the century, when most of them were torn down to make way for the present handsome buildings.

All in all, it seems clear that although there was an inevitable reaction to the fantastic boom of the previous year, 1859 may still be reckoned in many ways a year of economic advance.

In cultural matters, too, there was progress, as a wide variety of organizations made their appearance in Victoria. The local St. Andrew's Society was organized in 1859, mainly to aid Scots hard hit by the economic setback. Douglas consented to become its Honorary President, with Justices Cameron and Begbie as Honorary Vice-Presidents. The actual President was Gilbert M. Sproat.[28]

The Victoria Hebrew Benevolent Society was organized on June 4, 1859, and an account of the proceedings was given in the *Colonist* of June 6. A. Blackman was elected President, L. Davis Vice-President, and S. S. Hymes Secretary, while not long afterward the Society held an inaugural ball.[29]

A Masonic Lodge came into being on March 19, following a petition sent by a number of Masons to the Grand Lodge of England, asking for a charter. There was, however, a divergence from the beginning within the Masonic movement between those who favored lodges based on the British model and those who looked to the American movement for guidance in these matters.[30] Even in such matters was the early ambivalence of Victoria to be evidenced.

Nor were the arts neglected. The *Gazette* for January 29, 1859 carried a notice regarding a meeting of "the members of the Victoria Philharmonic Society", which, meeting at the house of Selim Franklin, elected its first officers. Matthew Begbie was chosen President, Selim Franklin[31] Vice-President, and Arthur Bushby[32] Secretary, and it is pleasant to record that they sang and played musical selections together before dispersing.[33] A second concert was held in May, the proceeds going to the new hospital. Some idea of the distance "the Fort" had travelled in twelve months may be gleaned from the report in the *Gazette* on May 24 that it was "attended by the beauty and fashion of the town". The *Colonist* reported on the 23rd of that month that the society now had nearly a hundred members.

Some of the most prominent citizens, we might note, prided themselves on their musical accomplishments. Augustus Pemberton, Commissioner of Police, had brought a flute from Ireland; B. W. Pearse the surveyor had a violin; the Rev. Cridge fancied himself on the cello; while a Mrs. Mowat joined them at the piano to make possible the playing of quartets.

On January 18 the *Gazette* declared that "a theatre and concert hall should be erected during the coming season in order that the recreation in search of which hundreds have departed in the last three months may be furnished here." In March, a group of actors from California visited Victoria. This was described as "the second theatrical company we have had in our town."[34]

More strenuous amusements were also available. On May 24 there were horse races on Beacon Hill, and in June a regatta in Esquimalt harbor, at which crews from H.M.S. *Pylades, Tribune* and *Satellite* displayed their prowess. Victoria's first cricket club had been formed on September 14, 1858, under the presidency of Thomas Harris, later to be the first mayor of the city. Matches were played at Beacon Hill and Colwood.[35]

Education, too, continued to receive attention. The Rev. Cridge, who acted as Superintendent of Education, made regular reports to the Colonial Secretary,[36] and though not all of these have survived, we can gain a fair picture of developments. There were two main government-operated schools at this time—the Victoria Colonial School, where in March 1859 W. H. Burr replaced Mr. Kennedy, and the Craigflower School, where Charles Clark was succeeded by Henry Claypole. Regarding the former, where in 1856 attendance had been a mere 17 boys, the Rev. Cridge now reported that between March 29, 1859 and November 29 of the same year, 64 boys and 13 girls had entered the school. He added some details which tend to put the theory that our ancestors underwent unimaginable hardships rather than miss a day's lessons in a somewhat doubtful light:

Of these about 7 were removed from various causes, one being a case of expulsion for immoral conduct. About 26 had left on account of the state of the weather, intending, as the teacher understood, to return in the spring.[37]

There was, however, a redeeming feature in this slightly spotty picture:

I am happy to learn that improper language, which at one time was painfully prevalent, is now becoming rare.[38]

The teachers at the two schools each received £150 a year, though a rise to £200 was envisioned. The Rev. Cridge was also considering the creation of "an elementary girls' school".[39]

There were also of course at this time numerous privately operated schools. On March 10, 1859, for example, the *Gazette* reported that Madame Pettibeau had opened a "Seminary for Young Ladies" on Fort Street, giving lessons in French and music, while on April 16 the *Colonist* reported:

Rev. Charles Vary will shortly open a school at the residence of Bishop De Mers. Instruction will be given in French and English. Judging from the well known learning of the Rev. gentleman the school cannot but prove a great acquisition.

Religion continued to thrive, as four Methodist ministers named Evans, White, Dobson and Browning arrived from Canada. No church building of their denomination yet existed, and they held their services at first "in the new brick Police Building on View Street, which His Excellency Gov. Douglas has kindly permitted to be used for Sabbath services until other arrangements are made."[40]

Anglicans also prospered. Not only had they a preferred position as—to employ a paradox—the unofficial state church, but they were aided by the gift of £15,000 (later increased to £25,000) from an English philanthropist, Miss Angela Burdett Coutts, with which to endow a bishopric. The first Anglican bishop of British Columbia, George Hills, was consecrated in Westminster Abbey on the 24th of February of this year, though he did not arrive in Victoria until January 6, 1860.[41]

St. Ann's Academy meanwhile continued to give instruction

and moral guidance to children of a wide variety of faiths and classes. An incident in the spring of 1859, however, caused a temporary setback in some respects. Girls enrolled at the Academy were strictly forbidden to attend dances. The Governor, on the other hand, in his official capacity had to appear at the more important ones, and he felt that his eldest daughters were under a public obligation to be present. The Sister Superior, nevertheless, would not relax the rules for even so distinguished a family, and the Governor felt himself forced, with profuse expressions of regret, to withdraw his daughters from the Academy. This decision was followed by similar ones on the part of those parents whose educational criteria were basically social.[41A] Undeterred by this contretemps, however, the energetic Sister Mary Providence rented a building on Broad Street for $20 a month and here classes were begun on December 19, 1859.

In this year, too, the Rev. Peter Rondeault began bringing the Catholic faith to other parts of the Island. Taking a breviary, a sack of flour and a gun, he went to Cowichan, where the natives, after considering this diverse equipment, accorded him a friendly reception. They built him a church and a log house and before long he had established the first school in the Cowichan area.[41B]

We might note that the question was already receiving consideration as to whether there should be government aid of any kind to Christian churches (it was taken for granted there should be none to synagogues, even though Jews made up a sizable proportion of the population), and whether the Anglican church should receive any sort of preferential treatment. When £400 was allotted by the administration of the Colony to the Church of England, the editor of the *Colonist* objected strongly. His remarks sum up so completely all that has been said in the subsequent century, at least on one side of the question, that they are perhaps worth quoting in full:

THE STATE CHURCH OF VANCOUVER ISLAND

An application was made yesterday to the Assembly by the Rev. Mr. Cridge to be continued as Colonial Chaplain, the five years for which he was engaged having ended, or being near its termination. This brings at once before the country the important questions, whether religion shall be supported by governmental aid? Whether one sect of Christians shall receive support, and the other none? Hitherto this colony has annually appropriated some £400 for the support of the incumbent of Victoria Church, whilst none has been extended to the Catholic Church, the first here, and the only one, besides the Rev. Mr. Cridge's, till lately. By this means we have virtually a State Church. Notwithstanding the injustice which has consequently been done hitherto to the Catholics, and which is apparent to every one who takes a correct view of the question, the Assembly is now asked to perpetuate the system. Is the country prepared to do it? We have no hesitation in saying that it is not, nor will not; that the principle of supporting religion by government subsidies is entirely wrong; that it is right that it should rely on voluntary aid, and none other; and that if an attempt is made to build up a minority church at the expense of the majority, it will embitter public feeling, create discord instead of harmony, and obstruct the great mission of Christianity in the Colony. Our revenue is too small; the demands on it too great, to think of it for one moment. But even had we a large and surplus revenue, still it would not be sound policy to grant one penny to support any church. The spirit of the age is opposed to it; pure religion does not require it; and now that the question is brought prominently before the country, it should be met, and our state church shaken off at once and forever.

Religious questions are always perplexing to the state, and the churchmen and laymen who will try to fasten them on this colony must bear the reproach of fanaticism, injustice, or bigotry, with the certainty of the attempt being met by defeat. To press the question into the area of politics will only be to urge it to a more speedy, but not less certain doom, and, with all, rack the community by the jarring of sectarianism without any good results. What! shall £400 be given to the minister of the Church of England and other denominations receive nothing? Shall the Methodists, the Catholics, the Congregationalists, who have an equal right to a proportionate share of the revenue, be treated as inferior, and the Established Church as a favorite? Such a proposition bears upon its face such rank bigotry and injustice, that were it not necessary to make some allowance for the force of

education, we would doubt whether any true follower of the
lowly Jesus could ever originate it. To avoid then the
injustice of giving to one and not to the other, shall all be
subsidized? No! Let us lay down the principles, and adhere
to them, that churches must depend on their congregations
for financial support; and that no state Church shall ever be
allowed to exist in Vancouver Island.[42]

Arguments over the use of the Bible (and what edition of it)
in the schools also entered at this time upon their long, indeed
apparently interminable career.

It is fair to state that here and there in the *Colonist* one detects
signs that the faith of some residents of Victoria was less fervent
than that of others, and that De Cosmos was perhaps to be
numbered with the lukewarm. When his paper on May 30 reported
that an unnamed member of the House of Assembly had declared
that "bishops were, perhaps, necessary evils", its editor added the
comment that "there are public secrets as well as private ones."
The same journal not long before had printed the following
jocosity:

"Tommy, my son", said a fond mother, "do you say your
prayers night and day?"
"Yes'm, that is nights; but any smart boy can take care of
himself in the day time."

(We might note in passing that 1859 was also the year that
saw the appearance of Charles Darwin's *Origin of Species,* a
work giving a picture of the past history and future prospects of
life on this planet at considerable variance from that expounded
by contemporary representatives of the cloth. The difference, at
first puzzling, is presumably accounted for by Darwin's being
deprived of the blessings of revelation.)

We have left the political affairs of the colony during 1859 to
the last. These were by no means quiescent, due mainly to the
rapid drum-fire of criticism directed against the "establishment"
by Amor De Cosmos in his *British Colonist.* In his first editorial
(December 11, 1858) he had given a forthright exposition of the
principles and policies he proposed to champion:

We intend, with the help of a generous public, to make

the *British Colonist* an independent paper, the organ of no clique or party—a true index of public opinion.

In our National politics we shall ever foster that loyalty which is due to the parent government, and determinedly oppose every influence tending to undermine or subvert the existing connection between the colonies and the mother country.

We shall give a careful summary of intercolonial politics and news. The great colonial issues of the day will from time to time engage our attention. Particular interest will be taken in the absorbing issues now before the British North American colonies: the union of these colonies, representation in the imperial parliament, the Pacific railroad, and the overland wagon road and telegraph.

In our local politics we shall be found the sure friend of reform. We shall aim at introducing such reforms as will tend to government according to the well understood wishes of the people. It will be a primary object with us to advocate such changes as will tend to establish self-government. The present Constitution we hold is radically defective, and unsuited to the advanced condition of this colony. We shall counsel the introduction of responsible government—a system long established in British America, by which the people will have the whole and sole control over the local affairs of the colony. In short we shall advocate a Constitution modelled after the British, and similar to that of Canada.

De Cosmos had then gone on to rake over what most people would have considered the dead ashes of the past. Speaking of the Governor, he declared:

He wanted to serve his country with honor, and at the same time preserve the grasping interests of the Hudson's Bay Company inviolate. In trying to serve two masters he was unsuccessful as a statesman.[43]

De Cosmos also somewhat belatedly attacked Douglas's proclamation of May 8, 1858, maintaining that the mainland should have been thrown open to all comers at that time with no restrictions whatever.

On December 18, 1858, the fiery editor demanded "the immediate establishment of self-government", and on December 25, ignoring the customary asmosphere of the season, he attacked Douglas for appointing Dr. Kennedy to be the member for Nanaimo without first holding an election in that constituency. As the new year opened, De Cosmos roundly declared Douglas "unsuited for the office of Chief Magistrate of these colonies".[44] and deplored the habit of choosing governors "from among men who have been all their lives among Indians, swapping baubles and blankets for furs at two thousand per cent profit . . ."[45]

On February 12, 1859, the *Colonist* published a list of key figures in the Colony, demonstrating, surely to no one's surprise, that nearly all of them had been associated in the past with the HBC. He then showed his lack of emotional balance[46] by declaring:

> In fact we honestly believe that the man who will not ask Her Majesty's Government to remove Gov. Douglas is a traitor to his country, and unworthy of her protection,—and blind to his own interests."[47]

Not content with this, De Cosmos on February 12 and again on February 19 demanded the removal of Chief Justice Cameron, as not qualified for his high position. He was, as De Cosmos, returning to the attack, declared on March 19, only "a clerk to a coal company".

There can be little doubt that Douglas and his circle were nettled by these attacks. Probably by way of retaliation, the Governor issued a proclamation on the 30th of March, 1859, requiring newspapers to put up sureties before being permitted to publish. This did little to deter De Cosmos, and may have gained him some sympathy; at all events, at a public meeting held on April 4, a resolution was passed that the required money (£800) should be raised by public subscription, which was speedily done.

Some of De Cosmos' sting was drawn by the end of the HBC monopoly of trade with the Indians on May 30, 1859. He continued, however, to find other targets for his indignation, and was soon one of the settlement's most noted figures, with a reputation which his unusual name and striking appearance did nothing to diminish.

Meanwhile, under the eye of not only De Cosmos and Governor Douglas but the rest of the community, the seven-man House of Assembly dealt with the problems and issues of the day. The assembly consisted of Yates, McKay, J. D. Pemberton, Skinner, Kennedy and Muir, with J. S. Helmcken as Speaker; Muir's attendance was noticeably infrequent, while Dr. Kennedy died in early April. In April it passed a bill for the protection of game and voted money to pave the streets;[48] it also made U.S. currency legal tender in the colony. A bill was passed in May "for the removal of dead bodies from the deserted Johnson street burial ground";[49] considerable time was devoted to establishing the qualifications for voters and candidates in the next general election; too complex to list here in detail, we may note that they by no means provided for universal manhood suffrage.[50] In October, speed demons had their activities curtailed, as it was enacted that "any person who shall hereafter ride, or drive any vehicle over any wooden bridge or causeway in Vancouver Island at a pace greater than a foot pace, shall be liable to a fine not exceeding £5, or in default of the payment of such fine to an imprisonment for a term of not more than seven days".[51] After some discussion, the term "a walking pace" was substituted for "a foot-pace".[52]

Only once in this period did the shadow of war fall for a moment across the colony. The ownership of San Juan Island was still in dispute between Great Britain and the United States. On the basis that American squatters needed the protection of the Stars and Stripes, an American force was sent in 1859 to occupy the Island. Douglas, realizing that his own island might be said to be largely populated by American squatters, feared yet a further extension of "manifest destiny". Always a man of action and decision, he resolved on a pre-emptive strike. His intention was to overwhelm the American forces on San Juan with the much stronger force under his own command, and only the intervention of higher authority prevented him from doing so. Dr. Helmcken in later years gave his own recollection of the matter:

> I know there would have been a collision and the island would have been captured had Governor Douglas had his own way—but altho he was Vice Admiral the commanders of

H.M. ships were dubious and wanted plain orders. Fortunately or unfortunately the British Admiral just then arrived—so he superseded the authority of Governor Douglas and would not embroil the nations in war on any account—there should be no bloodshed about the matter as far as he was concerned— he would await instructions.

Governor Douglas was no little chagrined at this, and subsequently told me if he had had his own way the affair would have been quickly settled, the island occupied by the British and the diplomacy would have settled the matter—he thought possession of great importance.[53]

Another question with more than parochial implications was also sometimes referred to in this period. On February 15 the *Gazette* in an editorial discussed the possibility of a confederation of all the British North American colonies and spoke of:

> . . . the certainty that, at no distant day, the high road of communication between the Pacific and the Atlantic will pass through the fertile valleys and prairies of our remote western districts; and there is little doubt that such a railway is destined to bind firmly together these disjoined divisions.

This survey of 1859 may perhaps be concluded with some mention of those destined not to see the dawn of 1860. Among them was Andrew Muir, Sheriff of Vancouver Island, whose passing was recorded in terms more candid than our own age is accustomed to:

> Andrew Muir, the deceased, was a native of Scotland, aged about 35 years, and had been the Sheriff of Vancouver Island for the term expiring on the day before his death. There can be no doubt that his fatal illness was brought on by long habits of intemperance. He leaves a father and mother and an only child to mourn his loss.[54]

March of the same year saw the funeral of Captain William Brotchie, Harbor Master of the Port of Victoria, who died on February 28. Born in 1799 at Caithness, Scotland, he had earlier in his career on the northwest coast commanded the HBC brigantine *Cadboro* and the barques *Nereid* and *Cowlitz*. He had been on board the barque *Albion* when it struck a reef off Dallas Road, Victoria, in 1849, on account of which mishap the reef was later named Brotchie Ledge. Appointed Harbor-Master in 1858, he was a member of the Pioneer Cricket Club, and was described as a portly, good-natured, even-tempered man.[55]

The year 1859 also saw the death, late in November, of Douglas's sister, Mrs. Cameron, wife of the Chief Justice.[56]

One of the journals in which these deaths were recorded now underwent its own demise. The *Gazette* had begun to take an unpopular pro-American "line" (especially in connection with the San Juan dispute), and this, coupled with loss of supporting readers through the departure of so many Americans and others from the Colony, forced it to suspend publication. The final issue was dated November 26, 1859.

The [*British*] *Colonist,* however, continued to flourish, and the events of 1860, notably the election of that year, found it pawing the ground and eager for the fray.

It had not long to wait. The year opened in an aura of excitement, as the campaign began which was to culminate in the selection of a new House of Assembly. The former (the first expression of democracy west of the Great Lakes), with its tiny membership of seven, had been dissolved the previous autumn, after an existence of three years. Now an enlarged membership of thirteen, representing nine constituencies, was to be chosen, and, stimulated no doubt by the economic transformation since 1856 and the presence since late 1858 of a vigorously independent daily newspaper, interest ran high.

In several respects the election differed markedly from similar contests today. There was no secret ballot, voters having to declare their preferences openly; moreover, the electorate was very small. There was a property qualification, and of course women did not participate.

None of this, however, prevented the generation of considerable excitement. There were no political parties, but candidates were thought of as either friendly or hostile to "the Company".

De Cosmos in his columns hewed vigorously to this line, declaring on December 3, 1859:

It is an old scriptural adage:—"No man can serve two masters, He will hate the one and love the other." A man cannot serve the Hudson's Bay Company and the Public in the Assembly . . . The magnitude of the questions at stake demand the election of men who are independent of the Company in every way.

His own campaign, however, for one of the two seats in Victoria City, was unsuccessful, possibly for reasons later recorded by Dr. Helmcken:

> On one occasion De Cosmos appeared on this stage[57]— performed all sorts of semi-theatrical attitudes—boasted of travelling through California with a revolver in each boot or something of this kind—was vainglorious and egoistic to the utmost degree. The theatre was crowded—De Cosmos was drunk! This settled the matter, he lost at the election . . .
>
> One newspaper made the remark that they could not report De Cosmos' speech in full because they had not a sufficient number of Capital I's![58]

When the final count was made, the results were as follows: Cary[59] 137; Franklin, S. 106; De Cosmos 91.

De Cosmos, much chagrined, attributed his defeat to "some eighteen votes improperly cast by colored foreigners",[60] and tried for some time without success to have the election nullified.

Other candidates, thought to be sympathetic to the HBC, were were also returned, though here and there its opponents were successful. In Esquimalt and Metchosin (two to be elected) the vote was: Helmcken 36; Cooper 22; Skinner 21; while in Victoria County (three to be elected) the verdict was: Tolmie[61] 44; Crease[62] 39; Waddington 35; Yates 14; Bayley 14.

A by-election in Esquimalt in August 1860 gave De Cosmos a chance to try again, but produced the following baffling result: Gordon 11, Smith, commonly known as De Cosmos, 10; De Cosmos 1. It was subsequently held that though De Cosmos, considered collectively, had not been defeated, his component parts had been, a verdict no doubt highly galling to his "constituents".

On Salt Spring Island, which still had fewer than a hundred white inhabitants, the results were: Southgate[63] 11; Copland 4.

On the first of March in the newly completed "birdcages", the new House assembled with considerable ceremony. Dr. Helmcken was again chosen Speaker, and Governor Douglas addressed the members in a speech full of confidence as to the future.

Selim Franklin, however, had difficulty in being seated, since he refused as a Jew to take the traditional oath "on the true faith of a Christian". After much discussion he was allowed to take his seat without making this declaration, and the House proceeded for the balance of the year to consider the colony's affairs.

These included such matters as "the formation of a public road from Saanich to Cowitchan", the construction of light-houses at Race Rocks and Fisgard Island,[64] the regulation of the medical and legal professions, a tax on the value of real estate, and the removal of the old Victoria Bridge. The "Victoria Gas Company Act" was passed in November. There was also much discussion throughout the year of the terms under which a final settlement with the HBC should be made.

Meanwhile, signs were appearing that the confidence of the Governor was justified. Early in January he had declared Victoria a free port, a distinction it shared at that time with Labuan and Hong Kong, and this no doubt was a stimulus to trade. Certainly a definite revival of business became apparent, and the *Colonist* reported on June 2:

> Lots in the suburbs, 60 x 120 feet, which could have been purchased three months since for $100 and $150, are now held at $300 and $400 . . . Beautiful cottages dot the roads leading into the country, and smiling gardens are noticeable where one year ago appeared only wild, unbroken tracts of underbrush.

The essential organs of civilization continued to develop.[65] Two volunteer fire companies were formed, the "Deluge Engine Company No. 1" and the "Tiger Engine Company No. 2", which vied with each other to reach conflagrations first.

First tentative moves made in the direction of independent civic government for Victoria occurred in 1860. The Attorney-General, Mr. Cary, gave notice in the Assembly on March 12 of "A Bill to Provide for the Incorporation of the Town of Victoria". The bill was introduced some six weeks later, and on May 10 given a second reading and then referred to a "Select Committee". This was, however, apparently as far as it got; the *Colonist* reported late in October that it was still in Committee and on December 11 noted that whenever the matter was brought up, enough members would leave the Assembly to prevent a quorum. At prorogation on February 3, 1861, despite the fact that the proposed bill had been on the order paper for over ten months, no progress had been made. The reasons for this calculated procrastination are not certain, but it seems likely that behind it were those who feared any extension of the democratic process as possibly leading to a "take-over" by the overwhelmingly American population of the colony.

Nevertheless, despite these attempts to hold back the clock of history, it continued to move forward. As a symbol of the great change that was relentlessly taking place, during the year the northeast bastion at the corner of View and Government Streets was demolished. The *Colonist* for December 15, 1860, pronounced its obituary:

> The old picket fence that has so long surrounded the fort yard is fast disappearing. Piece after piece it is taken down, sawed up, and piled away for firewood. Yesterday afternoon workmen commenced removing the old bastion at the corner of View and Government streets, and before today's sun gilds the western horizon, the wood comprising it will no doubt have shared the ignoble fate of the unfortunate pickets. Alas! poor bastion. Thy removal should be enough to break the heart of every Hudson Bay man in the country.

While old structures were disappearing, new ones were rising to replace them. The cornerstone of St. John's Anglican church was laid by Douglas on April 13, 1860,[66] and Bishop Hills preached the sermon at its consecration in September[67]. A Congregational church was opened early in the year, while a New Wesleyan Methodist church was dedicated on May 21.

An elementary form of "medicare" got under way, organized by the French Benevolent and Mutual Society. Members paid a dollar a month for the benefits of hospitalization.[68]

Social and cultural affairs also prospered. On January 25 a Burns dinner was held at the Colonial Hotel;[69] in February the press reported "three theatres in full blast", and late in the year the townsfolk were treated to a performance of "Othello". The Victoria Philharmonic Society continued to favor the musically inclined with concerts which were received with general enthusiasm.

Among other events of 1860 we may note the destruction by the police of all Indian tents and shanties on "this side of the Bay", the *Colonist* of April 28 reporting that "there is not now an Indian camp in the northern section of the city. The savages took it all in good part . . . "[70] In June there was a sale of cattle at the corner of Broad and Yates, while on July 10 the *Colonist* reported that "our streets are crowded with Celestials bound for the British Columbia mines. From China and from California, they continue to pour in at the rate of 500 weekly, and lose no time in making arrangements for transportation to the gold regions." In October James Yates, who had arrived in Victoria in June 1849 and was now one of the town's richest inhabitants, left for England, and workmen "commenced to grade and macadamize Yates street from Government to Douglas". In November, a deeper note was struck, when the election of Abraham Lincoln as President of the United States suddenly brought to the attention of Victoria citizens (the majority of them still recent arrivals from that country) the possibility of an American civil war.

So 1860, a year of cautious recovery, gave way to 1861. A New Year's editorial in the *Colonist* set the keynote for the next twelve months:

> The vague fears that haunted our people as to the stability of our gold mines, and the permanency of the fair towns and cities that have risen up like magic where two short years ago appeared barren wastes, or dense forests, have all "vanished into thin air", and a confidence never before felt here has assumed its sway.

This estimate was to prove a sound one, as the settlement continued to develop. The discovery of new coal fields at Nanaimo[71] and important new gold fields in the interior near Quesnel[72] undoubtedly proved a considerable stimulus. The year was, however, perhaps the least eventful since the founding of the Fort—a sharp contrast to the neighboring United States, where the republic established eighty years before seemed about to disintegrate. Civil war broke out there in April, and though strict neutrality was the official watchword in Victoria, this did not prevent its citizens from following the progress of the conflict eagerly, and on occasion displaying their sentiments.[73]

The town continued its steady though cautious expansion. The old bridge across the harbor was becoming dangerous, and new ones were constructed to replace it. On April 24 the *Colonist* reported "The new bridges across Rock Bay and at Ellis' Point are rapidly approaching completion. As soon as they are opened, the present bridge will be pulled down and numbered among the things that were." Another link with the past was broken when the Governor's residence, where Richard Blanshard had once lived, was torn down to make way for new buildings.[74]

Attention was also given to the matter of cemeteries. Some scandal was being occasioned by the fact that pigs, allowed to forage at will in the old graveyard, were rooting up the corpses and eating them.[75] In consequence, some of the remains of Victoria's early pioneers were exhumed and transferred to the Quadra Street cemetery.

A public market for the sale of farm produce was built on Fort Street, and late in the year a new post office was under construction on Wharf Street. Yet another theatre was erected[76], and a "grand jury" visited the hospital, found thirteen patients there, and recommended improvements.[77]

The rural areas were being opened up. A letter in the *Colonist* for September 27 describes a pleasant ride through Saanich which took the writer at least 14 miles from the Fort. A proclamation by Douglas, lowering the price of country land to 4/2 an acre, was doubtless a stimulus to settlement.[78] An "Agricultural and Horticultural Association" was formed in May[79], and had its first annual show on the second of October. Thomas Harris, soon to be the city's first mayor, "exhibited three barrows, each about two years old, that were so fat as to be scarcely able to move, and would dress from 500 to 600 lbs. each", while Dr. Tolmie won a prize for his entry of a dozen eggs.[80]

Wages had become more stable. Masons and plasterers now

received $5 a day, carpenters $4 and laborers $3.[81] The Victoria Typographical Union was formed, with John Flint as its first president. Its declared aims were "maintaining a uniform scale of prices for printers' wages in this town, as well as to further the interests of the publishers".[82]

Educational and cultural matters also made modest progress. The sixth annual examination at the Victoria school took place on July 16; 53 pupils were present.[83] The Rev. Cridge presented his third annual report on August 27.[84] He noted that the Victoria school, which had only one teacher—Mr. W. H. Burr—had ten acres of land, including "about four acres under cultivation by the teachers".[85] At Craigflower, where the teacher was Mr. H. Claypole, an examination was also held and prizes presented. At Nanaimo, where Mr. Cornelius Bryant was in charge, progress was also observed. (Each of these three teachers received £150 per year, and pupils each paid £1 per year in fees). Altogether, Mr. Cridge noted 56 attendants at the Victoria school, 23 at Craigflower and 32 at Nanaimo, or a total of 111. He cautioned, however, against too high a pupil-teacher ratio:

> It cannot be expected that while from twenty five to fifty scholars are under the care of a single teacher without Assistants or Monitors, the schools should be in so efficient a state as could be desired.[86]

The Philharmonic Society continued to please the musically inclined; the Germans of the town formed a singing club. "Hamlet" was presented in the Victoria Theatre, followed, lest any should go home from the performance unduly subdued, by "the laughable farce of 'Raising the Wind' ".[87] One theatrical performance unfortunately resulted in a race riot.[88] A meeting was held to consider the establishment of a public library and reading room. A society for this purpose was organized on October 26; its entrance fee was to be $5 and dues a dollar a month.

Religion continued to play a major part in the life of the settlement. The first Presbyterian church service was held by the Rev. John Hall in Moore's Hall on April 20.[89] All government aid to churches was ended, partly as a result of the persistent objections of De Cosmos[90] and partly because of Bishop Hills' sturdy refusal to accept it.

Bishop Hills was also in the news in another connection, as the Catholic Bishop Demers brought suit against him regarding the right of way into the cemetery, which he claimed Bishop Hills had obstructed by some buildings. After much public acrimony between these two spiritual luminaries, all faithfully reported in detail in the daily press, the jury decided that Bishop Demers was in the right of it.[91]

The winds of change were also at this time beginning to blow through the quiet graveyard of theology. *The Origin of Species,* published in London in the fall of 1859, had apparently gone unnoticed on this distant shore; but the same could not be said of *Essays and Reviews,* a work now almost unknown but of much notoriety in its day. Written by a group of professors (some of them Doctors of Divinity) at Oxford and Cambridge, it sought to re-examine various traditional Christian teachings in the light of such rapidly advancing sciences as history, biology, geology and anthropology. The aim of the book (like that of *Honest to God* and similar works in our own day) was to rescue the permanent spiritual truths illuminated by the Old and New Testaments from the legends of the ancient Hebrews in which some of them were embedded.[92] The book, however, whose procedure the learned authors saw as essential if Christianity was not to become totally discredited in the eyes of educated people, caused great consternation and anguish to many readers throughout the English-speaking world, and even in this remote colony one can hear echoes of the resulting uproar. At least twice the *Colonist* gave considerable attention to the book. On April 27, after noting that "these distinguished doctors of divinity do not believe in the infallibility of the Bible any more than Protestants do in the infallibility of the Pope or the Church", it concluded that "such heretical opinions coming from professors in the two first schools of Protestant Christendom could not fail to strengthen heterodoxy". De Cosmos saw no reason, though, to conclude that the denunciations of the book by the Convocation of the Anglican Church would have the intended effect of ending discussion of the ideas contained in it.

"Shrewd observers imagine, however, that they will only render them more popular". Indeed, he reported, "the volume has passed its sixth edition already, and is a topic of general conversation throughout the three kingdoms".

On June 7, the *Colonist* informed its readers that no less a dignitary than the Archbishop of York had publicly denounced the book, calling it "a work calculated to undermine the foundations of the Christian faith", and expressing the hope "that it will please our Heavenly Father to overrule for good this unexpected assault upon the truths of revelation". On this, however, De Cosmos (feeling perhaps that the matter was thus now outside his jurisdiction) made no comment.

Political affairs continued fairly quiet, even though De Cosmos (who on August 1, 1860 had changed the name of his paper to *The Daily British Colonist*) continued to attack the government on every likely occasion. In January, for example, he described the Governor's Council as "a weazened contrivance . . . which has kept its doors so closed to the refreshing and invigorating popular breeze, that it has become asthmatic".[93] He also, however, championed some constructive causes: an editorial on March 2 attacked the nonsensical practice of imprisoning men for debt, while on June 14 he supported the Confederation of all the British North American colonies. In March, in a striking gesture, he printed Lincoln's First Inaugural Address in full in a special supplement.

The budget was before the House of Assembly in July, showing the main sources of revenue to be harbour dues, the sale of crown lands, trades and liquor licences and the real estate tax. Receipts were estimated at £21,148 12s 11d, and expenditures were proposed of £20,385.[94] An interesting feature of the accounts was the provision for stimulating the interest of investors and tourists in the colony; £500 was allotted "for diffusing information abroad about Vancouver Island".[95]

Among matters several times before the House, we may note the question of selling liquor to Indians, and of a proposal, to be fulfilled within a year—the incorporation of Victoria into a city.

The year also saw some personal vicissitudes for prominent members of the community. In January the individualistic Captain E. E.

Langford left for England. In August the Governor's daughter Alice, aged 17, suddenly eloped with Charles Good, son of the Rev. Henry Good. The impulsive pair were married at Port Townsend, U.S.A aboard the British schooner *Explorer* by an American Justice of the Peace. On their return to the colony, the bride's father insisted on a second ceremony.[96]

In October, a scandal occurred in the civil service, as the Postmaster-General of Vancouver Island, John D'Ewes, who had been deeply in debt, suddenly vanished from the colony.[97] Financial scandals, indeed, seemed notably frequent in this period of Victoria's history. In December, Capt. George T. Gordon, Treasurer of Vancouver Island, and his clerk, Henry B. Campbell, were charged with embezzlement.[98]

The closing months of 1861 saw some political changes. D. B. Ring was elected the member for Nanaimo, and Dr. Trimble and J. W. Trutch members for Victoria District. John Work, who had begun working for the HBC in 1814, and who was credited with establishing the first farm west of the Rockies, died at the age of 70.[99] To fill the vacancy thus created in his Legislative Council, Douglas appointed E. G. Alston, much to the disgust of De Cosmos.[100]

The year also saw another attempt to provide Victoria with local government. An incorporation bill was introduced in the Assembly, but after being read a second time in mid-July, it was referred to a Committee of the House, where it apparently languished and died.[101]

As the year ended, a new post office was being built on Wharf Street, and the first gas works was under construction at Rock Bay. A sampling of Vancouver Island products was being put aboard a ship bound for London, where they were to be publicly exhibited; they included minerals, timber, fruit from the orchards of Douglas and Dr. Helmcken, oats from Dr. Tolmie's farm, and a collection of stuffed birds.[102] The circulation of the *Colonist* as it entered its fourth year reached 4000,[103] and several lots in Victoria West fetched from $35 to $65.[104] A store offered for sale silks and ribbons "direct from Paris by Express", while a rival establishment, not to be outdone, was ready with supplies of ostrich feathers.[105] A large advertisement for yet a third merchant declared vehemently, though perhaps a trifle belatedly, on Dec. 30th, "Santa Claus is Coming!"[106]

The year 1862 entered amid chilly weather. It was from 7° to 9° above zero in the town, and there was 16 inches of snow in Saanich, while on one occasion De Cosmos "counted over a dozen sleighs gliding through the streets yesterday."

The death of Prince Albert came as a sudden shock to the community, and the columns of the *Colonist* were edged in black. After a decent interval, however, its editor resumed his attack on Governor Douglas and his appointed officials. On February 3 he declared:

> Sooner or later the administration of Gov. Douglas will break down—will end—and a new administration will be inaugurated in its place. The elements of dissolution abound. Its glaring blunders, its sins of omission and commission, and above all its scandalous disregard of moral and legal right, preclude the possibility of its ever becoming popular or successful; but, on the contrary, holds out the uninviting prospect of being continually and justly execrated.

The language of De Cosmos was of course intemperate; yet we must not overlook the fact that slowly but surely the lines were being drawn for a genuine "show-down". The Governor and his Council were neither elected by the residents of Vancouver Island nor responsible to them; the House of Assembly was chosen by a fairly wide franchise, but was not the supreme authority in the colony. Eventually, one of the two conceptions of government which these institutions embodied would have to give way to the other, and however much we may regret De Cosmos' blindness to Douglas' many great qualities, it must be conceded that the fiery editor saw the ultimate issue with clarity and was a resolute champion of what the whole spirit of the swelling century made certain would prove the winning cause.

This great question of representative government would reverberate and be discussed some years yet; in the meantime De Cosmos observed and commented on day to day events in the town. He interviewed a Cowichan Indian waiting to be hanged ("We visited him yesterday, and found him in good health and spirits and very communicative"),[107] and a few days later gave an account of his execution; he noted that American merchants, even though supporting opposite sides in the Civil War, all closed their stores for Washington's birthday; he demanded a road to Nanaimo, estimating its maximum cost at £5000;[108] he recorded the election of Thomas Harris as member for Esquimalt; and was forced to report yet another black sheep in high places; A. Marchand, an assayer of gold, had absconded with a considerable amount of the precious metal he was analyzing.[109]

In March, Governor Douglas opened a new session of the House. He suggested, among other things, the need to extinguish Indian claims in the Cowichan district and the usefulness of a thorough geological survey of the colony. He also expressed the hope that the coming session would see the incorporation of Victoria as a city.

It was while the members were duly deliberating these and other questions that their attention, or at least that of the townsfolk, was briefly distracted by two memorable sights. A Sunday in April witnessed the appearance of the first:

> On Sunday a presentable looking middle-aged lady was observed on Esquimalt wharf, about the time of the departure of the *Oregon,* wearing a complete suit of gentleman's clothes—breeches and all! After the steamer had cast off, she quietly mounted a fine horse, in true gentlemanly style — which means with a pedal extremity on either side of the animal—and rode off briskly toward Victoria, leaving a large and curious crowd of spectators to wonder as to who she was, whence she came, and whither she was bound . . . Her appearance created quite a sensation among the usually phlegmatic Esquimalters.[110]

Ten days later, an even more exotic form of life than the New Woman was on display. This time it was camels; destined for use in pack-trains on the Cariboo Road,[111] they had been imported from San Francisco, and many curious onlookers gathered to inspect the ungainly beasts including (surely an almost historic confrontation) the betrousered female.[112]

So Spring wore on toward summer. Despite high interest rates (ranging from 15% to 36% per annum),[113] business was reasonably prosperous; for this, the increasingly encouraging news from the Cariboo gold fields was largely responsible.[114] De Cosmos continued to champion a variety of causes. Full self-government was still the most important of these, but lesser matters did not escape his notice. He urged the removal to some safer spot of the seven tons of gunpowder stored in a warehouse at the foot of Johnson Street;[115] he also drew attention to the unequal arrangements of constituencies—Victoria Town, he pointed out, had 446 voters and elected two members, while Victoria County with 116 voters elected three.[116] Looking across the Rockies to the eastern edge of British North America (from which he himself had originally come), he applauded the "Intercolonial Railway" as prefiguring the transcontinental line of the future.[117]

Meanwhile, settlement was spreading northward into Saanich; the *Colonist* for June 3, 1862 reported the consecration of a new church "near the residence of Mr. Thomson", about twelve miles from town.

Nanaimo, too, was also slowly growing. An excursion there by steamer was organized (return fare, $3), and it was estimated that the town, which included 84 dwellings, now had from 350 to 400 white settlers.[118] An Anglican church was rapidly approaching completion.[119] It was still, however, a "Company Town"; everything in it, including the houses, was owned by the Nanaimo Coal Company, a subsidiary of the HBC.

It was in Victoria, of course, that the signs of progress were most noticeable. The old bridge across the harbor finally disappeared, and with adequate clearance ships were now able to sail above Johnson Street.[120] Two new public cisterns, capable of holding 60,000 gallons of water, were completed at a cost of $1400. The first bar of soap was manufactured on the Island at the "Esquimalt Soap Factory".[121] The *Colonist* itself installed new and more powerful presses,[122] and reported shortly afterwards that "the gas-works at Rock Bay are approaching completion, and shortly we hope to have the pleasure of announcing the lighting of the town with gas."[123] The House of Assembly voted £850 for the Fire Department, including £500 for a new engine.[124] The Queen's Birthday was celebrated with enthusiasm by all on May 24, while

Washington's birthday and the Fourth of July aroused emotions in at least American hearts. Although fire hazard was mainly involved, building restrictions and a tentative form of town planning were initiated when a bill was passed forbidding the construction of wooden buildings over 18 feet high, or of more than one storey, within the town. The latter was defined as the area bounded by Johnson, Douglas and Fort streets and the harbor's edge to the west of them.[125] Bishop Demers presided at the annual ceremonies at St. Ann's Convent, and presented prizes to deserving scholars.[126]

Even for the less virtuous, it was temporarily a propitious time. The clerk of the Police Court, Henry C. Owens, disappeared with £233, and Capt. Gordon, who we noted earlier had been imprisoned in the debtors' prison, escaped by means of a "false key".[127]

These, however, when all was said and done, were merely incidents. Now an event of another order was at hand, as the community which had successively been first a trading post, then a settlement, then a town, now advanced proudly to the dignity of a city. It was on the second of August, 1862 after it had been debated and passed in the House of Assembly, that Douglas had signed "An Act to Incorporate the City of Victoria"; the powers and duties of the new entity had been defined in it, and provision made for the election of a mayor and six aldermen. All that remained was for the electorate to decide which of their fellow-townsmen should merit the honour of becoming their first freely chosen rulers.

The campaign began on the 11th, with a public meeting at which all the candidates spoke. The leading contender for the mayoralty, Thomas Harris, made a forthright bid for the voters' support. He declared that:

> It might be thought presumptuous for him (a tradesman) to offer to stand for the office, but he was not ashamed to say that he was both a tradesman and a farmer, and, sometimes, when the chance offered, a contractor. (Laughter) He was not the man to wear kid gloves or look to the Government for support; he asked nothing of Government, and

supported his family by honest labor. If anybody present could say a word against him, he invited him to come forward and say it there. Knowingly he had never wronged a single man, and standing under the flag of Old England, he was not ashamed to look his fellow-citizens in the eyes and ask for their votes if they thought him worthy to represent them. If any other man more capable of filling the civic chair was found, however, let him be brought forward and he would withdraw.

Harris then outlined some of the duties which Victoria's first mayor and councillors would have to face. According to the account in the *Colonist*,[128] he "drew a comparison between the work which they would have to perform and the building of a house—the foundation stones should be properly laid and the walls would stand firm . . . "

Other speakers followed Harris. Messrs. Hicks and Searby, two of the candidates for the six aldermanic seats, solicited support but criticized some provisions of the act incorporating the city. They pointed out that there was no power given to raise loans or to enforce the collection of taxes. Searby went on to estimate that 3000 immigrants soon would be arriving from England and foresaw economic distress. He suggested that the city should at least receive the revenue from the licensing of liquor dealers, as it would soon in all likelihood have to pay the salaries of policemen and magistrates, and "it was liquor that gave them the most to do". A number of other speakers also addressed the meeting, including Mifflin Gibbs. De Cosmos, however, was still evidently rankling over his defeat in the election of 1860, and contented himself with asserting that the colored store-keeper "delivered a long-winded and flowery address".

On the following Saturday, the assembled voters publicly chose their Chief Magistrate:

> Saturday was a great day—a day "big with events" for our maiden town, which then added several inches to the length of her petticoats and donned crinoline and pantalettes for the first time in her life. The 16th day of August, A.D. 1862, will be recorded in the annals of Victoria as the day on which our first Municipal Election took place—when our

worthy fellow-citizen, THOMAS HARRIS, ESQ., late M.P.P. for Esquimalt Town District, "an humble tradesman", as he delights to term himself, was by acclamation chosen to fill the chair—and right nobly will he fill it—of first Mayor of Victoria—the Queen City of the Pacific Possessions of Her Majesty, Queen Victoria.

Long before the hour set for the commencement of the business of the day had arrived, groups of people assembled at the hustings, and by noon the number present could not have been less than 600. At precisely 12 o'clock, the Sheriff mounted the stand and announced that he was prepared to proceed with the nomination of Mayor and Councillors for the City of Victoria. Mr. C. B. Young nominated Mr. Alfred Waddington, and Mr. Trimble, M.P.P., nominated Mr. Thomas Harris. A show of hands revealed the fact that but four or five electors were in favor of Mr. Waddington, while a perfect forest of hands were shown above the heads of the crowd when the vote on Mr. Harris was called for. The friends of Mr. Waddington demanded no poll, and, amid the wildest excitement and most vociferous cheering, the Sheriff declared Thomas Harris elected first Mayor of Victoria. Mr. Harris, being called for, came forward and briefly thanked the people for the honor conferred and retired— "three times three" being given as he left the stand.[129]

It had been hoped that Victoria's first six aldermen would also be chosen at the same time and in the same manner. Shows of hands, however, proved inconclusive, and the Sheriff was forced to declare that a formal election would be held on the following Monday.

When Monday came, there was a steady stream of Victorians to the polls, there to have their names and choices publicly entered in the record. Interim totals were announced from time to time, and for a while it appeared that Gibbs, despite the disapproval of De Cosmos, would gain a seat. The final tally, however, was as follows: John Copland 114; James Reid 113; N. M. Hicks 111; Wm. E. Stronach 107; Wm. M. Searby 104; Richard Lewis 98; M. W. Gibbs 94; James Thorne 70; Wm. Leigh 61; John G. McKay 57; David Leneveu 53; Geo. E. Dennis 30; Malcolm Munro 12; Alfred Fellows 1.[130]

And thus a great watershed in the history of Victoria was safely crossed. A few days later, on August 25, the new City Council met for the first time; as no regular meeting-place had been provided for it, it was forced to convene in the Police Barracks. No striking resolutions were passed; the appointment of Algernon Austen as clerk pro tem. (confirmed shortly afterwards) was one of the few steps taken. Yet these faltering beginnings could not disguise the fact that Victoria had passed irrevocably from one chapter of its life story to another. De Cosmos marked the moment in an editorial on August 27:

> The first meeting of the only City Council in Vancouver Island has taken place. Another step in the course of civilization has been made. Who among those whose lot it was to visit this lone spot some years ago, would have thought, as they beheld its pine-covered rocks, oak openings and dusky savages — and when they considered the remoteness from the great centres of population—that the forms and relations of civilized society were so soon to obtain, and displace the primitive inhabitants and their lowly abodes by the regular and well ordered edifices and institutions of the superior race?

The city, then, was now a reality; expectation had become accomplishment. Yet two ties still linked it with its first beginnings. One was the man who had stepped ashore at Clover Point less than twenty years before to found a fur-trading post. His connections with "the Company" were long since severed, and he sat now in the Governor's chair; moreover, the advancing tide of democracy was eroding his once almost absolute powers. Yet, like one of the mighty trees that still surrounded the city on all sides, he towered, majestic and unrivalled, above the underbrush of local politicians, and was recognized, while still daily visible in the flesh, as already a part of history.

Nor was the Governor the only reminder to Victorians of their earliest days. A few of the old Fort buildings still stood, and though in their time they had fulfilled a useful function, now, in the opinion of most citizens, they were merely a picturesque nuisance.

It was clear, then, that these two institutions, so long a familiar and seemingly essential a part of Victoria, were soon to pass into time's advancing shadow. Two years still remained to them, years marked by modest progress in the direction of the city we know today. Then the final formal break with the age of the first pioneers would be made; the Governor, his merits now perceived by even his bitterest critics, would retire into private life, and the last Fort buildings, whose construction he had supervised, would be dismantled. It is to these closing scenes in the drama of "The Fort" that—perhaps with a certain melancholy— we now must turn our attention.

FOOTNOTES

[1] Helmcken, *Reminiscences,* IV, p. 13. A letter in the *Gazette* for April 2, 1859, suggests the population of Victoria in 1859 was approximately 3,000. The same journal on November 22, 1859, reckoned there were 40 people living on Salt Spring Island.

[2] *Ibid.,* IV, p. 14.

[3] Macfie, *Vancouver Island and British Columbia,* London, 1865, p. 74.

[4] The Union Hotel at this time was charging a dollar a day for room and board. It boasted "wash rooms, bath rooms, and a select private reading room". (*Gazette,* April 16, 1859).

[5] *Gazette,* February 22, 1859. On May 20, 1859, the *Colonist* reported that "Hibben & Co. are erecting a capacious brick store on Yates Street".

[6] *Colonist,* October 28, 1859.

[7] For further details, see Cecil Maiden, *Lighted Journey,* B.C. Electric Railway Company, Vancouver, 1948.

[8] We might note that "watermen" were still delivering water at five cents a bucketful to private homes from a well on Yates Street. (Walden, *A Social History of Victoria,* p. 71).

[9] "It was customary for the 'chain gang' to emerge every morning from a side gate of the jail yard on Bastion Street and march to Government Street to the music of their chains, with two guards in the rear with loaded shotguns . . . The uniform consisted of moleskin trousers with V.P., a checked cotton shirt and a blue cloth cap." (Fawcett, *Some Reminiscences of Old Victoria,* Toronto, 1912).

[10] It is remarkable how small a role was assigned in this period to the "public sector". For example, even money for building bridges was sometimes provided by public subscription and sometimes by government grant (see *Colonist* for January 15, 1859). The Colonial Surveyor asserted on another occasion his belief that once the government had built a street, it was up to those who lived on it to maintain it (*Minutes of the House of Assembly* for February 15, 1859). Hospitals were also part of the "private

sector", the House of Assembly going on record as stating that " . . . the House does not consider that such an institution should be supported by the Colonial Government, but think(s) that such benevolent objects should be left to the good feeling and charity of the public . . . " (*Minutes of the House of Assembly* for August 17, 1858).

[11] For further details, see F. W.Laing and W. K. Lamb, Fire Companies of Old Victoria", *BCHQ*, Vol. X, No. 1, January, 1946. Also *Colonist* for January 12, 1860.

[12] *Gazette,* June 16, 1859.

[13] *Gazette,* April 16, 1859.

[14] *Gazette,* June 2, 1859.

[15] Walden, *Social History of Victoria,* p. 79. The *Gazette* for October 25, 1859, would suggest the sum was £250.

[16] Dr. Trimble represented Victoria in the B.C. Legislature from 1871 to 1876, during which time he was its Speaker. He died January 1, 1885, in Victoria. A street in Vancouver is named after him.

[17] For further details, see H. H. Murphy, *Royal Jubilee Hospital, 1858-1958,* Hebden Printing Company, Victoria, 1858. Also A. S. Munro, *The Medical History of British Columbia,* reprinted from the Canadian Medical Assn. Journal for 1931-32.

[18] Scholefield and Howay, *British Columbia from the Earliest Times to the Present,* Vancouver, 1914, Vol. 2, p. 153.

[19] *Gazette,* January 8, 1859. Victoria's original cemetery, at the southwest corner of Douglas and Johnson Streets, was shut down in the early 1860's. A letter by Edgar Fawcett in the *Victoria Times* for May 14, 1909, describes how as a boy he witnessed the cemetery being dug up in 1859 by the "chain-gang" and corpses and coffins being taken in carts to be re-interred in the Quadra Street Cemetery. (See also *Colonist* for 18 October, 1860, and 6 July, 1861). There were no more burials in the Quadra Street Cemetery after 1873, the ground for Ross Bay Cemetery being acquired in 1872. It would seem that burials continued in the grounds of St. Ann's Academy until well into the present century. The Jewish Cemetery was consecrated in 1860 (*Colonist,* February 7, 1860). Dr. Helmcken buried two of his children in his garden: "Daisy was a little blue eyed, flaxen haired, fair child—full of pleasant tricks, and always hid herself behind the door in order to frighten me when she heard me coming in. Poor little thing, she was a pet and methinks I see her now. We buried the poor little thing in the garden and I made an oval of white daiseys with a cross in the centre over the grave. The holly stands there now—my firstborn was buried there also." *Reminiscences,* V, pp. 1-2. When Helmcken's wife died, the bodies of the two children were removed to the Quadra Street Cemetery).
See also in this connection an article by Cecil ffrench, "The Burial Places of Early Victoria", in *Island Events,* (Victoria), for July 23, July 30, August 6 and December 10, 1948.

[20] H. H. Murphy, *Royal Jubilee Hospital, 1858-1958.* Hebden Printing Company, Victoria, 1958, p. 80.
Sometimes in this first democratic body west of the Great Lakes, "the Speaker and honorable members might be seen carrying in armfuls of bark to light the fire." (*Colonist,* May 3, 1862.)

[21] *Gazette,* May 12, 1859.

[22] *Loc. cit.*

[23] *Gazette,* May 12, 1859.

[24] The first pedestrian, a Mr. Josiah Wash, crossed the bridge on June 7, 1859. Readers even at this late date will doubtless be relieved to know that the feat was "accomplished in perfect safety and without extraordinary exertion or fatigue." (*Gazette,* June 7, 1859).

[25] *Gazette,* May 19, 1859.

[26] *Gazette,* September 20, 1859.

[27] See W. G. Shelton (ed.), *British Columbia and Confederation,* Morriss Printers, Victoria, 1967, p. 167.
The *Colonist* of April 5, 1864, calls the main building "a pagoda wigwam".

[28] F. E. Walden, *The Social History of Victoria, 1858-1871,* B.A. Thesis, UBC, 1951, p. 112.

[29] *Gazette,* June 18, 1859.

[30] See Walden, *Social History of Victoria,* pp. 116-120. Also Thomas Shotbolt, *An Account of the Establishment and Subsequent Progress of Freemasonry in the Colony of British Columbia from its Origin in 1859 to 1871,* British Colonist Press, 1871.

[31] His brother, Lumley Franklin, was a man of parts. Not only did he become Mayor of Victoria in 1865, but he was a composer of some merit, and in the same year sang some of his own works at a public concert (*Colonist,* May 9, 1865). One suspects that no subsequent mayor has duplicated this feat.

[32] Arthur Bushby (1835-1875) married Douglas' daughter Agnes, whom he described as "a stunning girl—black eye & hair & larking like the devil" (*BCHQ,* Vol. XXI, p. 87).
The marriage in Christ Church Cathedral on May 8, 1862, was a major social event. There were five children of this marriage, of whom one lived till 1944 (*Ibid.,* p. 95).

[33] *Gazette,* February 1, 1859.

[34] *Colonist,* March 12, 1859.

[35] Walden, *Social History of Victoria,* p. 155.

[36] W. A. G. Young (1827-1885) had arrived in Victoria on the *Satellite.* On March 20, 1858, he married Cecilia Cameron, step-daughter of Chief Justice Cameron and niece of Governor Douglas. Early in 1859 he was appointed Colonial Secretary for B.C. and Acting Colonial Secretary for Vancouver Island. When the two colonies were united he continued in office. At the time of his death he was Governor of the Gold Coast.

[37] D. L. Maclaurin, *The History of Education in the Crown Colonies of Vancouver Island and British Columbia and in the Province of British Columbia,* Ph.D. Thesis, U. of Washington, 1936, p. 34.

[38] *Loc. cit.*

[39] *Ibid.,* p. 36.

[40] *Gazette,* 12 February, 1859.

[41] The first Anglican cathedral in Victoria was consecrated on December 7, 1865. Bishop Hills eventually left Victoria on November 3, 1892, and died

on December 10, 1895. He is buried in the churchyard at Parham-in-Hacheston, Suffolk, England.

41A Douglas's letter to the Sister Superior, written in French and dated March 17, 1859, is in the archives of the Academy. An English translation is to be found on p. 38 of *A Century of Service* by Sister Mary Margaret Down (Morriss Printers, Victoria, 1966).

41B Down, *op. cit.*, p. 53.

42 *Colonist*, September 14, 1859. All government assistance to the Church of England ended in August, 1861. See F. H. Johnson, *A History of Public Education in British Columbia*, UBC, 1964, p. 27.

43 *Colonist*, December 11, 1858.

44 *Colonist*, January 8, 1859.

45 *Loc. cit.*

46 De Cosmos eventually died insane.

47 *Colonist*, February 12, 1859.

48 *Gazette*, April 6, 1869.

49 *Gazette*, May 12, 1859.

50 *Gazette*, October 6, 1859.

51 *Gazette*, October 4, 1859.

52 *Gazette*, October 8, 1859.

53 J. S. Helmcken, *Reminiscences*, IV, pp. 19-20.

54 *Gazette*, January 13, 1859.

55 *Gazette*, March 3, 1859. See also Walbran, *British Columbia Coast Names*, pp. 64-65.

56 *Colonist*, November 29, 1859.

57 An all-candidates meeting took place in the Victoria Theatre.

58 J. S. Helmcken, *Reminiscences*, IV, pp. 45-46.

59 George Hunter Cary was appointed early in 1859 to be the first Attorney-General of the united colonies of Vancouver Island and British Columbia. In this capacity he became the first (though not the last) British Columbia cabinet minister to have trouble obeying his own traffic regulations. He was arrested for "furious riding" on the new James Bay Bridge, but acquitted. In 1860 he was again arrested for riding his horse on the Fort Street footpath, and this time found guilty and fined. He later tried to build a castle, but ran out of funds. This building eventually became the first Government House of B.C. Cary's mind finally went, and he died insane in England in 1866, aged only 34.

60 *Colonist*, January 10, 1860.

61 William Fraser Tolmie, M.D., was born in Inverness, Scotland, in 1812 and came to Fort Vancouver in 1833. He became a Chief Factor of the HBC, and came to Victoria in 1858. He was a member of the first Board of Education, and compiled a dictionary of the Haida language. He died in Victoria in 1886. His diary was published by Mitchell Press Limited, Vancouver, in 1963, under title: *William Fraser Tolmie, Physician and Fur Trader*.

62 H. P. P. Crease was born in Cornwall in 1823. He was called to the bar in England and practised at Lincoln's Inn. He arrived in Victoria on

December 15, 1858, and was the first practising barrister on Vancouver Island. He was a member of the House of Assembly 1860-1861, and in July 1861 became Attorney-General for B.C. He took a prominent part in bringing about the eventual union with Canada. He retired and was knighted in 1896, and died in 1905.

[63] J. J. Southgate was a staunch supporter of the HBC. He was also the first Worshipful Master of the Victoria Lodge of the Masons (which had been organized on August 20, 1860), and was re-elected in 1861. At a later period he was the member for Nanaimo. He died in 1894. Southgate Street, Victoria, Southgate River in Bute Inlet, and the Southgate group of the Queen Charlotte Islands are named after him. See article by J. K. Nesbitt in the *Colonist* for December 11, 1949.

[64] On June 9, 1860, the *Colonist* reported the Fisgard light-house almost finished, and the one at Race Rocks under construction.

[65] A most useful work to examine in this connection is Edward Mallandaine's *First Victoria Directory,* published in Victoria in 1860. It lists all the officials of the colony, as well as its schools, hotels and restaurants, the rates of postage to foreign countries, and a complete voters' list.

[66] On April 19, however, De Cosmos vigorously attacked "the church monopoly", declaring that "the followers of the lowly Jesus are certainly well treated in this Ultima Thule".

[07] Some of Bishop Hills' first impressions of Victoria, written on January 13, 1860, are worth recording: "Victoria must be, I think, the most lovely and beautifully situated place in the world. I never saw anything before like it. In the summer it must be exquisite. I was agreeably struck with it altogether; there is every sort of scenery. Sublime mountains, placid sea, noble forest trees, undulating park-like glades, interspersed with venerable oaks, inland lakes and rivers abounding with fish . . . On the whole I was surprised to see the size and rapid growth of the town . . . It will be a large city ere a few years are over." (*Colonist,* January 13, 1929.)

[68] This society was later merged with the Royal Jubliee Hospital.

[69] For an account, see *Colonist* for January 28, 1860.

[70] The "credibility gap" is not necessarily a modern invention.

[71] *Colonist,* March 1, 1861.

[72] *Colonist,* April 5 and 6, 1861.

[73] "The first news was in favor of the South and great was the rejoicing of the Southerners . . . As a rule North and South in Victoria lived quietly, without public demonstration, but there were some hot headed fellows who would not be controlled—the confederate flag was hoisted in Langley St. after a battle and the North cut it down and vice versa, leading to a fight or two, a few only however taking part in it. However it was soon understood that such must not take place in a neutral British Colony."— J. S. Helmcken, *Reminiscences,* IV, pp. 57-58.

[74] *Colonist,* August 10, 1861.

[75] *Colonist*, August 9, 1861. See also Fawcett, *Some Reminiscences of Old Victoria,* Toronto, William Briggs, 1912, pp. 129 and 142.

[76] *Colonist,* May 17, 1861.

[77] H. H. Murphy, *Royal Jubilee Hospital, 1858-1958*, Hebden Printing Co., Victoria, 1958, p. 3.

[78] *Colonist*, March 7, 1861.

[79] *Colonist*, May 20, 1861.

[80] *Colonist*, October 1, 1861.

[81] *Colonist*, September 20, 1861.

[82] *Colonist*, April 2, 1861.

[83] Maclaurin, D. L., *The History of Education in the Crown Colonies of Vancouver Island and British Columbia and in the Province of British Columbia*, PhD Thesis, U. of Washington, 1936, p. 38.

[84] Published in full in the *Colonist* for September 3, 1861.

[85] Maclaurin, *op. cit.*, p. 38.

[86] *Ibid.*, p. 41.

[87] *Colonist*, January 23, 1861.

[88] J. W. Pilton, *Negro Settlement in British Columbia 1858-1871*, M.A. Thesis, UBC, 1951, pp. 187-191. Also *Colonist*, Nov. 7, 1860.

[89] Walden, *Social History of Victoria*, p. 146.

[90] See for example his editorial in the *Colonist* for July 16, 1861, in which he attacks Douglas for appropriating £100 for an Episcopal church at Port Douglas and £100 for the church at Cayoosh.

[91] *Colonist*, May 3, 1861.

[92] The matters on which the writers expressed intellectual uneasiness included the miracles recorded in the Bible. Some of them also had doubts as to whether the birth of Christ was foretold by various prophecies in the Old Testament, and even questioned "the descent of all mankind from Adam". (See article in the *Colonist* for May 9, 1862, entitled "The New Theology".)

[93] *Colonist*, January 24, 1861.

[94] It has not proved possible to hold the budget at this level. Premier Bennett, in his speech to the B.C. Legislature on February 9, 1968, estimated the needs of the province for the year 1968/69 at $866,021,000 and foresaw the early advent of the "billion-dollar budget" for the province.

[95] *Colonist*, August 12, 1861.

[96] The marriage, despite its romantic beginnings and double tying of the knot, was a failure. The couple had three children, after which they went their separate ways. Good went to England and Alice to San Francisco, where she obtained an American divorce and remarried. The English courts would not recognize the divorce, and Good in consequence divorced his wife. Douglas' comment on all this was "Had she trusted her Father more, and put less faith in Good, how different, and how much more happy, would her lot in life have been." Alice lived on till 1913. See *BCHQ*, Vol. XXI, pp. 174-5.

[97] He eventually committed suicide in Germany. See *Colonist* for April 30, 1862.

[98] *Colonist*, December 27, 1861. Gordon was acquitted of embezzlement, but immediately confined in the Debtor's prison.

[99] *Colonist,* December 21, 1861.

[100] *Colonist,* January 3, 1862. The "Notes and Remarks" of Mrs. E. G. Alston (1837-1915), contain some interesting sidelights on life in early Victoria. (MS in PABC.)

[101] The full text of the bill is given in the *Victoria Daily Press* for July 9, 1861.

[102] *Colonist,* January 21, 1862.

[103] *Colonist,* December 11, 1861.

[104] *Colonist,* November 26, 1861.

[105] *Colonist,* December 30, 1861.

[106] *Colonist,* December 30, 1861.

[107] *Colonist,* February 8, 1862. The bodies of executed criminals were buried in the Fort Yard, and there, somewhere in the vicinity of Bastion Square, their bones remain to this day.

[108] *Colonist,* May 9, 1862. On May 20, the House of Assembly passed a resolution recommending the opening of a road to "Comax" (*Colonist,* May 21, 1862). An editorial in the *Colonist* for July 15, 1862 is headed "Nanaimo and Comax—good places for farmers".

[109] *Colonist,* April 7, 1862.

[110] *Colonist,* April 15, 1862. It is a commentary on the earliest journalism that the mysterious lady does not appear to have been asked who she was and why she was thus attired and what were her immediate plans!

[111] An advertisement in the *Colonist* for April 24 by a private contractor asked for "1000 laborers . . . to work on the Great Trunk Road from Yale to Cariboo".

[112] See *Colonist* for April 25, May 2 and May 3, 1862.

[113] *Colonist,* July 9, 1862.

[114] "Within a few weeks we have received quite a large addition to our population from the States and Canada. Naturally enough the destination of nearly every one who arrives is the Cariboo mines . . ." (*Colonist,* May 1, 1862.)

[115] *Colonist,* May 6, 1862.

[116] *Colonist,* June 12, 1862.

[117] *Colonist,* June 18, 1862.

[118] *Colonist,* June 10, 1862.

[119] *Colonist,* May 13, 1862.

[120] *Colonist,* May 14, 1862.

[121] *Colonist,* June 21, 1862.

[122] *Colonist,* July 14, 1862.

[123] *Colonist,* July 28, 1862.

[124] *Colonist,* July 23, 1862.

[125] The "Victoria Fire Limit Act of 1862" is printed in full in the *Colonist* for July 12, 1862.

[126] *Colonist,* July 30, 1862.

[127] *Colonist,* May 19, 1862. In an editorial on August 6, De Cosmos, hardly surprisingly, spoke of "the vice of embezzlement and corruption which seem almost chronic in certain other quarters, and have well nigh exhausted our patience."

[128] *Colonist,* August 12, 1862.

[129] *Colonist,* August 18, 1862.

[130] *Colonist,* August 19, 1862. It was estimated at the time that only one out of every six British subjects over 21 was qualified to vote, and that of these 400, only 213 made use of their franchise. (See Victoria *Daily Press,* August 19, 1862.)

CHAPTER EIGHT

The End
of
The Old Order

Victoria, founded less than twenty years before as a fur-trading post, was now a city, and its citizens rejoiced in their new dignity and walked with a prouder step. Maturity, however, had brought not only new rights but new responsibilities, and it was in dealing with these in the circumstances of the year 1862 that awkward problems were soon facing Mayor Harris and his six councillors.

One difficulty was, in the nature of the case, inevitable: those entrusted with the direction of the city's affairs lacked previous experience in their duties. It was not easy for them to decide immediately which tasks should be tackled first, what resources should be allotted to them, and what personnel would need to be employed. A further complication was that although the Crown Grant of Vancouver Island to the Hudson's Bay Company had expired, a considerable portion of the land on which the city was rising undoubtedly still belonged to the Company; its exact extent, however, was far from clear. Finally, it was discovered before long that the act passed by the House of Assembly incorporating the city had not been drawn with sufficient care or foresight; it appeared that Victoria lacked legal power not only to borrow money but even to levy a tax on real estate. Much of the first year of the city's existence was to be bedevilled by complexities arising from these obstacles to progress; they were perhaps augmented by the rapidly shifting nature of the population, as waves of miners came and went between the coast and the gold-fields, and by the fact that Victoria was also the seat of the House of Assembly, the senior authority both in years and jurisdiction, while behind both loomed the formidable figure of the old Governor. Douglas still retained among his formal powers that of the right to veto any act of either body.

Nevertheless, the city's business had to be carried on, and the mayor and his associates tackled their new duties without delay. De Cosmos, in editorial written shortly before the first civic election, had enumerated what he believed to be the most urgent of them:

> The first thing to be done is to take steps for cleansing the town and making the streets passable in bad weather; further, measures which have been long and shamefully neglected, such as the storage of gunpowder, sanitary regulations, the building of wooden houses of a limited size in certain localities, and the introduction of water will require immediate attention.
>
> Considerable taxes must be imposed to effect these improvements. This we believe the inhabitants will cheerfully submit to: all they will require will be that the money should be honestly and judiciously applied.[1]

A few days after the election De Cosmos made some further comments:

> Our City Fathers will find that they have got no sincecure in the posts which they have been called by their fellow-citizens to fill. For the first year, long and arduous will be the duties they will have to perform. They will have to lay the foundation broad and deep of our municipal career. To them, in a large measure, future generations will owe a large part of our municipal system, for they must fight the battle which must be fought for such alterations and improvements as are necessary in our City Charter.[2]

The opening session of Victoria's first City Council, held at 7 p.m. on August 25, 1862 in the Police Barracks in the presence of about fifty spectators, was comparatively uneventful. Mr. Algernon Austen was appointed clerk of the council pro tem., and various councillors gave notice of motions to appoint committees to report on such matters as bridges, public nuisances and finance. A matter that was to vex the city fathers for some time to come also made its appearance on this first evening, as notice was given by Councillor Stronach of a motion to set up a committee to interview Governor Douglas and to ascertain from him "what portion of the public lands were to be given the city, and also what claims the Government had to the improvements already placed on the public property." It is significant, as showing that this was already seen as an important issue, that at this point the *Colonist's* report of the proceedings (printed in its issue of August 26) noticed "applause". The mayor was also requested "to advertise for proposals for the best design for a seal".

By early September, the city government was well into harness. At a meeting on September 4, a "Committee on Nuisances" made a detailed report concerning aspects of the city which they felt were in need of improvement; a few of its provisions will show that civilization, here as everywhere, had brought mixed blessings:

> We found, on the south side of Yates street, near the Bank of British North America, a very disagreeable stench arising from stagnant water in that neighbourhood, proceeding from a drain connecting with the Colonial Hotel and the Gipsey House baths, on Government street.
>
> We found, on the corner of Douglas and View streets, in the center of the highway, filthy puddles, caused by a flow of dirty water proceeding from a Bath House on the easterly corner of said streets, which causes great difficulty to vehicles in passing along Douglas street.
>
> We found that a number of pigs were kept in the space between Government, Johnson, Wharf and Yates streets, to the great nuisance and annoyance of the citizens resident on those streets, and the danger of the health of the City at large.
>
> We found the sidewalk on Yates street in front of Langley street in a broken and dilapidated condition, to the danger of passers by.
>
> We found also a number of houses of ill-fame on Humboldt, with Indian women . . . The neighbors complain of habitual drunkenness and disgusting language being continually made use of.

Before the City Council had been in existence for a month, however, it found itself suddenly facing an unexpected crisis in which high constitutional issues and farce were nicely blended. On September 15, proceeding to their customary meeting-place in the Police Barracks, the city fathers found it occupied by a session of the police court. Rather than disrupt the proceedings, the mayor and his councillors climbed the stairs to a smaller room on the upper floor. From this vantage point they attempted to salve their wounded feelings by sending a message to the Police Commissioner, Augustus Pemberton, suggesting that he should move his assemblage of constables, lawyers and malefactors elsewhere. The Commissioner, however, no doubt having heard in the course of his career the dictum about possession being nine points of the law, declined, and an embarrassing deadlock was created.

One of the councillors, N. M. Hicks, then suggested a means of breaking it. His proposal was that the mayor should swear in forty "special policemen" and with this newly created force drive the offending magistrate in disarray from his stronghold. Mayor Harris, however, declined to initiate an adventure so unpredictable in its outcome, and prudently adjourned the Council to some more propitious time and place.[3]

The editor of the *Colonist* lost no time in extracting from this series of events what he conceived to be its moral. It was, predictably, all the fault of Governor Douglas for not providing a Council Chamber. "The Governor must have foreseen that we would before long be a city, and must have known that the civic public would require lands and buildings for corporation purposes. Yet in the face of that, not a single step did he take to have land set aside for that purpose."[4]

Despite this contretemps, the Council in its first few months of office achieved quite a creditable record. Algernon Austen was confirmed in his office of city clerk,[5] and soon afterward F. W. Green was chosen as city surveyor.[6] Ordinances were passed regulating some activities which might prove a nuisance to others: no slaughterhouses or tanneries were to be allowed within the city limits; no guns, pistols or fire-crackers were to be set off; pigs and goats running at large were to be impounded.[7]

Later in the month this list was extended: eight miles per hour was fixed as the maximum speed which even so headlong a century as the nineteenth was prepared to tolerate within the city limits, and it was decided that drivers must keep to the left of the road.[8] Here was a beginning at traffic control.

It appeared that an awkward source of possible controversy had been cleared up when the townsite claims of the Hudson's Bay Company were settled by an agreement between the Company and the British Government, dated February 3, 1862. The Company was to retain the "Uplands Farm" of 1144 acres and the "North Dairy Farm" of 724 acres; also the Fort property except for a small portion reserved for the Harbormaster and the Police Barracks. All land sales made by the Company before January 1, 1862 were to be considered as valid, and the Company could keep the money it had received for them.[9] As the year ended, the Council was forbidding Sunday trading[10] and considering numbering the streets.[11]

All these changes, however, took place in the shadow of a controversial issue that was long to haunt those guiding Victoria's destiny. The exact financial powers of the city were far from clear, and this was soon to be the source of numerous disputes and difficulties. The Incorporation Act had declared that on the petition of 70% by value of the owners of real property on any street, the Council might "grade, macadamize, pave, drain or otherwise improve" it, and levy an appropriate tax on all the real property abutting on it. This provision appeared harmless, indeed useful, until it was made by some the legal basis for challenging the power of the Council to levy a general tax on real estate. Their contention was that the Act had named the only conditions under which such a tax might be levied and that under any other conditions it was of necessity illegal. As early as August 14, 1862, the *Colonist* had pointed out that nowhere was it specifically and unequivocally stated in the city charter that the mayor and council had "the power to collect money from the person or property of the inhabitants for municipal purposes generally", and a few weeks later D. B. Ring was stating unequivocally that the Council had no legal right to levy a general tax in any form.[12]

Those of a contrary view, however, pointed out that the Incorporation Act did state (Section 24) that "The Council may . . . direct in what manner the funds required for the municipal purposes shall be raised" and that "not more than one-half of the proposed annual revenue shall be raised by an assessment on freehold and leasehold property". This to them suggested clearly that the City had the general power to tax property or anything else.[13]

These two points of view were clearly irreconcilable, and the necessity seemed clear for a decision by the courts as to which was legally correct. This was, however, to be a considerable time in coming to pass, and in the meantime the City fathers coped as best they could. In the latter months of 1862 they drew up a schedule of trades licence fees or taxes; these were to vary from £50 for banks and printers to £2 for dentists and fishmongers. There was also to be a sales tax amounting to one-quarter of one per cent on wholesale sales, one half of one percent on sales by auction, and one sixteenth of one per cent on amounts loaned, exclusive of bank loans. This system of fees and taxes received its third reading in committee on November 24, 1862, but, as we shall see, was disallowed early in the following year (probably on the advice of Attorney-General Cary) by Governor Douglas, an action which naturally did little to resolve the Council's difficulties.

Despite this complex and vital problem, the economic life of Victoria continued to expand. There were, however, shifts in the relative price levels of various commodities and services. One writer tells us that not long before this period wages were from $3 to $5 a day,[14] and that suburban lots were generally £20 an acre,[15] while property in Saanich could be bought for £2 - £3 an acre.[16] The same observer reported the price of a two-pound loaf of bread as 6d, butter at 1/3 to 2/- a lb., eggs 1s to 2s per dozen and whiskey at 2s a quart.[17] In 1862, however, the *Colonist* reported day labor as bringing only $1.25 a day.[18]

Land prices, in contrast, had advanced drastically. On October 30, the *Colonist* took note of a lot which had sold in June of the same year for $700 now changing hands for $3050, and commented "this is a striking proof of the rapid advance in the value of real estate in the city and of the confidence felt by men of capital in our future prosperity."

Much of this economic well-being was connected with the encouraging news from the Cariboo gold fields. Fresh strikes had sent new waves of hopeful miners in pursuit of fortune; the results of their labors were soon being carried back across the straits in the steamer *Enterprise*. On one occasion alone it arrived from New Westminster with $250,000 worth of gold dust.[19] A series of letters in the *Times* of London, extolling the new colony on the rim of the Pacific, undoubtedly emboldened many adventurous souls to try their luck in the New World.[20]

Road-building on the Island also went forward. Late in October Mr. Cary reported to the House of Assembly that it would soon be possible to drive cattle from Nanaimo to Victoria,[21] and in November the *Colonist* announced that one could now ride from the capital city as far as Cowichan.[22]

In the city itself, signs of progress multiplied. Perhaps the most noticeable was the beginning of the lighting of the major streets by gas. The laying of the necessary mains had commenced in March,[23] and late in September the first lamp was lit. Its location was "in front of Caroll's liquor store on Yates Street".[24] Early in October the *Colonist* was able to declare:

> Several stores and saloons are now lighted with gas. Considerable air is in the mains and service pipes, and prevents the gas from burning with as bright and steady a flame as desirable, but in a few days this difficulty, like all the other mountains of trouble which have from time to time beset the operations of the Company, will be overcome, and the quality of gas supplied be equal to that furnished by similar works in any part of the world.[25]

The Company, meanwhile, anxious no doubt to build goodwill, gave its subscribers useful advice regarding the smooth functioning of the new apparatus. If the gas meters froze during the approaching winter, it was suggested that they be thawed out by putting whiskey in them.[26]

The possibility of a really serious fire was ever in the minds of those guiding the city's destinies, and appropriate action was taken to avert such a disaster.[27] On July 9, 1862, Douglas had signed "An Act to Establish Fire Limits Within the Town of Victoria"; these were defined as the area bounded by Johnson, Broad, Fort and the Harbour.[28] A new fire engine arrived in September 1862.[29] The fire department, however, was still independent of the civic government, although it did receive a grant from the city toward its expenses.

The problem of an adequate supply of water for the city in the years to come also was much discussed, as reliance on local wells was seen to be increasingly impractical. Inevitably, Elk Lake, only eight miles from the city, suggested itself, and editorials in the *Colonist* for October 31 and November 28, 1862, dealt with the question. On the latter occasion, after noting that "at present the town (*sic*) is supplied by water-carriers at the rate of two buckets a day for a week for fifty cents," it estimated that some day there would be from fifty thousand to a hundred thousand people in the area. This suggested to De Cosmos the necessity for obtaining the city's water from Elk Lake, with a big reservoir at Spring Ridge to contain two million gallons of water.[30] De Cosmos supported the idea of a private company to develop the project, with the proviso that the city should have the right to buy out the owners if it felt such a move appropriate.

Agriculture, too, made steady progress. The annual fall fair was held on the first of October, and Governor Douglas showed his versatility by winning a prize for some Muscovy ducks.

Meanwhile, there were also changes in those areas of life not immediately concerned with the physical necessities of existence. Religion in Victoria enjoyed a comparatively quiet year: the columns of the *Colonist* noted the continuing uproar in far-away England occasioned by the publication of the controversial *Essays and Reviews;* some of its authors were being summoned before a special tribunal known as the "Rolls Court".[31] Unperturbed by this dispute, however, the Presbyterians of Victoria bought a lot at the corner of Pandora and Blanshard, and announced their intention of erecting a new church on it.[32]

Social and cultural affairs exhibited considerable vitality in the latter months of 1862. Horse racing continued on Beacon Hill; a singer named Lulu Sweet came to town, and the bachelor editor of the *Colonist* pronounced her "a charming little actress".[33] A meeting was held on September 29 to organize "A Temperance Society and Debating Club"; the occasion was slightly marred by the chairman, only identified in the *Colonist* as "a certain well-known citizen", being drunk, and further proceedings were postponed to a more propitious occasion.[34] A rival newspaper to the *Colonist,* the *Press,* succumbed in October, but later in the same month the *Chronicle* made its appearance. Twenty-seven patients were reported in the hospital, "nine more than the capacity of the building will accommodate with any degree of comfort".[35] De Cosmos in his columns urged that all accounts in the colony should be kept in decimal currency,[36] and his cause was to triumph before many months had passed. He was not, however, to live to see what to him seemed an equally logical step: the establishment of the metric system. A committee of the City Council, set up to consider a standard system of weights and measures, recommended in November that it should be adopted,[37] and in an editorial on November 17 De Cosmos declared that it "must ultimately obtain in all civilized countries". His fellow-citizens, however, were evidently unwilling to exchange rods, poles and perches for the uncertain glories of milligrammes and hectolitres, and the proposal languished.[38]

Perhaps the most striking events of the closing months of 1862 came in September. On the 16th of that month, the Russian corvette *Kalevala* dropped anchor in Esquimalt harbor. She was on a courtesy visit from Sitka, Alaska, and for several days the city took on a slightly exotic aspect, as the bearded foreign sailors strolled about its streets.[39]

The seventeenth of the same month, however, was an even more memorable day in the history of Victoria. After a long voyage around the Horn, the *Tynemouth* sailed into the harbor; it brought with it from England about 270 passengers, and of these 62 were unmarried women anxious to find employment or husbands in the new colony. De Cosmos was apparently unable to await their disembarkation, and recounted his prompt investigations with some candor:

> As a matter of course, we went aboard the steamer yester-day morning and had a good look at the lady passengers. They are mostly cleanly, well-built, pretty looking young women—ages varying from fourteen to an uncertain figure; a few are young widows who have seen better days. Most appear to have been well raised and generally they seem a superior lot to the women usually met with on emigrant vessels.[40]

About thirty of the new arrivals were quickly engaged as servants, and after "a large and anxious crowd of breeches-wearing bipeds assembled to see the women disembark",[41] the remainder were quartered at the Marine Barracks.

One result of this invasion, one would gather, was a sartorial revolution. One merchant, at least, hastened to proclaim and to profit by it:

> Good news! The girls have arrived! And A. J. BRUNN has reduced the price of his well-selected stock of fashionable clothing, shirts, hats, caps and furnishing goods.[42]

Others besides haberdashers saw their duty clearly. The following Sunday at Christ Church the Rev. Scott preached to the massed ranks of femininity, pointing out that even in this Pacific Eden the Tempter might lurk disguised:

> The reverend gentleman exhorted the immigrants to re-member their religious duties and their duties to their em-ployers, always and under any circumstances to shape their conduct so that they might prove a credit to their English mothers, from whom many were now separated forever; and when beset by sin and temptation to rely on a kind Providence for aid and comfort . . . The poor girls wept freely during the delivery of the sermon, and there was scarcely a dry eye in the congregation.[43]

Surprisingly, in view of these auspicious beginnings, it was not long before one virgin heart, at least, was corrupted; one of the girls was discovered in the act of—talking through the fence to a young man! De Cosmos supplied his readers with fuller details, though his account seems to carry a hint here and there that he was not so impressed as he might have been with the gravity of the offence or the motives of those who uncovered it:

> The melancholy discovery was made by two clergymen and a naval officer—who, for the purpose of making "assurance doubly sure", crawled behind a water-butt, with necks outstretched to their utmost length—eyes starting from their sockets with expressions of eager expectancy—hats off—and their bald heads glistening beneath the fierce rays of the sun —all for the sake of morality.[44]

The "bride ship" was perhaps the high point of the period, but the remainder of 1862 saw some interesting events. The 21st birthday of the Prince of Wales on November 10 was celebrated with a big parade, horse races and a public holiday. The *Colonist* estimated that there were perhaps 4000 people in Beacon Hill Park for the occasion.[45]

Toward the end of the year camels once more ambled awkwardly through the pages of the city's history. A young one with its mother was observed on the Cadboro Bay Road,[46] and in the same month a boy, sent by his parents to collect firewood, was terrified by "two wild beasts—bigger nor horses, with humps on their backs".[47]

As the year closed, the Rev. Cridge presented his report on the schools at Victoria, Craigflower and Nanaimo. He estimated that the total income from fees for the three schools would be £90, and that the total expenses would be £675 10/-, a sum which included the services of three teachers at £200 per annum.[48]

All in all, it had been a remarkable year. The population of the city had perhaps doubled in a twelvemonth;[49] land prices were soaring ("lots that a few months ago could be bought for $3000 or $5000, cannot now be had for twice, nay three times these sums"), and De Cosmos was urging the creation of a Board of Trade.[50]

Moreover, it was beginning to be realized that a city should be not merely a place in which to make money but also a visible embodiment of the aspirations of the human spirit. Less than a month after Mayor Harris first assumed office, De Cosmos was asking:

> Who that has beheld the beautiful squares that adorn the great cities of Europe like so many oases, does not long to see so laudable an institution perpetuated out here in the Queen City of the Pacific . . . Now is the time to make such a provision while the city is young.[51]

In another striking suggestion, De Cosmos urged that the city should have its own "day", devoted to general celebrations of its existence. He suggested that the day Douglas had first landed in the area would be the most appropriate choice.[52]

The need for preserving the early records of the city was also urged by De Cosmos on his fellow citizens:

> . . . it is not long—not very many years—before all those who came hither in 1842 will lay their bones in the silent grave. The pioneers will be gone, no more to return. Victoria —the Colony—will live and grow whilst the Island remains anchored in the sea; but the men who made her—who first raised our flag here—who gave her language, laws, religion and the Anglo-Saxon race but twenty years ago, will soon be gone. Whilst they live and we live, we owe a duty to posterity to mark the era of the settlement of our adopted country. Who will take the initiative?[53]

A week later, in a moment of exuberance, De Cosmos pulled out all the stops:

> What with gas companies, water companies, railway companies and mining companies, one commences to ask himself if he is in a four-year-old town, or in a large European city.[54]

This was, if one reflected soberly—even if one looked about at the muddy streets where livestock still wandered at will—no very difficult question to answer. Nevertheless, even when one allows for the enthusiasm of De Cosmos for his adopted home, there was an element of truth in it. The foundations had indeed been firmly laid, and it was with a deserved pride that Victorians, the year of their incorporation safely traversed, now looked forward into 1863.[55]

The new year opened auspiciously with an address by Governor Douglas to the new session of the Legislature.[56] He spoke of "the recently formed settlements at Cowichan and Comax", and urged that provision be made not only for their protection but for "the secular and religious instruction of the settlers in those districts".[57] He reported that "a highly respectable English association is about to form a settlement at Quatseeno, on the West Coast of Vancouver Island. They propose to open mines of coal, establish fisheries, to embark largely in the export of deals and ship's spars, and in other branches of trade that promise remunerative employment for capital". He drew attention to the need for a thorough geological survey of the colony, declaring that "the mountain ranges which now so unprofitably occupy a large portion of the Island, are, with good reason, supposed to abound in valuable minerals". He requested financial aid for "encouraging the taking of cod and other fish on the coast of the Island", and also a subsidy for "a steam vessel to ply at stated intervals between Comax and Victoria, touching at Cowichan, Salt Spring, Nanaimo, and the intermediate settlements."

The Governor's encouraging message was abundantly confirmed by other sources. A "commercial review" in the *Colonist* on January 6 noted that "the Alberni saw-mills on Barclay Sound are continually loading vessels with lumber and spars for market in Australia and China. A shipment is also occasionally made from the mills in Sooke Inlet . . . " Exports of fur and coal were estimated at $750,000 annually, and the amount of gold dust passing through Victoria from the gold fields in 1862 was reckoned at $2,500,000.

Immigration continued to augment the population. A second "bride ship", the *Robert Lowe,* arrived with 180 passengers early in 1863; these included 36 young females. These latter had arrived, as it were, intact, since they had "occupied a separate compartment, never being allowed to mingle with the other passengers".[58] A thousand people watched the disembarkation, which was, however, somewhat undignified, since "the girls had to run the gauntlet through them amid the utterance of coarse jokes and personalities".[59]

Other signs of new growth soon appeared. The same month, it was reported that the trail to Nanaimo was now open for traffic.[60] An article in the *Colonist* for January 31 reported that town as having 250 buildings and 403 white inhabitants. (A letter to the editor shortly afterwards took issue with this latter figure, estimating the population as 892). Fur and coal were reported as the main exports; a shipyard and a saw-mill were in operation, and as evidence of high thinking and plain living, the town could boast both a "Literary Institute" and a "Total Abstinence Society". The colonial (non-sectarian) school had enrolled 19 boys and 9 girls, for a total of 28.

Meanwhile, the Cornishmen of Victoria held a banquet at which 85 persons were present; St. David's Charitable Society was formed by the local Welsh "for the purpose of mutually assisting those who are in real distress and want"; money was raised for the "Lancashire Relief Fund", and a public meeting was held on January 23 at the church in Esquimalt "with the view of discussing the project of establishing a free school in that town".[61]

This latter project soon took shape, for February 17 saw the opening of the desired school. Thirteen children were enrolled under the instruction of a Mrs. Partridge.[62] Later in the year a school was opened at Cedar Hill, with Thomas Nicholson as teacher.[63]

Some features of the city of today had their beginnings at this time. The Chamber of Commerce held its first meeting and chose Robert Burnaby as president.[64] The House of Assembly appropriated $1000 toward a library for its members,[65] and discussed the improvements that should be made to the network of roads now radiating from the centre of town. It was proposed to widen the East Saanich Road to 16 feet, to build three bridges on the West Saanich Road, to improve the Sooke, Cowichan and Metchosin Roads, and to do some work on the Victoria South Coast or Fowl (*sic*) Bay Road.[66] During this year, also, Richard Carr built a fine house of California redwood at what is now 207 Government street. Here his daughter Emily, destined to become Victoria's most celebrated artist, would one day be born.[67]

The city, because of its ambiguous charter, was still having difficulties with its financial affairs. As we saw earlier, the efforts of the Council to raise funds through a general tax on real estate were considered by many to be illegal; indeed, before the year was out, it was to meet with a deliberate refusal to pay such a tax. Moreover, the system of trades licences which it had instituted in November 1862 had been disallowed by Douglas in February 1863, also on the grounds of its doubtful legality. This resulted in a vigorous attack on the Governor by the *Colonist,* which on February 16 accused him of bowing to what it termed "the obstructionists". Fortunately, the Incorporation Act had provided for a referendum on doubtful issues, and this the Colonial Government now ordered. In the voting on March 28, the trades licence system was supported by 157 votes to 116.

This had at least a temporary effect on the city's fiscal dilemma. The Council had been anxious to borrow £5000 from the Bank of British Columbia; the sceptical financiers in charge of it, however, were unwilling to part with any funds unless and until the financial position of the city seemed more secure. A few days after the referendum, the bank agreed to lend the city £5000 at 12 percent per annum, nearly all of which was soon spent on improving the streets.

The legal status of the tax on real estate remained obscure, however; nor was even its fairness universally admitted. In an editorial on April 3, 1863, the *Colonist* declared:

> There are those who think that real estate should bear all the taxes; because the revenue raised is chiefly laid out in improving the streets, and consequently the property taxed. We disagree with that notion entirely. We believe that the taxes ought to be fairly distributed over all classes of property, so as not to fall too heavily anywhere; and we certainly cannot perceive any good reason why real estate should bear an unusual share of the public burdens. All classes of citizens enjoy in common the benefits arising from city improvements, and consequently it would be unfair to make one class pay and exempt the other.[68]

Despite this continuing controversy, new enterprises continued to appear. In May the James Bay Brewery operated by A. J. Welch, was reported in full production,[69] while in the same month the Albion Iron Works was founded at Chatham and Discovery Streets.[70]

The religious life of the community also made good progress. The cornerstone of the new Presbyterian church was laid on the 9th of April by Chief Justice Cameron. The cost of the building was estimated at $6000, and a full description of it was given in the *Colonist* the next day. The first of June saw the foundation stone of the Synagogue put in place. The occasion was noticeably ecumenical in character: the Freemasons attended in full regalia; the Hebrew Benevolent Society, the French Benevolent Society and St. Andrew's Society were all well represented. The band of H.M.S. *Topaze* rendered musical selections, and the Germania Sing Verein added their voices to the ceremony.[71]

A few days later a branch was formed of the British and Foreign Bible Society,[72] while in August a new brick building was under construction on Pandora Street. Of two and a half storeys and costing between $4000 and $5000, it was to be used by the Oblate Fathers as a college for young male Roman Catholics.

Aspiring scholars of the fair sex were also provided for. St. Ann's School for Young Ladies, in an advertisement in the *Colonist* for September 19, 1863, gave some account of that institution:

> The discipline of the School is mild, but firm and regular; strict attention to its regulations required at all times. The emulation of the pupils will be excited by every gentle means, and their success rewarded by an annual distribution of premiums, previous to the vacation, which will commence July 15th. The Scholastic year will open on the first of September.
>
> Difference of religion is no obstacle to admission into the institution . . .
>
> The uniform consists of a light muslin dress, and one of light blue merino for summer, and a dark blue dress for winter, with capes of the same material, a straw bonnet trimmed with light blue, and one trimmed with dark blue. The uniform is obligatory only on Sundays and festivals.

In October, a Rev. Mr. Nimmo was sent out to Vancouver Island by the General Assembly of the Church of Scotland, and since there was as yet no Presbyterian church in the city, held services in the council chamber.[73] The first church of his denomination was, however, opened the following month, and Mr. Nimmo again officiated.[74]

Meanwhile, an increasing amount of space was being given in the press to religious news of another sort. Bishop Colenso of Natal, South Africa, was formally censured by the assembled bishops of the Church of England, headed by the Archbishop of Canterbury, on the grounds that he had declared publicly that he was unable to take literally every statement in the Bible. The bishops spoke to their errant brother of "your method of handling that Bible which we believe to be the Word of Christ, and on the truth of which rest all our hopes for eternity", and declared that his attitude was causing "great pain and grievous scandal to the Church".[75]

Bishop Colenso, however, had decided, even in the face of the massed phalanxes of episcopacy, to stand his ground, and had retorted:

> I trust that I yield to none of your Lordships in a heart-felt reverence for the Holy Scriptures. But certainly I do not believe, as the words of the address seem to imply . . . that "all our hopes for eternity rest" on the literal historical truth of such a narrative as the scriptural account of the Noachian Deluge.

Moreover, he went on, in an exposition of the crux of the matter which would still be relevant a century later:

> I venture to add that the progress of true religion appears to me to be grievously impeded in the country by the contradictions which undeniably exist between the traditional notion of the historical truth of all the narratives contained in the Pentateuch and the conclusions of science, as now brought within the comprehension, even of the youth of both sexes, by the general extension of education.[76]

Attention was, however, diverted for a time from these high matters by events in which the military rather than the clergy took the leading roles. In May, a Grand Naval Ball was given by Commodore Spencer on H.M.S. *Topaze* in Esquimalt Harbour;[77] in the following month a court-martial aboard the same ship sentenced thirteen deserters from H.M.S. *Cameleon* to from 24 to 48 lashes each.[78] A few weeks later, the decisive battle of the American Civil War was fought near the little town of Gettysburg.

A country scarcely within the ken of most Victorians now made its appearance in the news columns. Japan, it was felt in some quarters, was needlessly obstructing the opening of trade relations with the West, and De Cosmos gave an analysis of the situation which some American pundits, considering appropriate attitudes toward the China of a century later, might well have applauded:

> There seems to be a difference of opinion as to the ability of the Allies to bring the Japanese to terms. The number, intelligence and independent disposition of the Islanders make them no mean enemy, even when opposed to the civilized and powerful nations of the west . . . Their conduct on the field of battle has yet to be tested; but that had better be done now than a few years hence, when they will have acquired a better knowledge of the military system of the western nations, and thus be in a better position to resist them.[79]

Difficulties with the mysterious East were apparently resolved, however, for later the same month we read of Japanese goods on sale in Victoria. These were at first "magnificent cabinets", but later they were joined by tea.[80]

Elections for a new House of Assembly now engrossed the public attention. Nomination day was July 17, and candidacies for the city of Victoria were declared in front of the sheriff in the Fort yard at the corner of Government and Fort at 11 A.M. The aspirants for office then addressed the voters, and the election on the 20th revealed the verdict of the citizenry. Final figures were as follows: A. G. Young 229; A. De Cosmos 211; J. W. Powell 203; J. C. Ridge 183; Selim Franklin 133; J. C. Pidwell 91.[81]

The top four were declared elected; of these Young was considered an "establishment" supporter, while the other three were thought of as independents. De Cosmos in an editorial on July 20 hailed the result as a great victory for the popular cause and a signal defeat for his great "bogey", the HBC. Not all districts voted on the same day, but when the smoke of battle had cleared, a new House of Assembly was in existence. Among the members we may note Capt. James Duncan, unopposed in Lake District, Dr. Helmcken and Robert Burnaby chosen for Esquimalt & Metchosin, and Dr. Tolmie as one of the three members for "Victoria District". Charles Street was unopposed in Saanich, Charles Bayley defeated Mr. Ring in Nanaimo by five votes to three, and G. E. Dennes became the member for Salt Spring Island.

The new House did not, however, convene until September, and the warm days of summer saw several events of interest in the city. The first of August was celebrated, as it was for several years, by the colored people of the town; two days later the Governor invited 300 citizens "including all the elite of Victoria and the neighborhood" to a luncheon in his private garden in James Bay. The band of H.M.S. *Sutlej* was in attendance, and there was dancing and general merriment.

The outlying districts were meanwhile prospering. The stage coach to Saanich, which had previously run every other day, now became a daily service. The horses left their stables at 8 a.m., proceeded by way of the West Road to North Saanich and returned by the East Road, being back in the city by 6 p.m.[82] A little later, De Cosmos was suggesting a ferry from North Saanich to a suitable spot higher up the Island. This, he declared, "would enable settlers to get up to Cowichan Bay with their cattle and wagons in one day with ease from Victoria"; he assumed that some sort of government subsidy would be necessary.[83]

Meanwhile, De Cosmos continued both to survey the passing scene and to relate it to the larger drama of the years. In an editorial on August 13, he pointed out the need to collect the accounts of the early Spanish, Russian and British explorers of the area, and to preserve them in the parliamentary library for the use of later generations:

> Is it not time, then, that we should make some effort to collect and preserve the past history of these colonies? The Spaniards must surely have learnt considerable respecting

the topography and resources of this Island, for instance, during their occupation. They had posts here, let us find out who governed them. Those in charge of them no doubt sent descriptions of the country and their actions to their superiors. These descriptions still exist either in print or in manuscript in the archives of Mexico or Spain. Through them we might derive hints that would be of inestimable value to us and aid us in acquiring more knowledge of our country than we now possess.

A few weeks later, the editor of the *Colonist* noted the first anniversary of Victoria's existence as a city:

The Council found the streets of mud and they will leave them, if not paved with marble, at least of good solid macadam. Instead of trails, crossing many a puddle for footpaths, they have given us good plank walks and have made Victoria look something else than an Indian village.[84]

Early in September, the Governor opened the new House of Assembly with an encouraging speech. He noted a considerable rise in the colony's revenue; he also took note of the marriage of the Prince of Wales and of a proposal that had been made for the establishment of telegraphic and postal communication between British Columbia and the head of Lake Superior. He told the members that the British Government had decided that the two colonies on the Pacific should be under separate governors, and he reported that a union of all the British North American colonies was looked upon favorably in London.[85]

The mention of two new governors inevitably focused attention on the fact—to many, no doubt, the unbelievable fact—that Douglas would soon be retiring from direction of the affairs of the two colonies. Some found this prospect so alarming that they took steps to prevent it, and a memorial was sent to the Colonial Secretary, the Duke of Newcastle, asking that the decision of the British Government be reconsidered. The document said, in part:

During the unusually protracted period of his administration, the colony has witnessed and enjoyed an unparalleled amount of prosperity, which is seen and felt everywhere in the activity of trade and commerce, which have grown and flourished to an extent such as no colony has hitherto seen in the same space of time.

His Excellency has devoted his sterling good sense, sound judgment, practical experience, moderation and uprightness of character, unremittingly to expand the resources of the Island.

Your memorialists are gratified to learn that Your Grace has placed a proper estimate upon the aspersions sought to be cast upon the Chief Executive; but at the same time express sincere regret that Your Grace deems it expedient, in conformity with established usage, to relieve Governor Douglas at a time when his invaluable services are most required.[86]

Douglas, however, in a letter to the *Colonist* on September 23, after expressing gratification at the trust reposed in him by the signers of the memorial, affirmed his irrevocable decision to retire from public life.

His services had not gone unnoticed by his superiors, however, and the *Colonist* for October 8 reported that the *London Gazette* for August 14 had announced that the retiring Governor was to become "an ordinary member of the Civil Division of the Second Class of Knight Commander of the Most Honorable Order of the Bath", and could thus henceforth style himself Sir James Douglas, K.C.B.

On this the *Colonist* (now under new management, De Cosmos having retired due to "delicate health, arising from over-application to the duties of a laborious profession"[87]) made a fitting comment:

His services to his country as Governor of these colonies will not be forgotten for many years to come, and we believe that nothing will be remembered of his administration of the government that will tend to tarnish the name of Douglas. Her Majesty, in conferring the honor of knighthood upon our Governor, has paid him a well-deserved compliment, which the colony will thoroughly appreciate.[88]

So the year waned into autumn, and lesser events continued to take place within the shadow of the great impending change. In September a Sunday excursion to San Juan Island was announced, and a letter to the *Colonist* protested against "such Sabbath desecration".[89] A circus arrived in the city from San Francisco.[90] The city council found itself plagued with fresh woes resulting from its defective charter, when at its meeting of September 14 it was announced by the City Assessor that D. B. Ring had refused to pay his license fee as a barrister on the ground that the city had no legal authority to impose such a tax.[91]

This was recognized to be a test case, and as such was laid before Chief Justice Cameron for a final decision. On December 16 he decided in favor of Ring, asserting that the City Council had no right to levy any sort of general taxes. The reasons for his decision[92] were not, perhaps, either to his listeners or to us, irresistible in their logic, but this did not alter the fact that from his decision there was no appeal. The Council was left in the unenviable position of apparently having collected more than $12,000 by means of an illegal tax—thus raising the question of possible demands for refunds. The best it could do was make an appeal to the public to continue paying their assessments out of sheer good will— which, remarkably, many persons did.[93]

Despite these awkward impediments to the efficient conduct of its affairs, however, the daily life of the city continued fairly smoothly. On September 24 the *Colonist* reprinted an article which had appeared in the *Times* of London for August 8. It suggested that those unemployed in the British cotton industry could easily find employment in the two colonies. Miners, it reported, were earning £2 a day, but were forced to spend £1 of this for board and lodging. It contained one sentence, however, which may have raised a few colonial hackles: "What England was 1000 or 1500 years ago, British Columbia seems to be now."

In an editorial the next day, De Cosmos deplored the lack of a lunatic asylum, expressing the belief that the current practice of shipping the mentally ill back to England was not in the long run very practical.[94]

Other deficiences in Victoria's daily life also engaged the attention of the *Colonist*. On the 28th of September, it stressed the need for a smaller coin than the "bit"; while on the 3rd of October it complained of "the inconvenience of the very limited supply which the miserable water-cart system affords", and suggested that the approaching civic elections would provide an opportunity for rectifying the situation. "Let a company, guaranteeing a plentiful supply of pure water, be set on foot before the municipal elections take place, and we are quite sure that there will be a sufficient water power to wash out of the Council all those candidates for seats in it who desire to keep up the monopoly of water carts."

These remarks evidently produced some effect, for later that month it was reported that a survey was under way to decide the best way of conveying water to the city from Elk Lake.[95]

This same month also saw William Wilson of Government Street informing the public that he had "on hand a most complete stock of superior winter clothes, which he is selling at lower prices than any other store in Victoria."[96] It also, as we have noted, saw De Cosmos transferring his ownership of the *Colonist* to Messrs. Harries, Mitchell, McKenzie, Oughton and Lawrie, all employees of the paper. Gold was discovered "on a stream flowing into Gold or Deadman's Creek, about two or three miles from Langford's Lake".[97] The House of Assembly passed a bill putting lawyers trained in the colonies on the same footing as those trained in the United Kingdom,[98] and also a bill designed to amend the unfortunate Incorporation Act.

November brought a reminder of the Civil War still raging below the border, as *Uncle Tom's Cabin* was presented at the Victoria Theatre.[99] Drama, indeed, appears to have flourished with unusual vigor at this time; the same month saw performances of *Romeo and Juliet, Macbeth, Camille* and *East Lynne.* On the 6th of the same month it was reported that "a commencement has at length been made towards the establishment of a Museum and Library in this city". Civic elections were held, Mayor Harris easily defeating John Copland, despite the latter's modest plea that "it required no ordinary man to fill the position of mayor for next year". The Mayor and his six aldermen (Lewis, Stronach, McDonald, Grahamslaw, Wallace and Ewing) were promptly presented with a petition asking that the prison (which also housed the insane) should be moved to the Indian Reserve.[100]

The *Colonist* approved strongly of this project, noting that:

We have confined in the common prison several dangerous

lunatics, and the idea that these unfortunate beings should be kept in a situation where their shouts and screams may be heard in some of the principal streets of the city is, to say the least of it, discreditable to our government and to the colony generally.[101]

November also saw the sudden death of Mr. James McQuade, a native of Galway, Ireland, who had come to Victoria in 1858 and become one of its leading merchants. He was buried in the "vaults beneath the Catholic Church".[102]

It was perhaps in this month, too, that the long shadow of a still distant universal war first fell across the city. Prussia, in its quest for world mastery, had selected the conquest of Schleswig-Holstein from unoffending Denmark as its opening move, and its threats against the Danes were daily more menacing. With remarkable prescience the *Colonist* suggested that Prussia's actions might yet cause "a general continental and world-wide war", and asked:

> Ought we not to ask from the Home Government for an armed force, and for a fleet of some strength to protect our homes and our trade? Our local Parliament would, we are confident, be warmly supported in any steps they may take to give more security to the Island.[103]

This crisis, however, remained for a few months yet just short of war, and Victorians in the last few months of 1863 were able to turn their attention to more local matters. Alberni was given representation in the House of Assembly;[104] the city was divided into four wards around the Government and Yates axis for fire protection purposes;[105] and an employment agency office was opened. A real estate tax was passed by the city fathers, amounting to one half of one per cent of the market value of property; the *Colonist* was "glad to notice a movement on foot for the establishment of a Library and Scientific Institution in Victoria";[106] and *Hamlet* was presented for thoughtful theatre-goers.

As the year ended, a local stock exchange had been opened; hopeful speculators were now able to discover by a glance at their newspaper the current value, or at least quotation, of the Sooke Mining Company, the Sangster Copper Company and the Queen

Charlotte Mining Company, and wonder what 1864 would hold in store for them.

It did not, in fact, open too auspiciously; three inches of ice covered lakes and ponds in the area, and on January 8 the House of Assembly added to the difficulties of Victoria's mayor and council by deferring for six months a bill legalizing the collection of general taxes by the city. This resulted in a further series of complexities. Some aldermen refused to attend council meetings on the grounds that perhaps the city itself had no legal existence; one (Alderman Lewis) went so far as to resign and was replaced by James Bunting. Faced with a drastic need for retrenchment, the Council on February 8 dismissed all city officials but the City Clerk, asked for a reduction in the rent of the council chamber from $100 to $70 a month, and ordered (despite its apparent lack of legal authority to do so) that the Real Estate Tax should be enforced.

January did see, however, some constructive development: the *Colonist* gave strong support for a trans-Canada railroad, and Mr. Selim Franklin was elected to fill a vacant Victoria seat in the Assembly.

Governor Douglas was at this time on the mainland, where the month saw the beginnings of democracy in the other coastal colony. A British Order-in-council, dated June 11, 1863 had provided for the establishment of a partly elected, partly appointed "Legislative council", and on January 21, 1864 Douglas opened its first session at New Westminster with at least outward signs of approval, declaring:

> . . . I offer you and the people of the colony at large my sincere congratulations on this event, the first step toward a perfect form of representative Government, and the establishment of those popular institutions which we all revere as our birth-right and inheritance, and which Her Majesty's Government saw fit to withold in the infancy of the colony, only from a sincere regard for its happiness and prosperity.[107]

The Governor in his address laid great stress on the function of roads in the mainland colony, and reported that £83,937 had been spent on them in 1863 out of a total expenditure of £192,860.

That its sister colony was also prospering was evidenced by figures appearing in a supplement to the *Colonist* in early February. They showed that whereas imports through Victoria into Vancouver Island for 1861 had been $2,018,424, in 1862 they had risen to $2,550,242 and in 1863 to $3,860,430. It was estimated that over ten million dollars of gold had been exported through Victoria to this time.

So winter gave way to spring. In February the *Colonist* displayed advertisements for valentines, both sentimental and comic, and early in March De Cosmos moved in the Assembly that an address be presented to the Governor, asking that Mount Douglas be preserved for public use forever. A bill was also passed by the Assembly to provide a pension for Chief Justice Cameron, now about to retire.

It was in this season too, that Prussia took the first of the long series of moves that were to hold the world in fretful awe until the sound of guns finally died away amid the ruins of Berlin in the spring of 1945.[108] German troops invaded Schleswig-Holstein in what was to prove a successful attempt to wrench that area from Danish control. There was much fluttering in diplomatic dovecotes, but it was soon apparent that no serious effort would be made to halt the advance of this newest addition to the ranks of the major powers.

More and more, it was becoming evident that the pioneer days were yielding to the onrush of what was, till the dawn of our own, the most headlong of all centuries. In an editorial on March 7, the *Colonist* reflected on the great and continuing change:

> We have passed through the bustle and excitement of first emerging into the outer world, shining with the reflected light of the gold of the Upper Fraser and its tributaries, and we have survived the reaction which was the inevitable consequence of the first excitement, and are now settling down in earnest to take our proper place in the world as a thriving mercantile colony; the steady increase of buildings in our city and its vicinity, the constant though gradual addition of villas with a fair show of comfort in their menage, and the gradual introduction of those adjuncts to social life which of late years have become so necessary and essential to the

well-being of all towns, both as regards their commercial and social prosperity, the introduction of gas, water, and a telegraph system into our city are all steps in the right direction, and marks of civilization which we must all welcome with gratification.

Now, however, the clock of history was not merely moving faster; it was beginning to strike the end of the old order. On the tenth of March in the Victoria Theatre a grand farewell banquet was given for the old Governor.[109] All the leading figures of the colony were among the two hundred present—Judge Begbie, Judge Cameron, Mayor Harris and Drs. Helmcken and Tolmie were perhaps the most notable. Alfred Waddington was in the chair, with Douglas on his right. When it was the Governor's turn to speak, he declared that he

"would beg to thank the company most cordially for this sincere expression of their good will. It was highly gratifying to him to see so hearty a demonstration of approval of the policy of his government, and to know that the community approved of his course during the long term of his protracted administration · · · He felt that the community were disposed to place a higher value on his services than they deserved." (Loud cries of "no, no".) The progress was due rather to the effects of their highly patriotic legislature (applause). In closing his relations with the colony, he would ever retain a grateful recollection of this day's proceedings, and of the high honor conferred upon him, and in whatever part of the world he should spend the remainder of his days, he would ever rejoice to hear of the welfare and progress and prosperity of this colony. (Tremendous cheering).

Other speeches followed. Capt. Hardinge, R.N., spoke for the Navy, and Col. Foster for the Army; J. J. Southgate proposed a toast to "The Legislative Assembly"; Dr. Helmcken recalled that "he could recollect the time when the only means of mail communication we had with England was by a canoe across Puget Sound, and that only twelve short years ago". Dr. Tolmie proposed "The Bench and the Bar"; Chief Justice Cameron responded for the Bench and Mr. Cary for the Bar. Selim Franklin proposed a toast to "Our Sister Colony", and ascribed much of its progress to Governor Douglas; Mayor Harris and Judge Begbie also spoke, and D. B. Ring proposed "Our Foreign Residents". A. C. Anderson spoke for the agricultural interests, and P. M. Backus, speaking for the Americans in the colony, ventured on a pun (received, apparently, with uncontrollable hilarity), declaring that Vancouver Island was sure to go ahead "if we only had the wealth of old England to back us". All in all, the evening was a great success, as old grudges were forgotten and former factions dissolved in a common glow of general good will.

On the 12th of March, the *Colonist* passed its verdict on the Governor's long term of office. It defended him stoutly against any accusations that he had unduly favored the HBC since assuming the Governorship, declaring that the evidence was all to the contrary:

> The best answer to Sir James' accusers is the publication of the despatches relative to the Crown lands, which show how thoroughly the Governor performed his duty toward the Crown and the public of this Colony when the interests of the Hudson Bay Company came in conflict with those of the colonists. Many held the opinion, previously to the publication of these despatches, that the Governor had leaned toward the Hudson Bay Company more than his position as Governor justified him in doing. Human nature is weak, and those who were so ready to accuse Sir James of unpatriotic conduct, in all probability judged him by their own standard of morality, and did not give him credit for that zeal for the interests of the country, which it has since been proved that he warmly exerted upon this most trying and important occasion.

On the 14th of the month, the city and all the ships in the harbor were decked with flags. As the band played "For he's a jolly good fellow", Douglas went on board the *Enterprise* at the HBC wharf. Then to cheers from the crowd, salutes from the guns and the playing of "Auld Lang Syne", slowly the ship moved into the harbor and thence out to sea and New Westminster.[110] It had been twenty-one years almost to the hour since he had first set foot on this spot; so much had happened since then that the first days of "The Fort" seemed now to belong to an almost prehistoric time; but now — almost unbelievably — an era was suddenly over.[111]

In the ten days that were to elapse before the arrival of the new governor, the citizens of Victoria went about their daily duties, and even in this brief gap of time the evidence of social change continued. The bill passed by the Assembly to establish telegraphic communication by way of San Francisco with the outer world became law,[113] and a writer in the *Colonist* expressed the view that "we may before the close of the present year be enabled to exchange greetings with our Eastern neighbours and perhaps even with the old folks at home". It was announced that regular mail service to other parts of the Island would begin on the first of April; it was planned that a ship would call at Comox once a month, and at Nanaimo twice a month, with stops at Cowichan, Maple Bay, and Salt Spring Island.[114] Hickman, Tye and Co. advertised hardware, cutlery and mule shoes; Peter Lester and Mifflin Gibbs, colored merchants who had arrived with the first wave of newcomers in 1858, announced the dissolution of their partnership; while another firm offered paper collars at 25c a dozen. A cricket club arrived from the Cariboo (an area not instantly associated with the sport today) and subdued the more effete Victorians by 126 to 125.

All this, however, soon faded into the background as the day approached for the arrival of Governor Kennedy. The press pointed out the significance of the now imminent event, equating its place in the history of the colony with the position of the spring months in the calendar:

> Governor Kennedy arrives at the most important phase of our existence—the transforming period of youth to manhood. After the boisterous weather of our springtime—the gales and showers of a blustering March—we are gradually gliding to a more serene season, the summer of our political maturity.[114]

The duties which the Colonist deemed appropriate to the new Governor were also outlined:

> To aid and encourage the inhabitants in every laudable enterprise—to endeavour, in colonies where the population is

large, to remove by social reunions the ascerbities (*sic*) of political life—to give a tone to that society of which he should be the ornament and the head—and to look after the constitutionality of the acts of the Legislature, are really the duties pertaining to his office.[115]

A note of warning was sounded, however, by the *Colonist*:

The days of intermeddling Executives have, in nearly all the colonies, happily ceased, and the wise Governor, no more than Queen Victoria, attempts to interfere in the political affairs of the country.[116]

Finally the great day arrived; the booming of cannon announced the new Governor's approach. Immediately, "every vehicle in the city and every equine quadruped capable of locomotion was put in requisition, and hurried down to Esquimalt with the greatest possible expedition".[117] The Governor, however, sailed round to Victoria harbor in a small gun-boat, the *Grappler*. No sooner had he disembarked there than he struck a happy and encouraging note:

He had come to this country with a desire rather to serve the people than to rule over them; their interests were his, and he had no doubt that he would find the people of the colony ever ready to assist him in his endeavours for the general welfare.[118]

Then the new Governor, "seated in a carriage drawn by six splendid horses", took part in a large procession replete with bands supplied by the fire and police departments. His wife and two daughters, meanwhile, were taken to the St. George's Hotel.

On March 26, 1864 Governor Kennedy was officially inaugurated. He at once gave his audience some idea of what the colony might expect from him:

In the administration of the laws he knew neither class, creed, sect nor nationality (cheers)—all were equal in the eyes of the British law. He did not pretend to any degree of infallibility; on the contrary, being well aware of the difficulties of his position, he felt that he must of necessity be sometimes wrong, and would therefore claim the indulgence of the people. There was one thing, however, upon which they might firmly rely—his sincerity in doing everything for the best (cheers). If he did err he would do so earnestly and in good faith; for he was of opinion that it was much better to be decidedly wrong than undecidedly right (cheers).[119]

In the next few days, a variety of groups of citizens paid their respects to the new governor. Among these were the local Chinese, who expressed themselves well satisfied with the treatment they had received under Governor Douglas, and predicted that Victoria would eventually be as thriving a centre on the eastern shore of the Pacific as Canton was on the western.

The Governor in his reply declared that their address "showed a great knowledge of trade and commercial principles" and remarked that "he had always found the Chinese an orderly and industrious people, and he hoped they would keep up the same good reputation in this colony."[120]

It must have come as quite a shock when these sounds of harmony were almost immediately dissolved in discord. No suitable official residence as yet existed for the new Governor, and the House of Assembly, debating the matter, refused to provide one, on the grounds that this was the responsibility of the British Government. The *Colonist* undoubtedly voiced the views of many when on April 9 it declared:

> The refusal (after going into the question) to afford His Excellency a decent habitation, or his Private Secretary a salary, is about the most wanton piece of discourtesy that could be exhibited to an English Governor.

A "monster meeting" was speedily assembled, and many of those who had supported the action of the Assembly, notably Dr. Helmcken and Amor De Cosmos, were barely allowed to speak.[121] When tempers had somewhat cooled, a deputation headed by Mayor Harris called on the governor and apologized for the action of the House. The Governor, however, urbanely replied that he took no offence and had temporarily secured a house from Mr. Trutch. He hinted, though, that it was by no means impossible that he might shortly dissolve the Assembly and thus set in motion a new election.

Meanwhile, the daily life of the city continued to display vitality. The need for a free public school system was increasingly recognized, and a public meeting with Mayor Harris in the chair supported the following resolution:

That in the opinion of this meeting the wants of the city, too long neglected, imperatively demand the establishment of a free Common School in a central position, efficiently conducted, open to all classes of the community, and non-sectarian in the strictest sense of the term.[122]

A short time later, a deputation waited on the Governor to inform him that the House of Assembly had appropriated $5000 to build a school on the School Reserve, but asking him either to veto the action or else to see that the school was built nearer the centre of population.

Kennedy replied that although he had the power to disallow the expenditure, he had no authority to decide the location of the school. He quite agreed, however, that it should be non-denominational, saying that:

It was highly desirable that all classes should live in harmony, and he was decidedly of opinion that such feelings would not be advanced by allowing religious dissensions to creep into the public schools. He had been at school himself, and he had not found that attending chapel and lectures had done him much good, or indeed anyone else.[123]

Progress, however, was not rapid in these matters; an editorial the following month declared, "We have been, to our disgrace, up to the present time without any scheme of public education".[124] In June, Dr. Powell moved in the Assembly to appropriate $2500 for temporary school purposes, but this was voted down;[125] and so the problem continued to drag on.

Other difficulties were also still some distance from settlement, notably those arising out of defects in the city charter and those resulting from the tangled question of the ownership of the town-site. In April, the Assembly, debating a new Incorporation Act, added a section permitting the city to borrow a maximum of $10,000 at a maximum rate of 12% per annum. It also provided that the City should keep "clear and correct accounts" and publish a statement of its revenue and expenditure in the newspaper once a year.[126]

Bearing in mind the claim that had been put forward by some that the City had previously been raising money illegally, the House passed an amendment stating that all licence money paid to date had been legally collected.[127] In May, it was proposed that $6000 be borrowed from the administration so that the civic debt (estimated at $4990) could be paid off. It was pointed out by some of the more penetrating minds in the Assembly that borrowing was not really a method of extinguishing debt, and a motion was then moved by De Cosmos and passed that a tax of ½ of 1% on real estate in Victoria be legalized.[128]

It was also hoped by some that the agreement of 1862 between the British Government and the HBC might still in some way be invalidated. An editorial in the *Colonist* for May 7, 1864 gave expression to this somewhat vain hope:

> With a little honesty and ability on the part of the House of Assembly, the four-fifths of the present Victoria town-site might be wrested from the Company's grasp, despite the indenture of 1862, so culpably and so foolishly made by the Imperial authorities.

In June, the matter was gone into by a Committee of the House, which estimated that the Hudson's Bay Company owed about $765,000 to the Colonial Trust Fund, declared that the Indenture of 1862 should be annulled, and urged that a new agreement be drawn up based on the Royal Grant of January 13, 1849. Otherwise, the Committee declared, the Crown would lose well over a million dollars.[129]

Dr. Helmcken, on the other hand, defended the position of the Company and declared that in any case the whole matter was now past history.[130] Dr. Tolmie, speaking soon afterwards, also supported the claims of the HBC and maintained that the 3084 acres comprising the townsite of Victoria had never been Crown Lands.[131] This did not prevent the *Colonist* from declaring in an editorial that the agreement of 1862 should be cancelled, that "the colony has been virtually robbed of so many hundred thousands of dollars" and that a commission should be set up in the United Kingdom to re-open the entire question.[132]

Governor Kennedy made no response to this, but when addressing the Assembly in July he admitted the complexity of the questions involved, but observed that they "must be left in their present very unsatisfactory state, to the serious detriment of the best interests of the colony".[133]

In most other respects, however, the march of progress was evident. In May a meeting was held, presided over by Selim Franklin, to consider ways and means of exploring the lesser-known parts of the Island; it was decided that money for this purpose should be raised by public subscription.[134] The Governor expressed himself as gratified by this development, and promised that for every dollar raised in this manner, the administration would contribute two.[135]

Gold was found near Goldstream and on the Sooke River,[136] the *Colonist* reporting on July 29 "the whole city thrown into a state of excitement by the announcement of extensive surface diggings, of surprising richness, having been discovered by the exploration party on the Sooke and Leech Rivers". A few weeks later, the Governor himself visited the mines. Reflecting the economic activity of the district, a new magazine appeared: "The Mining News and Register of the Stock and Real Estate Markets".

Other signs of economic growth were apparent. A turpentine factory was opened in Saanich; the Singer Sewing Machine Company demonstrated its wares to awestruck housewives;[137] the Victoria Gas Company reported that it was doing well, and proved it by declaring a dividend;[138] street numbers made their appearance; and a meeting of the directors of the Spring Ridge Water Works Company resolved that iron pipes for city water mains should be forthwith ordered from Scotland.[139] A remarkable number of inns offered hospitality to the weary or merely thirsty traveller: among them we may note "The Willows", located "three miles from town on the Cadboro Bay Road", Fry's Hotel, at Arlington Farm, North Saanich, and the South Saanich Hotel. Governor Kennedy showed the editors of the *Colonist* a sketch of a proposed graving dock at Esquimalt, to be 1000 feet in length and 300 to 500 feet in width;[140] and there was much debate about the deepening of Victoria harbor.

The stars, too, received appropriate attention, the *Colonist* reporting on June 28 that "an observatory is about to be constructed in the gaol yard, under the superintendence of Dr. Walker. The necessary instruments are already in possession of the Government, and the men of the police force will be instructed by Dr. Walker in their use". The mainland made its contribution to Victoria's prosperity, it being possible to record on one occasion that "the sum of $300,000 has arrived in Victoria during the past week".[141] The permanent population was also rising, being estimated at approximately 6,550.[142]

It was small wonder, then, with eventual union of the two Pacific colonies widely debated, and the future Dominion of Canada already a ghostly outline in many minds, that an almost boundless era of prosperity was envisioned for the years ahead:

> With telegraphic and railway communcation from the one ocean to the other, and with a federal union that will collect and concentrate the colonial intellect representing the various colonial interests, what country can have a greater future before it than this gigantic confederacy with its illimitable and diversified resources?[143]

The upper parts of the Island also made progress. Bishop Demers visited Comox[144] in the summer, and reported that the crops were good. Governor Kennedy did not, however, see fit to grant either Comox or Cowichan representation in the House of Assembly. At Nanaimo, Robert Dunsmuir was presented with a gold watch and chain by the men employed in the mines.[146]

The spiritual side of life and its appointed guardians were from time to time in the news. In June, the Rev. Macfie left on a tour of eastern Canada and the British Isles. His purpose was to inform their inhabitants that the Kingdom of Heaven had been located on the shore of the Pacific, and that they would do well to emigrate forthwith. His expenses were to be paid by the Colony, and this brought protests from some who believed that the reverend lecturer might make use of the occasion to publicize the tenets of his own (Congregational) denomination. However, the objectors were overruled,[147] and Mr. Macfie commenced his lengthy journey.

Bishop Demers was also active. In October it was announced that he had "taken steps to establish an hospital for the use of all classes and creeds, on his property in Collinson street, in the rear of the Catholic Church".[148]

Theological developments in the homeland were also faithfully reported in the press. An outline of conditions to be expected beyond the grave was given by the Archbishop of Canterbury, who explained that "the eternity of punishment and the eternity of blessedness must both stand or fall together", and stressed that the Church of England "holds both doctrines clearly and decidedly".[149] The tribulations of Bishop Colenso of Natal, noted earlier, continued, as he refused to concede that the embracing of faith inevitably involved the rejection of intelligence, preferring instead to declare:

> I have no doubt whatever that the canonical books of Scripture do contain errors, and some very grave ones, in matters of fact, and that the historical narratives are not to be depended on as true in all their details.
> I have never stated this publicly, but surely in this age of critical inquiry every intelligent student of the Scriptures must be aware of the truth of what I say.[150]

This forthright declaration, however, failed to sit well with his fellow South African bishops, who decided that "the Bishop of Natal had wholly disqualified himself for bearing rule in the Church of God and for the cure of souls therein", and recommended that he be deprived of his see.[151]

The social history of the time also contains items of interest. The Victoria Rifle Corps was active, and regular drill nights were fixed for Monday and Thursday at 8 p.m. In May, the *Colonist* reported that "a large number of the Russian sailors were on shore yesterday from the *Bogatyz*. They are a bronzed wiry looking set of fellows, and present the appearance of able, effective seamen. They conducted themselves in a very orderly manner while in town."[152] The 24th of May was celebrated by horse-racing and dancing, and also witnessed the marriage of John S. Bowker to Mary, second daughter of the Hon. John Tod. The fourth of July also saw general festivities (although later in the year, Hallowe'en passed unnoticed). The Agricultural and Horticultural Society held its annual show on September 29 in the old

Fort Yard, while a meeting of the Amateur Dramatic Association was held in the Bee Hive Hotel.[153] A letter from Queen Victoria,
originally appearing in the *Times* of London, was reprinted in
the *Colonist;* in it, the mourning monarch explained that she was
unable to take part in more than the absolute minimum of public
functions.[154]

Advertisements of the day often provide interesting reading,
what a later generation would term "wonder drugs" being lavishly
represented in this period. Perhaps the most intriguing was "Constitution Water", which retailed for a dollar a bottle to "persons
about to marry, if conscious of any weakness". A vivid portrait of
a prospective piece of aisle-fodder, both before and after ingesting
the magical elixir, was painted for hesitant purchasers:

> The stooping, trembling victim of depression and debility
> becomes a new man; he stands erect, he moves with a firm
> step; his mind, which was previously sunk in gloom of an
> almost idiotic apathy, becomes bright and active; and he goes
> forth regenerated, conscious of new vigor.[155]

So, as events both great and small flowed into the larger stream
of the life of the city, the seasons came and went. In due course,
when their cycle was completed, a new year would arrive, but
there in this account we shall not follow. The story of Victoria, it
was decided, would be carried in this volume only as far as the
birth of the city, the end of Governor Douglas' long term of office,
and the final dismantling of the Fort. Two of these now lie behind
us, and it is time to turn our attention to the third.

It was in late November that the last remaining buildings were
demolished; the *Colonist* recorded some details:

> Bit by bit all traces of the Hudson Bay Company's old fort
> are being obliterated. The work of demolition of the remain-
> ing fort buildings has been going on gloriously during the
> past few days. Yesterday evening the last of the number, an
> old log house, adjoining the Globe Hotel, formerly used as
> a kitchen, was brought to the ground. The structure was very
> strongly put together, the wall being constructed of double
> rows of stout logs, and the interstices filled with beach shingle
> to render it bullet-proof. Intending purchasers at the great sale

to take place on the 30th will now have every opportunity of examining the lots before the sale.[156]

The lots were quickly sold, some fetching more then ten thousand dollars; where the old buildings once had stood, in due course rose new and more imposing ones; but the Fort, which in its twenty-one years had seen so much, was now no more.

It had been established by James Douglas when he was still a man of forty and only the trusted subordinate of a fur-trading company; it had witnessed the coming of Governor Blanshard and his uneasy term of office; it had seen Douglas combine for some years the duties of Governor and Chief Factor; and finally, the lesser of these two offices resigned, it had been guided by its founder while it evolved from a trading-post into a city, and until he himself was Sir James Douglas, K.C.B. Bullets had peppered its walls; ships had come to link it with the four quarters of the globe; it had girded itself for wars that never reached it. Some of those who had known its earliest years now slept in the Quadra Street cemetery; others had come here from distant lands to begin new lives; and already there were some who, born here, had known no other home. Founded by a company built on almost feudal lines, it had seen the beginnings of democracy; while, spartan in its original mode of life, it now aspired to participate in the commodous living which the burgeoning age made possible. Once it had been virtually isolated from the rest of humanity; then, step by step, tenuous links with the outside had grown strong; now, as the nineteenth century revolutionized communication and transportation, it was being drawn forever into the network of the larger world.

So, blow by blow, as the short November day waned, the old Fort succumbed to the workman's axe and the enterpriser's dream; and as night descended, it had been razed, to live henceforth but in memory.

Only a fragment survived, and does so yet. Whoever will wander through Bastion Square, where once the Fort stood, and down to the harbour's edge, will find, still fixed in the rocky slope against which the salt tide laps, two rings; nearby is a plaque that tells their story. Here once, long years ago, ships bringing news or supplies from the other side of the globe tied up; and here, when the nights are dark and foggy and the square deserted, perhaps they do so still.

FOOTNOTES

[1] *Colonist,* August 6, 1862.

[2] *Colonist,* August 20, 1862.

[3] *Colonist,* September 16, 1862.

[4] *Colonist,* September 17, 1862.

[5] *Colonist,* September 23, 1862.

[6] *Colonist,* October 4, 1862.

[7] *Colonist,* September 9, 1862.

[8] *Colonist,* September 23, 1862.

[9] *Colonist,* October 17, 1862. As we shall see, however, the controversy dragged on for a long time yet, mainly over the question of what balances were owing to whom. The subject is treated exhaustively in Wrinch, L. A., *Land Policy of the Colony of Vancouver Island 1849-1866,* M.A. Thesis, U.B.C., October 1932.

[10] De Cosmos in an editorial on February 16, 1863 criticized this decision, declaring: "If a greater than our legislative councillors could enter the corn fields of Judaea on the Sabbath Day in defiance of the Levitical Code, we fail to see so very great an evil in some of our own people entering a butchery, bakery, grocery or vegetable stall, early on the Sabbath, while the majority of church-going Christians are wrapped in sleep."

[11] *Colonist,* December 16, 1862.

[12] *Colonist,* September 30, 1862.

[13] With the exception of "personal estate . . . ships, shipping or passengers", a provision designed to prevent any sort of customs duties, which would in effect end Victoria's status as a free port.

[14] Alexander Rattray, *Vancouver Island and British Columbia,* London, 1862, p. 167.

[15] *Ibid.,* p. 71.

[16] *Ibid.,* p. 72.

[17] *Ibid.,* p. 168.

[18] *Colonist,* November 6, 1862.

[19] *Colonist,* October 20, 1862.

[20] "The letters of the 'Times' correspondent, published in 1862, excited great attention, and in that year several thousands were induced to visit the country from England, Canada, Australia and New Zealand." (Macfie, *Vancouver Island and British Columbia,* London, 1865, p. 75.)

[21] *Colonist,* October 30, 1862.

[22] *Colonist,* November 17, 1862.

[23] Cecil Maiden, *Lighted Journey,* B.C. Electric Railway, Vancouver, 1948, p. 7.

[24] Maiden, *Lighted Journey,* p. 7.

[25] *Colonist,* October 4, 1862.

[26] Maiden, *Lighted Journey,* p. 9.

[27] Some fires did occur from time to time. On December 1, 1862 the *Colonist* reported "The roof of a house of ill-fame on Broad street took fire again last Saturday morning".

[28] "Fire Companies of Old Victoria", by F. W. Laing and W. K. Lamb, *BCHQ,* Vol. X, January 1946, p. 64.

[29] *Ibid.,* p. 62.

[30] Spring Ridge was near the present site of Victoria High School.

[31] *Colonist,* August 23, 1862.

[32] *Colonist,* November 18, 1862.

[33] *Colonist,* August 25, 1862. It is almost certain that Lulu Island is named after her. See Walbran, *British Columbia Coast Names,* Ottawa, 1909, p. 309.

[34] *Colonist,* September 30, 1862.

[35] *Colonist,* September 8, 1862.

[36] *Colonist,* August 28, 1862.

[37] *Colonist,* November 14, 1862. Both the British and American gallons were in use in the colony, causing much confusion.

[38] See also the editorial in the *Colonist* for August 6, 1863.

[39] *Colonist,* September 19, 1862.

[40] *Colonist,* September 19, 1862.

[41] *Colonist,* September 20, 1862. It is hard to determine if this is Victorian humour or merely Victorian prose.

[42] *Colonist,* September 20, 1862.

[43] *Colonist,* September 22, 1862.

[44] *Colonist,* September 29, 1862. De Cosmos was, however, quite capable of upholding proper standards of public rectitude when the occasion clearly demanded it. When it was proposed to erect a dance hall in the city, he thundered: "On moral grounds, we can see no excuse for licensing such a hell-hole. Every instinct of morality denounces it, and as for necessity we fail to observe a solitary reason that can be offered in support of it." (*Colonist,* November 28, 1862.)

[45] *Colonist,* November 12, 1862.

[46] *Colonist,* November 24, 1862.

[47] *Colonist,* November 29, 1862.

[48] See *The History of Education in the Crown Colonies of Vancouver Island and British Columbia and in the Province of British Columbia,* by D. L. Maclaurin, PhD Thesis, U. of Washington, 1936, p. 42.

[49] *Colonist*, November 26, 1862.

[50] *Colonist*, October 30, 1862.

[51] *Colonist*, September 11, 1862. It is pleasant to be able to record that the city, after a century presumably devoted to considering the pros and cons of this proposition, has now put it into effect.

[52] *Colonist*, November 20, 1862.

[53] *Colonist*, November 20, 1862. It will be observed that De Cosmos was already uncertain of the exact date (1843) the settlement was founded.

[54] *Colonist*, November 26, 1862.

[55] Mallandaine's *Directory for 1863* (Victoria, 1863) gives a useful picture of the city's progress to this point.
It reports several brick hotels, among them the St. Nicholas, the St. George and the Royal, and five churches: two Anglican, one Roman Catholic, one Wesleyan and one Congregationalist. There were also two joint-stock banks (the Bank of British North America and the Bank of British Columbia) and three private banks. Three steamships a month connected the city with San Francisco.
The Directory also contains the full text of the Incorporation Act of 1862.

[56] *Colonist*, January 3, 1863.

[57] De Cosmos in an editorial on January 7, 1863, vigorously attacked this suggestion of state aid for religion. Among other things he declared "the union of Church and State may now be placed in the catalogue of exploded ideas".

[58] *Colonist*, January 12, 1863.

[59] *Colonist*, January 13, 1863.

[60] *Colonist*, January 14, 1863.

[61] *Colonist*, January 26, 1863.

[62] *Colonist*, February 18, 1863.

[63] *Maclaurin*, op. cit., p. 43.

[64] *Colonist*, February 12, 1863.

[65] *Colonist*, February 17, 1863.

[66] *Colonist*, February 26, 1863.
It should be noted that it was provided in the "Road Act of 1860" that property-owners were to contribute a certain amount of personal "statute labor" toward the maintenance of the roads. Public notice was given, for example, in June, 1863, ordering those living on Cadboro Bay Road, Cedar Hill Road, or in the "Lake District", to turn up for work at 7 a.m. on the 15th of the month "with the proper tools". (*Colonist*, June 6, 1863).

[67] On December 13, 1871.

[68] *Colonist*, April 3, 1863.

[69] *Colonist*, May 5, 1863.

[70] *Colonist*, May 21, 1863.

[71] A long account is given in the *Colonist* for June 3, 1863. The synagogue (on Cormorant Street) was consecrated on September 13, 1863 (see *Colonist* for September 14, 1863).

[72] *Colonist,* June 5, 1863.

[73] *Colonist,* October 26, 1863.

[74] *Colonist,* November 16, 1863.

[75] *Colonist,* May 13, 1863.

[76] *Loc. cit.* See also issues of June 8, 13 and 24, 1863.

[77] *Colonist,* May 29, 1863.

[78] *Colonist,* June 13, 1863.

[79] *Colonist,* July 4, 1863.

[80] *Colonist,* July 29, 1863.

[81] *Colonist,* July 20, 1863.

[82] *Colonist,* August 13, 1863.

[83] *Colonist,* September 18, 1863. It would seem from the account that a ferry service between these areas had already been tried, but had been discontinued for financial reasons.

[84] *Colonist,* August 26, 1863.

[85] *Colonist,* September 4, 1863.

[86] *Colonist,* September 16, 1863.

[87] The last issue edited by him was that of October 6, 1863.

[88] *Colonist,* October 13, 1863.

[89] *Colonist,* September 5, 1863.

[90] *Colonist,* September 9, 1863.

[91] *Colonist,* September 17, 1863.

[92] Outlined in the *Colonist* for December 17, 1863.

[93] See *Colonist* for December 31, 1863, and January 11, 1864.

[94] On September 16 the *Colonist* had reported the opening of a public subscription for a Mr. Templeton, who was in this unfortunate predicament. A one-way ticket was soon procured by this means, and the sufferer then disappears from the pages of history.

A passage from *Hamlet* may or may not be relevant in this connection:

Hamlet:	Why was he sent into England?
Gravedigger:	Why, because he was mad: he shall recover his wits there; or, if he do not, 'tis no great matter there.
Hamlet:	Why?
Gravedigger:	'Twill not be seen in him there; there the men are as mad as he. (V. 1).

[95] *Colonist,* October 12, 1863.

[96] *Colonist,* October 5, 1863.

[97] *Colonist,* October 19, 1863. See also issues for October 20 and 24.

[98] As we shall see, obstructions were placed in the way of this piece of legislation, and it was some time before it actually became law. See *Colonist* for July 9, 1864, where an article on the subject declares: "The idea that some pompous ninny from the English courts should strut about, like a king's jester or a pantomimic clown, with gown and wig, claiming a monopoly of legal acumen and learning, and shutting the door of the colonial courts in the face of men that have forgot more than the simpleton ever knew, is something so disgracefully preposterous,

that we are astonished the outrage has been allowed to exist in any one of the colonies for a single day."

99 *Colonist,* November 4, 1863.

100 *Colonist,* November 19, 1863.

101 *Colonist,* November 21, 1863.

102 *Colonist,* November 23, 1863.

103 *Colonist,* November 26, 1863.

104 *Colonist,* November 28, 1863.

105 *Colonist,* December 12, 1863.

106 *Colonist,* December 17, 1863.

107 *Colonist,* January 29, 1864.

108 As early as February 7, 1860, the *Colonist* had reported "Prussia is certainly arming."

109 Reported in detail in the *Colonist* for March 11, 1864.

110 A full account is given in the *Colonist* for March 15.

111 On May 14, Douglas, together with Mr. Young, the Colonial Secretary, left on the *Sierra Nevada* for England. On May 16 the *Colonist* reported "Sir James, we understand, purposes travelling through Europe, and will therefore probably be absent for a year or two." For an account of the remainder of Douglas' life, see W. N. Sage *Sir James Douglas and British Columbia,* U. of Toronto, 1930.

112 See editorial in the *Colonist* for March 18, 1864.
The United Kingdom government later insisted that such a line must take an "all-red" route; otherwise communications between London and British naval forces in the Pacific might be subject to "wire-tapping" by inquisitive Americans. (*Colonist,* August 24, 1864).

113 The steamer *Emily Harris* eventually received the contract, its owners being paid $194 a month. (*Colonist,* April 7, 1864).

114 *Colonist,* March 21, 1864.

115 *Loc. cit.*

116 *Loc. cit.*

117 *Colonist,* March 26, 1864.

118 *Loc. cit.*

119 *Colonist,* March 28, 1864.

120 *Colonist,* April 5, 1864.

121 *Colonist,* April 12, 1864.

122 *Colonist,* April 11, 1864.

123 *Colonist,* April 13, 1864.

124 *Colonist,* May 11, 1864.

125 *Colonist,* June 9, 1864.

126 *Colonist,* April 14, 1864.

127 *Colonist,* April 16, 1864.

128 *Colonist,* May 18, 1864.

129 *Colonist,* June 17, 1864.

130 *Loc. cit.*

131 *Colonist,* June 18, 1864.

[132] *Loc. cit.*

[133] *Colonist,* July 9, 1864.

[134] *Colonist,* April 29, 1864.

[135] *Colonist,* May 11, 1864. Preliminary reports by the exploring party are to be found in the *Colonist* for September 3 and October 13, 1864.
The Surveyor-General of the Colony at this time was J. D. Pemberton, who was succeeded by B. W. Pearse in October, 1864. In 1860, Pearse had built a fine stone house, which he named "Fernwood". He himself died in 1902, but his second wife, who had gone there as a bride in 1876, lived to be a hundred, dying on January 23, 1954. Pearse left $10,000 in his will "for the purpose of assisting in the establishment of a university or other institute for higher education in Victoria".

[136] *Colonist,* July 11 and 26, 1864.

[137] *Colonist,* October 13, 1864.

[138] *Colonist,* August 17, 1864.

[139] *Colonist,* August 20, 1864.

[140] *Colonist,* August 8, 1864.

[141] *Colonist,* June 20, 1864.

[142] *Colonist,* May 10, 1864. An editorial on May 20 stressed the need for accurate statistics on the colony, including the establishment of a registrar of births, marriages and deaths, and the taking of a census.

[143] *Colonist,* August 30, 1864. For a strong advocacy of Confederation, see the editorial in the *Colonist* for August 16, 1864.

[144] *Colonist,* July 15, 1864. This spelling of the name becomes invariable about this time.

[145] *Colonist,* April 23, 1864.
Much interesting material regarding the early days of Chemainus is given in W. H. Olsen's "Water Over the Wheel", (Peninsula Printing Co., Sidney, B.C., 1963). The Cowichan Valley is similarly treated in "The Warm Land" by E. B. Norcross (Evergreen Press, Nanaimo, 1959).

[146] " . . . the only real opposition comes in the form of clerical fulminations from one or two denominations that aim at guiding sinners aright in a little different manner from the system pursuant by the persuasion to which Mr. Macfie belongs". (*Colonist,* March 10, 1864).

[147] *Colonist,* October 25, 1864.

[148] *Colonist,* May 21, 1864.

[149] *Colonist,* March 30, 1864.

[150] Colenso was pronounced deposed by Bishop Gray, Metropolitan of Cape Town, on December 16, 1863; the judicial committee of the Privy Council subsequently declared the proceedings null and void and he resumed his position. He was, however, denied all financial support by both the Society for the Propagation of the Gospel and the Society for the Promotion of Christian Knowledge. He died on June 20, 1883.

[151] The *Bogatyz* was a steam corvette of 21 guns, carrying the flag of Admiral Popoff, Admiral of the Pacific Squadron. Prince Maksutoff, Governor of Russian America, was on board. (*Colonist,* May 19, 1864).

[152] *Colonist,* October 17, 1864.

[153] *Colonist,* May 23, 1864.

[154] *Colonist,* May 2, 1864.

[155] *Colonist,* November 25, 1864.

Epilogue

So, with the dismantling of the last remnants of the Fort, we reach the end of one phase of Victoria's story and the opening of another. Its pioneer days were over; its career as a modern city had been launched.

To sum up Victoria's history to this point would be difficult; but few will deny, surely, that it contained a remarkable variety of interesting characters and events—some of them of much more than local significance—and that its past had given promise that its future would be bright.

The next fifty years of Victoria's life-story would see the bursting buds of progress come to flower and fruit. The time, of course, was propitious: the half-century that ended in 1914 was perhaps the happiest fifty years that the western world had known since the fall of the Roman Empire. It was a time when it was believed that all the fundamental problems of human existence were either solved, on the way to solution, or imaginary; and that all efforts therefore could be devoted to the development of material prosperity. It was, as no age before it had been, and as no subsequent period seems likely to be, the age of the comfortable middle class. All this, however, will be dealt with in another place.

We who live in the flourishing capital city of today must not on that account despise "The Fort". In its day an outpost of civilization in the wilderness, a wink of light in the vast primeval darkness, as such it served both its time and our own. Now a new age was dawning, destined to carry the city from the days of skirmishes with the native tribes to the threshold of a world conflagration; but an age whose achievements would be based on foundations firmly laid. We should, I think, bear this reflection with us, as we come now to the last inevitable task: to bid farewell to "The Fort", as, like all things mortal in this transitory world, it slips below the horizon of the turning globe of time.

DEREK PETHICK
Saanich, B.C., 1968

Bibliography

Victoria newspapers:

The Colonist
The Gazette
The Press

Unpublished memoirs in Provincial Archives, Victoria:

ANDERSON, J. R., Notes and comments on early days and events in British Columbia, Washington and Oregon, 1925.

COOPER, James, Maritime matters on the Northwest Coast, 1878.

DEANS, James, The Settlement of Vancouver Island, 1878.

FINLAYSON, R., Biography, 1891.

————. History of Vancouver Island and the North West Coast, n.d.

HELMCKEN, J. S., Reminiscences, 1892.

TOD, John, History of New Caledonia and the North West Coast, 1878.

WILSON, C. W. (Sir), Journal of service with boundary commission April 20, 1858 to July 17, 1862.

Official Publications:

Papers relative to the affairs of British Columbia, four parts, London, Queen's Printer, 1859-1862.

Correspondence Relative to the Discovery of Gold in the Fraser's River District, London, Queen's Printer, 1858.

Great Britain, Colonial Office: Miscellaneous Papers Relating to Vancouver Island, 1848-1863.

Legislative Council of Vancouver Island, Minutes, 1851-1861, Victoria, King's Printer, 1918 (PABC Memoir No. 2).

Vancouver Island House of Assembly, Minutes, 1856-1858, Victoria, King's Printer, 1918 (PABC Memoir No. 3).

Unpublished Theses:

MACLAURIN, D. L., The History of Education in the Crown Colonies of Vancouver Island and British Columbia and in the Province of British Columbia, Ph.D. Thesis, U. of Washington, 1936.

PALMER, P., A Fiscal History of British Columbia in the Colonial Period, Ph.D. Dissertation, Stanford University, 1932.

PILTON, J. W., Negro Settlement in British Columbia, 1858-1871, M.A. Thesis, UBC, 1951.

WALDEN, F. E., The Social History of Victoria, 1858-1871, B.A. Thesis, UBC, 1951.

WRINCH, L. A., Land Policy of the Colony of Vancouver Island, 1849-1866, M.A. Thesis, UBC, October, 1932.

Books:

BANCROFT, H. H. *History of British Columbia, 1792-1887,* San Francisco, 1890.

————. *History of Alaska, 1730-1885,* San Francisco, 1886.

BARBEAU, M. *Totem Poles,* 2 vols., National Museum of Canada, Ottawa, 1950.

BARNETT, H. G. *The Coast Salish of British Columbia,* U. of Oregon Press, Eugene, 1955.

BARRETT-LENNARD, C. E. *Travels in British Columbia,* London, 1862.

BEGG, Alexander. *History of British Columbia From Its Earliest Discovery to the Present Time,* Toronto, 1894.

BOAS, F. Second General Report on the Indians of British Columbia, British Association for the Advancement of Science, *6th report on the North-Western Tribes of Canada,* London, 1890.

————. *The Kwakiutl of Vancouver Island,* American Museum of Natural History, Memoir No. 8, 1909.

————. *Primitive Art,* Cambridge, Mass. 1927. (Reprinted by Dover Publications, New York, 1955).

COOK, James. *The Three Famous Voyages of Captain James Cook Round the World,* Ward, Lock, Bowden and Co., London, n.d.

DAY, Patience. *Pioneer Days,* Colonist Press, Victoria, 1924.

DRIVER, H. *Indians of North America,* U. of Chicago Press, 1961.

DRUCKER, Philip. *Indians of Northwest Coast,* McGraw-Hill Book Co., 1955.

————. *The Northern and Central Nootkan Tribes,* Bureau of American Ethnology, Bulletin 144, Washington, 1951.

————. *Culture of the North Pacific Coast,* Chandler Publishing Co., San Francisco, 1965.

————. (with Robert F. Heizer) *To Make My Name Good,* U. of California Press, Berkeley and Los Angeles, 1967.

DUTHIE, D. (ed.). *A Bishop in the Rough,* London, 1909.

ESPINOSA Y TELLO, Jose. *Account of the Voyage made by the Schooners 'Sutil' and 'Mexicana',* Madrid, 1802. (trans. G. F. Barwick.)

FAWCETT, Edgar. *Some Reminiscences of Old Victoria,* Toronto, William Briggs, 1912.

GALBRAITH, J. S. *The Hudson's Bay Company as an Imperial Factor, 1821-1869,* U. of Toronto Press, 1957.

GIBBS, Mifflin. *Shadow and Light,* Washington, 1902.

GLAZEBROOK, G. P. (ed.). *The Hargrave Correspondence,* Toronto, The Champlain Society, 1938.

HAIG-BROWN, R. *Fur and Gold,* Longmans, Toronto, 1962.

HALLIDAY, W. M. *Potlatch and Totem,* Dent, London and Toronto, 1935.

HOLM, W. *Northwest Coast Indian Art: An analysis of form*, U. of Washington Press, 1966.

HOWAY, F. W. (ed.). *The Dixon-Meares Controversy*, Ryerson Press, Toronto, 1929.

HUTCHISON, B. *The Fraser*, Clarke Irwin, Toronto, 1950.

INVERARITY, R. B. *Art of the Northwest Coast Indians*, U. of California Press, Berkeley, 1950.

JENNESS, D. *The Indians of Canada*, National Musuem of Canada, Ottawa, 3rd edition, 1955.

JOHNSON, F. H. *A History of Public Education in British Columbia*, UBC, 1964.

KANE, Paul. *Wanderings of an Artist among the Indians of North America*, Radisson Society, Toronto, 1925.

LAMB, W. K. (ed.). *Letters and Journals of Simon Fraser, 1806-1808*, Toronto, Macmillan, 1960.

LEECHMAN, D. *Native Tribes of Canada*, W. J. Gage and Co., Toronto, n.d.

LONGSTAFF, F. V. *Esquimalt Naval Base: A History of its work and its defenses*, Clarke and Stuart, Vancouver, 1942.

LUGRIN, N. and HOSIE, J. *The Pioneer Women of Vancouver Island, 1843-1866*, Victoria, 1928.

MACDONALD, D. G. *British Columbia and Vancouver's Island*, London, 1862.

MACFIE, Matthew. *Vancouver Island and British Columbia*, London, 1865.

MACGOWAN, K. *Early Man in the New World*, Macmillan, New York, 1950.

MACKAY, D. *The Honourable Company*, McClelland and Stewart, Toronto, 1937.

McKELVIE, B. *Tales of Conflict*, Vancouver Daily Province, 1949.

————. *Maquinna the Magnificent*, Vancouver Daily Province, 1946.

McLEAN, John. *Notes of a Twenty-five years' service in the Hudson's Bay Territory*, London, 1849. Reprinted by the Champlain Society, Toronto, 1932.

MACLEOD, M. A. (ed.). *The Letters of Letitia Hargrave*, The Champlain Society, Toronto, 1947.

MAIDEN, Cecil. *Lighted Journey*, B.C. Electric Railway, Vancouver, 1948.

MALLANDAINE, Edward. *First Victoria Directory*, Victoria, 1860.

————. *Directory for 1863*, Victoria, 1863.

MARSHALL, J. S. and MARSHALL, C. *Vancouver's Voyage*, Mitchell Press Ltd., Vancouver, 1967.

MASTERSON, J. R. and BROWER D. *Bering's Successors 1745-1780*, U. of Washington Press, 1948.

MAYNE, R. C. *Four Years in British Columbia and Vancouver Island,* London, John Murray, 1862.

MONRO, A. S. *The Medical History of British Columbia,* 1932. (Reprinted from the Journal of the Canadian Medical Association for 1931-1932).

MORESBY, John. *Two Admirals,* London, John Murray, 1909.

MORICE, Rev. A. G. *The History of the Northern Interior of British Columbia, formerly New Caledonia, 1660 to 1880,* Toronto, 1904.

MURPHY, H. H. *Royal Jubilee Hospital, 1858-1958.* Hebden Printing Co., Victoria, 1958.

NORCROSS, E. B. *The Warm Land,* Evergreen Press, Nanaimo, 1959.

OLSEN, W. H. *Water over the Wheel,* Peninsula Printing Co., Sidney, B.C., 1963.

ORMSBY, Margaret. *British Columbia: A History,* Macmillan, 1958.

PEMBERTON, J. D. *Facts and Figures Relating to Vancouver Island and British Columbia,* London, Longman Green, 1860.

RAMSEY, B. *Ghost Towns of British Columbia,* Mitchell Press, Vancouver, 1963.

RATTRAY, A. *Vancouver Island and British Columbia,* London, 1862.

RICH, E. E. *The Letters of John McLoughlin,* 1st series, 1825-1838, Toronto, The Champlain Society, 1941.

ROBINSON, L. B. *Esquimalt, Place of Shoaling Waters,* Quality Press, Victoria, 1947.

ROME, David. *The First Two Years,* H. M. Caiserman, Montreal, 1942.

SAGE, W. N. *Sir James Douglas and British Columbia,* U. of Toronto, 1930.

SCHOLEFIELD, E. and HOWAY, F. *British Columbia from the earliest times to the present.* 4 vols., Vancouver, 1914.

SEEMANN, B. *Narrative of the Voyage of H.M.S. Herald,* 2 vols., Reeve and Co., London, 1853.

SHELTON, W. G. (ed.). *British Columbia and Confederation,* Morriss Printers, Victoria, 1967.

SIMPSON, Sir George, *Narrative of an overland journey round the world during the years 1841 and 1842.* 2 vols., London, 1847.

SMITH, D. B. (ed.). *James Douglas in California,* The Library's Press, Vancouver, 1965.

SMITH, Marian (ed.). *Indians of the Urban Northwest,* Columbia University Press,1949.

SPROAT, G. M. *Scenes and Studies of Savage Life,* London, 1868.

TOLMIE, Dr. W. F. *Physician and Fur Trader,* Mitchell Press, Vancouver, 1963.

WADDINGTON, A. *The Fraser Mines Vindicated,* Victoria, 1858.

WAGNER, H. R. *Spanish Exploration in the Strait of Juan de Fuca,* Fine Arts Press, Santa Ana, California, 1933.

WALBRAN, John T. *British Columbia Coast Names 1592-1906,* Ottawa, 1909.

WEBB, W. *The Great Frontier,* Houghton Mifflin, Boston, 1952.

WILLEY, G. *An Introduction to American Archaeology,* Prentice-Hall, Englewood Cliffs, New Jersey, 1966.

WOOLLACOTT, A. P. *Mackenzie and His Voyages, by Canoe to the Arctic and the Pacific 1789-1793,* J. M. Dent, London and Toronto, 1927.

WORMINGTON, H. M. *Ancient Man in North America,* 4th edition, Denver Museum of Natural History, Denver, Colorado, 1957.

ZWEIG, S. *Conqueror of the Seas,* Viking Press, New York, 1938.

Index